MAKING ENVIRONMENTAL LAWS WORK
—an Anglo American comparison
WILLIAM WILSON

Making Environmental Laws Work

—an Anglo American comparison

WILLIAM WILSON

·HART·
PUBLISHING
OXFORD
1999

Hart Publishing
Oxford
UK

Distributed in the United States by
International Specialized Book Services, Inc.
5804 N.E. Massalo St., Portland
Oregon 97213-3644 USA

Distributed in Australia and New Zealand by
Federation Press Pty Ltd
PO Box 45, Annandale
NSW 203, Australia

Distributed in the Netherlands, Belgium and Luxembourg by
Intersentia, Churchillaan 108
B2900 Schoten, Antwerpen
Belgium

Hart Publishing is a specialist legal publisher based in Oxford, England.
To order further copies of this book or to request a list of other
publications please write to:

Hart Publishing, 19 Whitehouse Road, Oxford, OX1 4PA
Telephone: +44 (0)1865 434459 or Fax: +44 (0)1865 794882
e-mail: hartpub@janep.demon.co.uk

British Library Cataloguing in Publication Data
Data Available
ISBN 1–901362–79–5

Typeset in 10.5pt Sabon
by Hope Services (Abingdon) Ltd.
Printed in Great Britain on acid-free paper
by Bookcraft Ltd., Midsomer Norton, Somerset

For Juliette, Samuel and Edward,
who shared and shaped this adventure.

Acknowledgements

I would like to make it clear that all opinions expressed in this book are my own. They are not necessarily those of my department, of any of those who kindly agreed to be interviewed while I was researching the book, or of anyone who commented on or corrected parts of the book.

While researching this book, I became very grateful for the American habit of courtesy and openness in responding to questions and visits from "visiting firemen". Many busy people took the time to see me or to provide information or material that I had asked for. I wish I could be sure that I had properly thanked them all.

My particular thanks are due to the following—

The Department of the Environment, Transport and the Regions for supporting my application for a Harkness Fellowship and allowing me to go to America on secondment; and particularly to Marilynne Morgan, then Solicitor and Legal Adviser; Michael Ross, Departmental Training Officer; John Featherstone and Bess Teeger, DETR Library;

The Commonwealth Fund of New York, for awarding me a Harkness Fellowship, and particularly to Genevieve Austin, Keith Kirby (Director), Lis Kirby, Robert Kostrzewa (Deputy Director), William Plowden (UK Director, Harkness Fellowships) and Carolyn Zafiros for all their help in moving to America with a young family, and for arranging the series of seminars in London, Rye, New Orleans, Washington D.C. and New York from which we learned so much;

The Northwestern School of Law of Lewis and Clark College, Portland, Oregon, for a base in America and a welcome, and in particular Carla Almaraz, Dean James Huffman, Dorothy Johnson, Pat Kraske, Daniel Rohlf, Adele Rolfe and Janice Weis (who included me in the LL.M seminars, the Federal judges' environmental law seminar and so many other activities at the school);

The Oregon Department of Environmental Quality, for allowing me to attend a range of hearings, and helping me to understand the enforcement of environmental law in Oregon, and in particular Tom Bispham, Paul Burnet, Leslie Carlough, Van Kollias, Langdon Marsh (Director, and a kind mentor) and Chris Rich; and

IN ARIZONA

Larry Hagy, Environmental Engineer, ASARCO Inc, Ray Complex copper mine and smelter, Hayden; Wayne H. Leipold, Senior Environmental Engineer, Cyprus Miami Mining Corporation, Claypool; Robert F. Ressler, Manager, Environmental Affairs & Land, Cyprus Miami Mining Corporation;

IN CALIFORNIA

David Chatfield, State Director, Clean Water Action, San Francisco; Lawrence E. Cowles, Environmental Health & Safety Manager, Read-Rite Corporation and Chair, Environmental Committee, Silicon Valley Manufacturing Group, Fremont; Ellen Hickey, Pesticide Action Network, San Francisco; Lee Neal, Division of Occupational Health, Safety and Environmental Programmes, Semiconductor Industry Association, San Jose; Isao Kobashi, Program Manager, Pollution Prevention Program, Santa Clara County; Carl Smith, Foundation for Advancements in Science and Education, Los Angeles; Ted Smith, Executive Director, Silicon Valley Toxics Coalition, San Jose;

IN CANADA

Beverley Hobby, Advocate, Environment Canada; Digby Keir Q.C., Department of Justice, Canada; Robert Martinolich, Head of Enforcement, Department of Fisheries and Oceans, Vancouver B.C.; James Riordan, Director, National Office of Pollution Prevention, Hull, Quebec; Gordon Thompson, Head of Investigations, Environment Canada, Vancouver B.C. (who came in on his day off to give me a valuable briefing on Canadian enforcement practice);

IN LOUISIANA

Professor Kirstin Engel, Tulane University Law School, New Orleans; William Fontenot, Public Protection Division, Louisiana Department of Justice (with special thanks for slides of Mississippi pollution); Harry Freeman, Louisiana Environmental Leadership Programme; Gary Johnson, Office of the Secretary, Louisiana Department of Environmental Quality;

Baton Rouge; Louis Johnson, water quality and Lake Ponchartrain project, Louisiana D.E.Q.; Charles Killebrew, Office of Secretary, Louisiana D.E.Q.; Professor Bob Kuehn, Tulane University Law School, New Orleans; Tania Matherne, Barrataria/Terrebonne project, Louisiana D.E.Q.; Mike McWilliams, Environmental Co-ordinator, Exxon Baton Rouge Refinery; Judith La Rosa, Tulane University (with special thanks for a memorable seminar); Dugan Sabins, Mississippi water quality, Louisiana D.E.Q.; April Snellgrove, Senior Attorney, Louisiana D.E.Q., Professor William Toscano, Department of Environmental Health Sciences, Tulane University Medical Center;

IN NEW YORK

Nancy Marks, Natural Resources Defense Council, for responding to my final Harkness Fellowship presentation in June 1997;

AT THE NATIONAL POLLUTION PREVENTION ROUNDTABLE CONFERENCE IN DENVER, COLORADO, FEBRUARY 1997

Walter L. McLeod, Senior Regulatory Analyst, American Petroleum Institute; Joncile Martin, Environmental Affairs, Texaco Inc.;

IN OREGON

Professor Donald Balmer of Lewis and Clark College for kind assistance on the political aspects of lawmaking, in whose wake I paid a memorable visit to the Oregon state legislature;

Judge Holland, Chief Federal District Court Judge, Anchorage, Alaska; James O. Luce, Assistant General Counsel, Bonneville Power Administration; Joseph Hobson, General Counsel, Oregon Farm Bureau; Phil Keisling, Secretary of State (visited with Donald Balmer); Lori Laws (for much kind help getting settled in America and making the most of Oregon and Washington); Governor John Kitzhaber (for kindly allowing me to sit in at his meeting with the Cabinet of natural resources agency chiefs); Larry Knudsen, Assistant Attorney General, State of Oregon Department of Justice; Judith Kobbervig, Chief, Civil Division, U.S. Attorney's Office; Bill Marlett, Oregon Natural Desert Association; David McMullen, Assistant Regional Director, U.S. Fish and Wildlife Service, U.S. Department of the Interior; James "Moose" Mojewski, Pacific Party, (for kindly allowing me to attend election meetings and learn more about grassroots environmental politics); Frank Noonan, Chief, Criminal Division, U.S. Attorney's Office; Anne Richardson, Office of Congresswoman Elizabeth Furse; Stanley Speaks, Area Director, Bureau of Indian Affairs, U.S. Department of the Interior;

IN TEXAS

Dr Frank Anderson, U.S. Environmental Protection Agency, Region 6, Dallas; Pat Baker, U.S. E.P.A. Region 6; Rob Borowski, Clean Industries 2000, Texas Natural Resources Conservation Commission, Austin; Dr Norman Dyer, U.S. E.P.A., Region 6; David W. Gray, Director, Office of External Affairs, U.S. E.P.A., Region 6 (who responded to a letter of inquiry with one with ten introductions in Texas and Louisiana, each of whom he had contacted for me); Dr Warren Layne, Toxicologist and Toxics Release Inventory co-ordinator, U.S. E.P.A. Region 6 (with thanks for all the TRI material about the top emitters of pollution); Pierre Lichaa, U.S./Mexico Pollution Prevention Asssistance to Maquiladora industries, TNRCC; Andrew Neblett, Director, Office of Pollution Prevention and Recycling, TNRCC and Chair, National Pollution Prevention Roundtable (with thanks for arranging my visit to the NPPR conference in Denver); Pat Rankin, U.S. E.P.A., Region 6; John A. Riley, Division Director, Litigation Support Division, TNRCC; Jerry Saunders, U.S. E.P.A., Region 6 ; Professor Gerald Torres, University of Texas at Austin;

IN WASHINGTON D.C.

Rosina Bierbaum, Acting Associate Director for the Environment, Office of Science and Technology Policy, Executive Office of the President ; Cynthia Cummis, Staff Advisor, U.S. Environmental Protection Agency; Earl Devaney, Director, Office of Criminal Enforcement, U.S. E.P.A.; Nancy Firestone, Deputy Assistant Attorney General, U.S. Department of Justice; Keith Laughlin, Assistant Director, Council on Environmental Quality, Executive Office of the President; Barbara D. Littell, Senior Staff, Brookings Institution, and colleagues (for a valuable seminar on "Understanding American Politics and Public Policy"); Jessica Tuchman Mathews, Washington Post; David Rejeski, then with Office of Science and Technology Policy; Jacob Scherr, Senior Attorney, Natural Resources Defense Council;

IN WASHINGTON STATE

Ron Kreizenbeck, Director, Office of Enforcement and Compliance, U.S. Environmental Protection Agency Region 10; Bill Renfroe, Environmental Affairs Manager, WaferTech, Camas-Washougal (for a memorable tour of a semiconductor manufacturing plant under construction);

AND IN BRITAIN

David Slater, lately Head of Her Majesty's Inspectorate of Pollution and a Director of the Environment Agency for England and Wales; my publisher Richard Hart for constructive criticism and encouragement; my copy editor Kate Elliott; my parents John and Shirley Moran for kindly reading and correcting drafts with much practised and well informed comment.

I owe a debt to my father for early lessons in environmental issues, and for being an authoritative point of reference on so many of them. He is equally at home discussing transport statistics, reasons for the decline of the song-thrush, the plight of lowland raised peat bogs or the prospects for basking sharks in the North Sea.

Finally, my grateful thanks to my wife Juliette, without whose real talent for exploration I would have seen and learned so much less.

Note on the Harkness Fellowships

This book is the product of a year spent in America undertaking a Harkness Fellowship. These fellowships have been run by the Commonwealth Fund of New York for over 72 years, bringing people mainly from Britain, Australia and New Zealand to pursue their studies in America and to learn more about that country. The Commonwealth Fund recently announced its intention to focus the fellowships on its domestic heath care priorities, replacing them with short term study visits for health care policy analysts, so our year was the about the last expression of biodiversity before the onset of mono-culture, and it was sad to be one of the last lawyers to be able to take advantage of such an opportunity. One great benefit of the way that the fellowships were then run was the requirement for the fellows to look beyond his or her own discipline and to attend seminars, with their families, across the United

States to learn more about current trends in politics, health care, welfare reform, demographics, race issues and economics as well as (in my case) law. No other introduction to life and ideas in America could have been quite as ambitious or comprehensive.

Edward Harkness' family had made a huge fortune through early investments in the Southern Pacific Railroad and in Standard Oil, backing the young Rockefeller when nobody else would, and receiving in return a major stake in the oil company that resulted. They proceeded to spend this fortune on philanthropic causes, and Edward Harkness' endowments led to the substantial rebuilding of Yale, Harvard, Columbia Medical School and Johns Hopkins University, to take a few examples.

Edward Harkness was one of the best friends and benefactors that Britain ever had in America. In the midst of the Great Depression he founded the Pilgrim Trust with $10 million for the relief of the unemployed and for the preservation of places of cultural importance. The church of St Mary-le-Strand in London, Darwin's house at Down, the field of the Battle of Bannockburn in Scotland, the chapter library of Westminster Abbey, St Mary's College by St David's Cathedral in Wales and the students' union at Queen's University in Belfast have all benefited as a result. With this and the Harkness Fellowships, Edward Harkness is in some ways comparable to the Briton, James Smithson, whose unexpected bequest to America 150 years ago led to what is now the Smithsonian Institution.

Contents

1

Introduction

"It may be true that morality cannot be legislated but behaviour can be regulated:
it may be true that the law cannot change the heart but it can restrain the heart-
less: it may be true that the law cannot make a man love me but it can restrain him
from lynching me—and I think that is pretty important also.
So while the law may not change the hearts of men it does change the habits of
men if it is vigorously enforced."

Dr Martin Luther King, on receiving an honorary degree of Doctor of Civil
Law, Newcastle University, England, November 1967.

WHY AMERICA?

On 9 July 1995 the Environment Act received Royal Assent and became law
in the United Kingdom. As a lawyer at the Department of the Environment
in England, I had lived with this piece of legislation for a long time. With
administrative colleagues on the Bill team, I worked on the provisions to set
up a new Environment Agency for England and Wales, and to combat air
pollution, and helped to co-ordinate the legal work on the Bill as a whole.
We tried to marshal the teams of policy officials and other lawyers with
knowledge of hedgerows, opencast mining, water pollution, contaminated
land, radioactivity, national parks and the other topics that the Bill covered,
and to ensure that they were in place to answer the huge variety of questions
and amendments thrown up by the parliamentary process. The long sessions
in committee stretching into the night, the preparation of Government
amendments and responses, meetings with ministers and parliamentary
draftsmen, lobbyists and Members of Parliament were an education.

But the parliamentary process itself is only one part of the story of what
makes a law effective. Working with environmental laws every day, I began
to think about the constitutional framework in which they are made, the
political climate in which they are passed, the means by which they are
enforced, and the extent to which the public supports them. All these factors
seemed just as capable of making a law a success or a failure as getting the
drafting right.

In 1996 the opportunity arose to apply for a Harkness Fellowship to go the United States for a year with my wife and two small sons. This was a chance to learn at first hand in the jurisdiction which had given rise to so many environmental laws and principles. The range of lawyers, judges, academics and Federal and state environmental agencies involved in applying environmental laws in America is huge. In Britain, a full-time professor of environmental law is still a relative novelty. At the Northwestern School of Law of Lewis and Clark College in Portland, Oregon, where I was based, as many as eight or ten professors teach different aspects of the subject. Furthermore, the main legislation governing environmental protection in America has in many cases been in place for longer, and there is therefore wider experience of its strong points and shortcomings. As we put the finishing touches to legislation combining three other bodies into an Environment Agency for England and Wales, the U.S. Environmental Protection Agency celebrated its twenty-fifth anniversary.

Like so much else in America, environmental issues and problems have a way of being bigger and better. Consumption of most raw materials is on an impressive scale. The United States, with 5 per cent of the world's population and 6 per cent of its forest cover, produces and consumes one third of the world's paper.[1] America has 50,000 square miles of lawns, an area larger than the state of Pennsylvania, and the chemicals used to treat them are a problem. Americans at the end of the 1980s drove some 87 percent more vehicle-miles travelled per person than the British, and in 1988, around 80 per cent of urban passenger trips in the United States were made by car.[2] These trips are not always made in fuel-efficient cars, and the Ford Motor Company in 1997 was reported to be bringing out a model of four wheel drive vehicle one foot longer than the popular Chevrolet Suburban, which itself has difficulty fitting inside a standard American garage.

America also produces waste on a heroic scale. Contractual advertisements in the *New York Times* in May 1997 referred to the Freshkills Landfill on Staten Island as still growing at the rate of 11,800 tons per day. Vice President Gore refers in his book, *Earth in the Balance*[3] to a study by *Newsday* which predicted that the pile of New York's garbage would soon become the highest point on the Eastern Seaboard south of Maine, and Gore adds that the Freshkills Landfill will soon legally require a Federal Aviation Administration permit as a threat to aircraft.

But equally remarkable is the American sense that problems can be tackled and solutions found. The same automobile manufacturers who predicted dire consequences if the Kyoto protocol on global warming was signed in December 1997 issued press releases days later about energy efficient alternatives and prototype vehicles. The 3M Corporation in California has found a way to analyse the emissions from the stacks at one of its plants by laser, with the resulting data being placed on the Internet almost simultaneously.

In February 1998, the League of Conservation Voters contacted supporters by E-mail with its latest "scorecard" of voting records of members of Congress. Recipients could check the deplorable record of their representative, then complete and send an E-mail message of indignation directly to his or her office, armed with all the facts. Whether it is in technological fixes, or new approaches to pollution prevention, or confidence in citizen power and the use of freedom of information legislation, America is not only a fascinating collection of environmental problems, but an invigorating source of ideas and confidence in new solutions.

To a much greater extent than I had appreciated from outside, environmental laws in America are passed and applied at state level, and this has important advantages for any visiting researcher. Fifty different states adopting somewhat different approaches offer a variety of "laboratories" from which to pick and choose ideas. Also, 1996 was a Presidential election year, and environmental laws turned out to be one of the issues debated by Republicans and Democrats. I had not expected to be able to attend a campaign rally, to see the top of some well known heads, and to hear the President and Vice President addressing the way that environmental laws should be applied.

But above all, undertaking a year's "free-range" research in America offered the chance to follow up questions as they arose, with research and interviews. Why is the computer industry in Seattle, Washington, or San Jose, California, not applying pollution prevention techniques that are already in use in Texas or Colorado? Why does a copper mine in Arizona have to report an ammonia leak to the U.S. Coastguard in California? When the headquarters of the U.S. Environmental Protection Agency tells you one thing about an initiative, how does that compare to the verdict from one of the Agency's regional offices? What does the management of pollution of the Mississippi River imply for the management of pollution of the Columbia River, or for that matter the Severn or the Mersey rivers, or is it the other way around? I tried to look at different angles on the subjects I was concerned with, using the neutral status of a visiting foreigner to try to talk to protagonists on both sides of an issue. Americans find it entirely understandable that people should come to their country to look for answers to such questions, and tend to assume that any answers worth having will be found in America. This faint incredulity that there is anything much to learn from experience elsewhere is also a feature of some European environmental lawyers, and once recognised need not be a problem. Everywhere that I went I benefited from the very great courtesy and patience with which Americans treat visitors with questions.[4]

PART OF THE PICTURE

It would not be possible in a book of this kind to address every aspect of the question of what makes environmental laws work well or badly. There are a number of subjects which might be thought to be part of this story, but which would each be worth a book in its own right. The use of economic instruments as an alternative to "command and control" regulation is one such topic, and the use of "alternative dispute resolution" in place of civil litigation is another. I have tried instead to focus on areas where I believe that insufficient account is taken of their importance, or where American practice might inform the ways in which we in the United Kingdom consider our own laws.

CIVIL LITIGATION: A NON-COMPARISON

There are also issues where the dissimilarity of practice in America and the United Kingdom limits the usefulness of a detailed comparison. One such is the use of civil litigation as a means to enforce environmental laws. In America, Congress quite often leaves it to individual citizens to enforce environmental laws by giving them rights in legislation to bring actions in the courts against those violating the laws,[5] sometimes adding the power to make grants to groups of individuals affected by, say, toxic releases, to help them to interpret technical information about the releases. This is judged to be more cost-effective than supporting very large staffs at regulatory agencies, and it is assumed that the people most affected by a violation will be the most keen to pursue the violator. But in America, damages are assessed by juries, and losing plaintiffs do not generally have to pay their opponents' costs. In the United Kingdom, the loser in a civil action routinely has to pay the other party's costs, and damages awards in civil cases are assessed by judges. At the time of writing, proposals are under consideration to permit litigation in the United Kingdom to proceed by way of the "contingency fee" arrangements known to American lawyers. These clearly permit large numbers of plaintiffs in America to embark upon litigation without the fear that they will be ruined by the costs if they do not succeed, and they sometimes do so in the hope of a "telephone number" award of damages from a jury.[6]

The current British arrangements avoid many of the excesses of the jury damages assessments in America that we enjoy reading about. British arrangements might be of interest to proponents of the reform of damages awards in America. But it must be said that, with the risks from costs and the level of damages awards, litigation is simply not a viable option for many middle-income individuals in Britain. What is gained in common sense is lost in access to justice. It is clear that you could not sensibly, any time soon, leave the enforcement of a United Kingdom environmental statute to be carried out by citizen suit. Few citizens would be willing to risk so much trying to enforce an environmental obligation when they might gain so little.

Litigation over violation or non-enforcement of environmental statutes in the United Kingdom therefore takes two main forms. First, there are the challenges to government or agency actions or inactions brought by the well-financed "non-governmental organisations". The English law reports have their clusters of cases brought by Greenpeace to challenge aspects of the government's nuclear policies,[7] by Friends of the Earth to challenge the way that the government has applied the European Community Drinking Water Directive[8] or by the Royal Society for the Protection of Birds to challenge the decision to allow a funicular railway to be constructed in the Cairngorm mountains of Scotland.[9]

Then, and very importantly, both these groups and individual citizens have the right to complain to the European Commission that the government of a Member State of the European Community has infringed or failed to apply a provision of Community law.[10] The European Commission investigates the issues raised, and can and does require information and explanations from the Member State in correspondence. The replies to such letters are detailed and carefully considered statements by the Member States, and for all that this process is slow and sometimes cumbersome, it can be a formidably effective way of calling the whole government of a country to account if the issue is one concerning Community law. Eventually, if the issues raised by the challenge are not satisfactorily answered or addressed, the case may be stated by the Commission as a Reasoned Opinion, and then be referred by the Commission for adjudication by the European Court of Justice. As the European Court of Justice struggles with its ever increasing case-load, there are sometimes calls for more of these cases to be decided by the national courts. But it is hard to think of an American comparison to the process whereby, for the initial price of a stamp to send a letter to the European Commission, a single individual can launch a process which can result in a Member State having an adverse judgment made against it in the European Court of Justice. To this extent, European Community law and institutions have provided a means of redress to individuals and organisations, for environmental cases as well as all other Community law cases, which the national courts have failed to provide.

WHO GETS TO SUE?

Another area where the courts of the two jurisdictions are far apart, and getting further apart, in their approach is in the rules of "standing" developed by the court to determine who can be allowed to bring an action in civil proceedings. Standing is an obscure but important topic as, without being able to persuade a court that they have a sufficient interest to bring a case, plaintiffs are not allowed to proceed with it.

In America, the Supreme Court used until recently to take a very relaxed view of "standing", and anyone who could argue even a remote interest in the subject matter of a suit was allowed to proceed with it. Perhaps the high point of the extension of standing to bring cases in America was the case in 1973 of *United States* v. *Students Challenging Regulatory Agency Procedures (SCRAP I)*.[11] A group of students brought an action challenging railroad fare increases on the grounds that the fare increases discouraged recycling. The students argued that this in turn would lead to an increase in litter. Some of the litter might end up in parks near the plaintiffs' houses. The Supreme Court allowed that the group had sufficient standing to challenge the decision.

In the Supreme Court in America in the 1990s, Justice Scalia, who is seldom feted by environmentalists, has led the efforts to restrict the more speculative assertion of rights to have standing to sue. In the case of *Lujan* v. *National Wildlife Federation*[12] in 1990, the plaintiffs were trying to challenge decisions by the Federal Bureau of Land Management which would have permitted mining on Federal lands. Justice Scalia concluded that the plaintiffs actually had to use the lands in question to have standing to bring the suit. A plaintiff could only challenge some "concrete action applying the regulation to the claimant's situation in a fashion that harms or threatens to harm him".

In the case of *Lujan* v. *Defenders of Wildlife*[13] in 1992, the plaintiffs wanted to prevent actions by the Federal government which they argued would cause damage to endangered species in Egypt and Sri Lanka. Justice Scalia declared that "It goes beyond the limit, and into pure speculation and fantasy, to say that anyone who observes or works with an endangered species, anywhere in the world, is appreciably harmed by a single project affecting some portion of that species with which he has not had more specific connection".

The practical effect of the Supreme Court's limitations of plaintiffs' standing is that it is harder to bring cases challenging the Federal government and its agencies. This is particularly the case where the object of a suit is to try to protect some part of the environment which is not owned, and in which it is hard to describe an individual's interest. If, for example, the Federal government were taking actions which damaged the upper atmosphere, it might be hard for any individual to establish to Justice Scalia's satisfaction that he had enough of a direct interest in the upper atmosphere to be allowed to bring any proceedings: perhaps an astronaut could qualify. Assuming the absence of many litigious astronauts, the Federal government might be free of challenge.

The European Court of Justice also takes a relatively narrow view of standing to sue, based on Article 173 of the Treaty of Rome. This Article allows a Member State, the Council of Ministers or the European Commission to bring an action to challenge the decisions of Community institutions for infringements of Community law. Individuals may challenge those decisions of Community institutions which are addressed to them. If the decisions are addressed to another person, then individuals may challenge them only if they can establish that the decisions are "of direct and individual concern to them", In the case of *Greenpeace International and others* v. *European Commission* on 2 April 1998,[14] the European Court of Justice ruled that Greenpeace did not have standing to challenge a decision of the European Commission concerning the use of Community structural funds for Spain to build two oil-fired power stations in the Canary Islands.

The English courts appear to be moving in the opposite direction. From the rather narrow and technical arguments over standing in earlier cases,[15] English judges seem much more pragmatic, and willing to hear argument from groups which are well established or active in a particular field of environmental protection if that is going to be the best way to have the arguments deployed (which it often is).[16] Lord Woolf, Master of the Rolls (and thus President of the Court of Appeal in England) recently remarked in a lecture:[17]

> "It is difficult, if not impossible, to find a case in which a case of merit is turned away from the courts because of lack of standing . . . On standing, I am in favour of a two track approach. A *right* to initiate proceedings if a party is directly affected and a *discretion* to do so when the individual is a concerned member of the public. The issues which can arise in environmental proceedings mean that the courts should welcome any assistance which is available."

Government departments in the United Kingdom are also reluctant to take too many artificial points on the issue of a plaintiff's standing if in practice the plaintiffs have some real interest in the case and the means to present substantial arguments on points of real importance.

DEFERENTIAL COURTS

There is another reason to concentrate on how environmental laws are made and enforced by agencies and governments, rather than the case law surrounding them. It is increasingly recognised by courts in both England and America that while they always assert the right to challenge unlawful administrative actions, courts are not necessarily best placed to determine technical decisions based on complex environmental legislation. In America, with the 1984 case of *Chevron U.S.A., Inc. v. Natural Resources Defense Council. Inc.*,[18] this has developed into a formal doctrine of "deference" towards an agency's determinations on the part of the courts. American courts after *Chevron* take the view that where Congress has delegated regulatory authority to an administrative agency, that agency should decide upon public policy in its area and not the judges. The courts will be prepared to intervene if the agency exceeds its statutory mandate, but otherwise its decisions will be entitled to a high level of deference. Agencies and government departments enjoy having their decisions treated with a high level of deference: whether it is good for them may be another matter.

While "deference" has not evolved into a formal doctrine in England, Lord Justice Goff's speech in 1993 in the leading environmental case of *Cambridge Water Co. Ltd. v. Eastern Counties Leather plc*[19] contains the following statement:

> "It is of particular relevance that the present case is concerned with environmental pollution. The protection and preservation of the environment is now perceived as being of crucial importance to the future of mankind; and public bodies, both national and international, are taking significant steps towards the establishment of legislation which will promote the protection of the environment, and make the polluter pay for damage to the environment for which he is responsible . . . But it does not follow from these developments that a common law principle . . . should be developed or rendered more strict to provide for liability in respect of such pollution. On the contrary, given that so much well-informed and carefully structured legislation is now being put in place for this purpose, there is less need for the courts to develop a common law principle to achieve the same end, and indeed it may well be undesirable that they should do so."

For some, this acknowledgement of the primacy of legislation in the environmental field, and the *de facto* deference of the courts to the expertise and scientific knowledge of the agencies that apply it, may seem to be a rather forlorn commentary on the state of the common law and its capacity to deliver results that will make a difference to environmental protection. In America, despite the *Chevron* case, the complaint is rather different. Policymakers and those in government decry the extent to which the aims and aspirations of environmental agencies are decided for them by the constant pressure of the lawsuits that they face. Kathleen A. McGinty, Chair of the Council on Environmental Quality in the Executive Office of the President has written that:[20]

". . . despite all our progress in 25 years, our common ground—the environment—has become a battleground. Somehow, nearly half of the Environmental Protection Agency's work is not the product of our collective will on the environment, but rather, the product of judicial decree. Somehow, we have become a country in receivership, with the courts managing our forests, our rivers and our rangelands."

The contrasting retreat of the English courts from wanting to second-guess the technical and scientific decisions of environmental agencies underlines the importance of environmental statutes themselves and the way that they are applied. It would seem that any study of ways to make those laws more effective will have to start there.

A CONSTITUTIONAL MISMATCH

The nature of law-making is of course largely determined by the constitutional arrangements applicable to that country or region. Time spent in America can begin to raise doubts whether one is comparing like with like in setting the United Kingdom against the United States. An American citizen starts with a distinct advantage in exercising his constitutional rights by having a reasonable chance of being able to find out what they are. The United States Constitution can be comfortably printed in a booklet the size of a passport.[21] It is taught in schools, there are special editions for Boy and Girl Scouts, and even eccentric militarists in the back country of Montana show signs of having read it. In the United Kingdom, the nature of the unwritten constitution has changed greatly in recent years, particularly since the country joined the European Community in 1973, but it appears that there is little or no concern among those involved in applying or amending the constitution to make its detailed provisions known to the public at large. A simple comparison can therefore rapidly become baffling.

For example, under the United States Constitution, all legislative powers are vested in a Congress consisting of a Senate and a House of Representatives.[22] In the United Kingdom today, legislative powers are vested in the Queen in Parliament: in effect the party with a governing majority forms the government and passes its own legislation. But the Commission of the European Community has exclusive powers to propose Community legislation[23] which can trump national legislation. The European Parliament has powers to call for legislative proposals from the Commission.[24] In future even the European Central Bank will have powers to make regulations binding upon all citizens of Member States of the European Union and to issue directives which Member States must transpose into national legislation and obey.[25]

Bills for raising revenue in the United States must all originate in the House of Representatives, although the Senate may amend them.[26] In the United Kingdom, the House of Commons has primacy in considering matters relating to public expenditure.[27] Yet Treaty provisions will now require that the European Central Bank be consulted about "draft legislative provisions" in its field of competence brought forward by national authorities, which will presumably include future national budgets of the United Kingdom[28] if and when the United Kingdom pound sterling becomes part of the single European currency, the Euro.

The judicial power in the United States is vested in the Supreme Court.[29] In the United Kingdom, the primacy of European Community law over national legislation was established by the accession of the United Kingdom to the Treaty of Rome, and the final judicial authority in any matter touching upon Community law is the European Court of Justice.[30]

Recent treaties amending the constitutional arrangements within the European Community and establishing the European Union, notably the Treaty of Maastricht[31] and the Treaty of Amsterdam,[32] have been written as amending texts. They are dense, impenetrable documents, impossible to understand without constant cross-reference to earlier texts. They contain a sometimes bizarre mixture of provisions and ideas. In the Treaty of Amsterdam, for example, provisions describing the formulation of a common foreign and security policy for Europe, with moves towards a common defence[33] are mixed up with provisions about paid holiday schemes,[34] and a Declaration Accompanying the Final Act that even contains exhortations about the importance of amateur sport.[35] Having got this out of the way (and repealed various provisions relating to tarriffs on coffee and bananas), the conference of the Treaty of Amsterdam adopted a further declaration exhorting the European Parliament, Council and Commission to establish "guidelines for improving the quality of drafting of Community legislation" and urged them to "make their best efforts to accelerate the codification of legislative texts".[36]

These treaties amount to very significant revisions of the constitution of the United Kingdom, and of all other Member States of the European Community and European Union. Unlike the United States, where amendments to the Constitution must be ratified by the legislatures of at least three-quarters[37] of all states, constitutional change in the United Kingdom can be accomplished by the passage of legislation incorporating a new treaty in the national Parliament at Westminster, where it cannot be amended. This happened, with much internal acrimony within the governing Conservative party, with legislation to incorporate the Treaty of Maastricht,[38] and in 1998 under the new Labour administration with legislation incorporating the Treaty of Amsterdam.[39]

The party of government in the United Kingdom can therefore also be the party that changes the constitution, underlining the vulnerability of constitutional arrangements that depend so heavily upon consensus. In the United Kingdom, given the nature of Treaty texts which are regarded as unknowable and occult, it is little wonder that people at large have little clear understanding of the way in which their constitutional arrangements are changing, or indeed what, exactly, they are.

The context for so much activity from negotiators of treaties is the gathering pace of European integration, and here a little reverse translation may be called for. An American trying to understand the scale of what is being attempted in terms of European integration should try to imagine the North American Free Trade Agreement "NAFTA"[40] extending not only to the United States, Canada and Mexico, but also to, say, 12 other countries. Then to imagine that it was not merely a trade pact, but entailed a single currency within the area controlled by a single central bank holding all the reserves of all participating countries, a commitment to "ever closer political union", a single court to enforce laws made centrally, the development of a common foreign and security policy leading to a common defence, common monetary and fiscal policies, harmonised taxation, a parliament, a powerful central bureaucracy with the exclusive right to propose and to police legislation for the area and much more. In effect, what is under construction is a single state. It would be hard to imagine the idea catching on on Capitol Hill.

The context for environmental legislation affecting the United Kingdom, therefore, is that an increasing amount of it is made through the constitutional machinery of the European Community. The constitutional arrangements that now apply in the United Kingdom certainly are not easy for the public to understand or use, and provide little encouragement to meaningful public participation, a fact that is explored in more detail in Chapter 3.

THE CHANGING UNITED KINGDOM

Europe is a dominant factor in British politics, and will remain so for the foreseeable future. But it is not the only aspect of the constitution of the United Kingdom of Great Britain and Northern Ireland which is undergoing rapid and fundamental change. The first of May 1997 saw the election of the Labour Party in Britain with a huge parliamentary majority after 18 years of government by the Conservative party. The new government set about tackling its manifesto commitments, several of which will have a very significant impact on the way that environmental issues are dealt with in future.

Referendums were held in Scotland and Wales to decide on proposals for a Scottish Parliament and a Welsh Assembly. The Scots voted "yes" to the first by a large majority, and the Welsh "yes" to the second by a small majority. Legislation to give effect to these votes was swiftly introduced, and it is clear that in both cases the government envisages that the environment will be one of the issues for which responsibility will be transferred from the Secretary of State to the representative assembly for each country. For example, the Government of Wales Act 1998[41] envisages that the Secretary of State for Wales will make orders transferring to the Welsh Assembly his responsibilities for agriculture, fisheries and food, the environment, health and health services, town and country planning, water and flood defence, which covers most of the aspects of the natural environment handled by central government. The Scottish Parliament is likely to be able to pass Acts on any matter not reserved to the United Kingdom Parliament, including nearly all aspects of the environment.[42] In Northern Ireland, the agreement reached in multi-party negotiations on Good Friday 1998 allowed for the establishment of a Northern Ireland Assembly, for which elections took place on 22 May 1998. The "Good Friday Agreement" envisaged that the Assembly would take on all legislative and executive authority for matters within the responsibility of the existing six Northern Ireland government departments,[43] except where powers and duties are specifically reserved. This will probably result in the functions of those departments covering the environment being transferred to the Assembly. Legislation to implement the powers of the new Assembly was introduced in the Northern Ireland Bill in July 1998.

This devolution of power to smaller national assemblies seems likely to result in a re-ordering of many priorities in the environmental field. The Welsh and Northern Ireland Assemblies, the Scottish Parliament and the United Kingdom as a whole will remain subject to European Community law. But politicians from Scotland, Wales and Northern Ireland will be taking very important decisions on the environment, and be accountable for them to an electorate nearer to home. In many respects, government within Wales, Scotland and Northern Ireland will become more closely analogous to that within an American state, and, as with American states, it is quite possible that uniformity of approach will be a thing of the past. Certainly it will be impossible to describe the ways that environmental laws are made within the United Kingdom without reference to the legislative record of both these new assemblies. It may also be that those assemblies will start to explore ways of encouraging public participation in environmental law making, the absence of which is one of the chief concerns of Chapter 3 of this book. Whatever decisions these assemblies take in the short term, in the longer term it seems likely that their elected representatives will find it harder to hide from their electorate than, perhaps, United Kingdom ministers and officials. Decisions made closer to home may thereby move closer towards what local electorates understand and accept.

There are many other proposals to change the way that the United Kingdom is governed. Legislation proposed or already being introduced will affect the government of cities,[44] local governments, regions, the reform of the national Parliament itself and the incorporation into national law of the provisions of the European Convention on Human Rights.[45] It is a heady time in which to take an interest in constitutional law and reform in the United Kingdom, and it sometimes serves to be reminded of the first principles.

In a remarkable speech at a lunch to celebrate her Golden Wedding given by the British Prime Minister at the Banqueting House in London on 20 November 1997, Queen Elizabeth II said:

> ". . . despite the huge constitutional difference between a hereditary monarchy and an elected government, in reality, the gulf is not so wide. They are complementary institutions, each with its own role to play. And each, in its different way, exists only with the support and consent of the people."

Outside the window of the very room where this speech was made, King Charles I of England went to his death on the scaffold denying that public consent mattered.

The Queen's speech almost echoed the American Declaration of Independence, written at a time when King George III underestimated the importance of the consent of the governed. To live in America is to be reminded daily of the ways in which such consent is not taken for granted. Returning to the United Kingdom, one cannot but observe that some ways in which laws are made have begun to neglect this principle.

THE INFLUENCE OF SCALE

Environmental laws in the United Kingdom are coloured by the fact that Britain is a very small and overcrowded island, about the size of Oregon. Regulation and law so often step in to adjudicate between competing claims. There is a higher tolerance of government prescription. Our priorities are often dictated by the density and proximity in which we live. Land-use planning issues in Britain are keenly contested. Noise is a problem where you are likely to hear your neighbour. The Afrikaner principle that your neighbour is too close if you can see the smoke from his chimney is hard to apply in London and the South East of England (much of which will be a smoke free zone in any event). Traffic volumes and the pressures of development are acute.

America's environmental laws are in part a product of the scale of the country. Mining laws there are a remnant of the unreconstructed policies for opening up the West. Even today, certainly in the West, environmental debates are affected by the fact that over half of the land west of the Rockies belongs to the Federal government. Environmentalists struggle for influence over the Federal departments and agencies that administer this land against the strong vested interests of those accustomed to use it at relatively low cost—loggers, miners and ranchers. One such environmental group has argued that it costs between two and seven times more to feed a hamster than it costs a rancher, subsidised by low grazing fees, to feed a cow on Federal lands.

It used to take 110 days or more to travel by covered wagon from Missouri to California, and emigrants were advised to take:

> "150 lbs of flour, or its equivalent in hard bread;
> 25 lbs of bacon or pork, and enough fresh beef to be driven on the hoof to make up the meat component of the ration;
> 15 lbs of coffee; and
> 25 lbs of sugar; also
> a quantity of saleratus or yeast powders for making bread, and salt and pepper."[46]

And that was just to cross this extraordinary country. Today the same journey across the vastness of the plains can be accomplished in a few comfortable hours sitting in an aeroplane, or a few days of some of the best train journeys in the world. But the sense of scale and the attitudes necessary to deal with it have not disappeared from American life. There is a sense of optimism, there is an openness to new ideas, and it is a time and place of very rapid technological progress. America is a good place to go fishing for ideas for ways to make environmental laws work better.

SUMMARY OF CONTENTS

The first half of this book deals generally with the ways that environmental laws are made for the United Kingdom and some of the factors which influence their content. Chapter 2 deals with politics and environmental laws, and considers in particular some of the possible lessons from the treatment of the environment as a political issue in the 1996 American Presidential election. These include the Democrats' capture of a public mood to defend environmental laws against the efforts of a Republican Congress to cut them back: but also the way in which Republican ideas of smaller government are now part of the rhetoric of both main parties in America.

Chapter 3 deals with the way in which environmental laws are actually made in, or for, the United Kingdom, contrasting this with the American ballot measure process. Primary legislation made by the United Kingdom Parliament at Westminster, secondary legislation drafted within government departments, and directives negotiated in Brussels all become part of the body of national laws. The chapter advances the argument that the absence of effective public participation in the lawmaking process causes the distance between legislators and the governed to grow ever wider.

Chapter 4 considers the issue of the public and science. "Sound science" is supposed to form the basis of much of environmental law, together with risk assessment and, increasingly, cost and benefit analysis. The chapter considers whether new science, or all science, is always good science, and what weight should be given to public concerns about new scientific developments and research.

Chapter 5 looks for common themes in three striking but different environmental issues: environmental degradation in Russia, the environmental justice movement in America and water pollution in the Mississippi River. It speculates as to how these themes might apply to three current environmental issues: pressures of development in Britain and America, traffic growth and global warming. It argues that when measures necessary to address these issues entail an extensive infringement of people's freedoms and way of life, much more has to be done to explain the issues to the public and to seek consensus about the means to address them.

The second half of the book concentrates more on the means to enforce environmental laws, and considers some important differences in the American approach. Chapter 6 deals with the use of the criminal law in America as a means to enforce environmental obligations. At both Federal and state level the criminal law is used very selectively, and only aimed at the most serious violations of environmental statutes. In the United Kingdom, by contrast, every sort of trivial infraction is made a criminal offence. The chapter considers some of the reasons for this and its consequences.

Chapter 7 contains a more detailed account of civil and administrative law enforcement, particularly in the state of Oregon. This will be the area of environmental law enforcement least familiar to the United Kingdom. It offers a number of significant advantages in terms of predictability, better assessment of penalties, and more appropriate tribunals.

Chapter 8 reviews some current initiatives in the field of pollution prevention as a possible alternative to prescriptive regulation and its enforcement. The chapter takes two Federal pollution prevention initiatives that have worked spectacularly well, and two others that have had much more modest success, and considers possible reasons for the difference. It also addresses the question of "regulating high tech", and the implications of high technology industries such as the American computer industry for traditional approaches to regulation.

Chapter 9 returns to issues of opinion and perception, and considers the need for optimism in approaching environmental laws. It suggests that environmentalists may need to do more than to sound the alarm and to dwell on failures if more people are to feel that the environment is their issue too, and that there are steps which they can take as individuals which will make a real difference.

REFERENCES

1. Union of Concerned Scientists, Briefing Paper, *U.S. Consumption and the Environment*, February 1994.
2. *Ibid.*
3. At 151.
4. Having what was regarded as an outlandish accent was also a great help.
5. An example would be the citizens' suits provisions of the Comprehensive Environmental Response, Compensation and Liability Act of 1980, "CERCLA" ("Superfund"), sect. 9659, See also sect. 9617 of that Act for the technical assistance grants "TAGs" which may be made to groups affected by actual or threatened releases from any regulated facility, to help them to interpret technical information about the releases.
6. For an eye-opening account of environmental litigation in America based on contingency fees, see *A Civil Action* by Jonathan Harr (Vintage: 1995). This bestselling story of litigation over contaminated water supplies in Woburn, Mass. in the 1980s starts with harrowing accounts of victims of leukaemia clusters, and then rather disappears into the legal machinations of the trials and how many millions the heroic lawyer for the plaintiffs will settle for.
7. See e.g. *R*. v. *Secretary of State for the Environment and others, ex parte Greenpeace Limited and another*, Potts J. QBD, 8 Mar. 1994 [1994] 4 Env. L.R. 401.
8. *R*. v. *Secretary of State for the Environment, ex parte Friends of the Earth Limited*, Schiemann J., Mar. 1994, QBD [1995] 1 Env. L.R. 11; *R*. v. *Secretary of State for the Environment, ex parte Friends of the Earth and another*, C.A. (Civil Division), 25 May 1995; *Independent*, 7 June 1995; *Times*, 8 June 1995.
9. See *Financial Times*, 21 Apr. 1998, "Legal Battle Resumes over funicular plan", an article about the RSPB's case before the Court of Session in Edinburgh, Scotland.
10. See Art. 169 Treaty of Rome: to become Art. 226 Treaty of Rome as amended by the Treaty of Amsterdam.
    Formally, Art. 169 Treaty establishing the European Community (signed in Rome on 25 Mar. 1957) "the Treaty of Rome"; as amended by the Treaty on

European Union (signed in Maastricht on 7 Feb. 1992) "the Maastricht Treaty"; as prospectively amended by the Treaty of Amsterdam amending the Treaty on European Union, the Treaties establishing the European Communities and certain related Acts (signed in Amsterdam on 2 Oct. 1997: but, as at May 1998, yet to be generally in force) "the Treaty of Amsterdam"; as no doubt to be amended further at future intergovernmental conferences.

The Treaty of Amsterdam causes strong men to weep by changing the number of most Arts. in other treaties that have finally become familiar. It does, however, contain a table of old and new numbers, for those sufficiently interested.

For the environment in the treaties, see Title VII of the Treaty of Rome, Title XVI of the Treaty of Maastricht and Title XIX of the Treaty of Rome as amended by the Treaty of Amsterdam.

Hugh Brogan, in his *Penguin History of the United States*, when describing some of the more obscure tenets of the Mormon faith, quoted the entertainer Anna Russell: "I am not making this up, you know."

11. 412 U.S. 669, 93 S.Ct. 2405 (1973).
12. 497 U.S. 871; 110 S.Ct. 3177; 111 L.Ed 2d 695 (1990).
13. 504 U.S. 555; 112 S.Ct. 2130; 119 L.Ed. 2d 351 (1992).
14. Case C–321/95 P, ECJ, 2 Apr. 1998; see report by Prof. Richard Macrory in *ENDS*, Report 279, Apr. 1998..
15. See e.g. *R. v. Secretary of State for the Environment, ex parte Rose Theatre Trust Co.* [1990] 1 All E.R. 754.
16. See e.g. the terms in which Otton J. granted standing to Greenpeace to challenge the construction of the Thermal Oxide Reprocessing Plant (for nuclear reprocessing) at Sellafield, Cumbria, in *R. v. H.M Inspectorate of Pollution and Ministry of Agriculture, Fisheries and Food, ex parte Greenpeace*, QBD, 29 Sept. 1993 [1994] 1 Env. L.R. 76.
17. "The Courts' Role in Achieving Environmental Justice": Lord Morris Memorial Lecture, Friday, 31 Oct. 1997, University of Aberystwyth, Wales, Rt. Hon. Lord Woolf, M.R.
18. 467 U.S. 837; 104 S.Ct. 2778; 81 L.Ed.2d 694 (1984).
19. First instance: *The Times*, 23 Oct. 1991, (judgment 31 July 1991). C.A. Civil Div. (19 Nov. 1992) [1994] 1 All E.R. 53; H.L. (9 Dec. 1993) [1994] 2 A.C. 264, [1994] 1 All E.R. 53. Lord Goff's comments are taken from the H.L. judgment [1994] 1 All E.R. 53, at 76.
20. The Council on Environmental Quality, *Environment Quality—25th Anniversary Report*, (CEQ reports for 1994 and 1995, with some material from 1996), "Statement from the Chair", p. ix.
21. My copy runs to 46 pages, including all the Amendments, and index and the Declaration of Independence, with its several pages on the awfulness of the English Crown.
22. Art. 1, Sect. 1, U.S. Constitution.
23. See, e.g. Art. 100 Treaty of Rome, to become Art. 94 Treaty of Rome (as amended by the Treaty of Amsterdam).

24. Art. 138b Treaty of Rome (as amended by the Treaty of Maastricht): to become Art. 192 of the Treaty of Rome (as amended by the Treaty of Amsterdam).
25. Art. 34, Prot. (No 3) on the Statute of the European System of Central Banks and of the European Central Bank, Treaty of Rome (as inserted by the Treaty of Maastricht): to become Prot. (No 18) to the Treaty of Rome (as amended by the Treaty of Amsterdam).
26. Art. 1, Sect. 7, U.S. Constitution.
27. See, e.g., "Restrictions under Constitutional Usage—Basis of modern practice with respect to privilege", Erskine May, *Parliamentary Practice* (22nd edn., Butterworths, London, 1997), 797.
28. Art. 105(4) Treaty of Rome (as amended by the Treaty of Maastricht): to remain Art. 105(4) even after the Treaty of Amsterdam.
29. Art. III, Sect. 1, U.S. Constitution.
30. European Communities Act 1972: and see, e.g., Art. 171 Treaty of Rome, to become Art. 228 Treaty of Rome (as amended by Treaty of Amsterdam).
31. See n. 10 above.
32. See *ibid*.
33. Title V, Art. 11 *et seq.*, Treaty of Maastricht as amended by Treaty of Amsterdam.
34. Art. 119a/Art. 120 Treaty of Rome as amended by Treaty of Maastricht: to become Art. 142 Treaty of Rome (as amended by Treaty of Amsterdam).
35. Declaration 29 accompanying the Final Act, Treaty of Amsterdam.
36. Declaration 39 accompanying the Final Act, Treaty of Amsterdam.
37. Art. V U.S. Constitution.
38. European Communities (Amendment) Act 1993 (c.32).
39. European Communities (Amendment) Act 1998 (c.21) incorporates into law in the United Kingdom, by amendment of the European Communities Act 1972, most of the Amsterdam Treaty.
40. The North American Free Trade Agreement signed by Prime Minister Brian Mulroney of Canada, President Carlos Salinas de Gortari of Mexico and President George Bush of America on 17 Dec. 1992. The agreement came into force on 1 Jan. 1994, and will eliminate many tariffs on trade in qualifying goods between these countries.
41. c.38, s. 22 and Sched. 2.
42. Scotland Bill, House of Commons Bill 104, 17 Dec. 1997: see cll. 27, 28 and Sched. 5.
43. Strand One, "Democratic Institutions in Northern Ireland", para. 3, *The Agreement—Agreement Reached in Multi-party Negotiations* (Cm 3883, HMSO, London, 1998). The Northern Ireland Bill is H.C. [Bill 229], printed 15 July 1998 (HMSO, London, 1998).
44. S. 4(3), Greater London Authority (Referendum) Act 1998, and the Greater London Authority (Referendum Arrangements) Order 1998, SI 1998/746.
45. Human Rights Bill (H.L. Bill 38, 23 Oct. 1997).
46. Randolph B. Marcy, Captain, U.S. Army, *The Prairie Traveller* (Perigee Books (first published 1859), New York, n.d. for this edn.).

2

Politics and Environmental Laws

Towards the end of 1997, the representatives of 150 nations gathered in Kyoto, Japan, to try to negotiate a convention to tackle the problem of global warming. There was never a better example of the central place of politics in the making or unmaking of environmental laws.

Scientific understanding of global warming has come a long way since the pioneering work and studies on Man's impact on climate undertaken by the Massachusetts Institute of Technology in the 1970s. While still not sufficiently clear to persuade the most sceptical,[1] the scientific consensus is clearly in favour of the view that an unprecedented warming in global temperatures is already under way as a result of man's activities on the planet, notably in the release of carbon dioxide and other emissions to the atmosphere. The Second Assessment Report of the Intergovernmental Panel on Climate Change, prepared by 2,500 of the world's leading experts on climate change, provided a lengthy review of the health, environmental and economic impacts of climate change, and concluded "the balance of evidence suggests a discernible human influence on global climate".[2]

Climate change was predicted to continue to occur, and the Report added that of the various alternative scenarios "in all cases the average rate of warming would probably be greater than any seen in the last 10,000 years". That scientific consensus, which played a significant part in enabling the conference to be held in the first place, also predicts widely variable but significant consequences from global warming. Some countries may experience flooding as sea levels rise, some low-lying countries and islands may disappear altogether, others will experience more frequent storms or violent weather patterns and dramatic shifts in the viability of different kinds of agriculture within their frontiers.

If the same 2,500 scientists who prepared the Second Assessment Report had been left to decide by argument and consensus what action should be taken as a result of their findings, would they ever have come up with the highly complex system of emissions trading between countries contained in the Kyoto protocol? It seems unlikely, but then national politics had intervened.

While the effects of global warming may be scattered across the whole globe, its causes stem principally from the emissions made by the major industrialised nations in the Northern Hemisphere, although some of the developing nations aspire to be able to cause equal or greater amounts of damage. Each nation represented at Kyoto had in its different way to address not just the scientific assessments about global warming, or the legal problems of constructing a coherent treaty mechanism to address it, but the political realities back home.

Developing countries were quick to challenge any infringement of their sovereignty from enforcement machinery within the protocol which might have made it more workable. They were keen to resist any limitations on the development of their industries imposed by developed countries which had already done their bit for global pollution. The European Union was firm in its insistence that the Americans must do more to cut their emissions, but less firm about Spain and Portugal, which were apparently to be allowed to increase theirs. The American delegation was prodded from behind by industry lobbyists from oil companies and automobile manufacturers pressing them to reject a deal, and by implacable opponents in the Senate and Congress.

The industrial firms lobbying against the convention were themselves the target of environmentalists' protests, and after reading about the convention in piles of press cuttings thousands of miles from Kyoto, I could walk down Victoria Street in London past the headquarters of Exxon, where Greenpeace and Friends of the Earth were picketing the building and handing out campaign literature denouncing the company's part in trying to sabotage the convention. Even Vice President Gore, who had spoken in almost apocalyptic terms about the problem in his book *Earth in the Balance*,[3] was the same Vice President Gore who intends to run for U.S. President in the year 2000, and who sounded notably more robust in his defence of American industrial heartlands as a result.

At the time of writing, it is still unclear whether the American Congress can be persuaded to ratify the convention, and if it does not, the complex formulae agreed at Kyoto may yet unravel.[4] To come into force, the convention must be signed by 55 countries representing 55 per cent of global emissions.[5] As America accounts for over 30 per cent of these emissions, without American ratification there may be no effective convention. The achievement of that ratification will necessitate a vigorous campaign by the American administration to persuade representatives from the Congress and the Senate that industry in America in general, and in their states and Congressional regions in particular, will not suffer an unfair or disproportionate burden as a result of the convention, and that America too has an interest in halting the present shift towards climate modification.

Whatever the laws say and whatever the Senate and Congress do about ratification of the Kyoto protocol, America will, after all, not escape the effects of global warming. Even the Alaskan delegation to Congress could not bring that about. America's own experts are warning that temperature trends in the United States are consistent with the Intergovernmental Panel on Climate Change's climate model predictions, that rainfall is tending to become more concentrated in heavy downpours, and that sea level is rising along the U.S. coast, with 30 miles of shoreline in Maryland alone being replaced each year by rock revetments.[6] There probably will come a point when the political voices of those Americans affected by global warming will become louder than those of Americans with a vested interest in denying that the phenomenon exists.

It is unlikely that full agreement will be achieved on the necessary steps to address global warming at one, or even several, international conventions. But law makers' scope to negotiate at international conventions depends ultimately upon what their domestic public opinion will accommodate. That in turn depends upon the assessments of politicians.

THE 104TH CONGRESS AND THE REPUBLICAN "CONTRACT WITH AMERICA"

The election of the 104th Congress in America in 1994 brought to power a majority of Republican freshmen with the Republican "Contract with America" as their manifesto. Environmental protection did not rank high on their list of priorities. In their eyes, environmental protection and the agencies which enforced it had become part of "big government", which they saw themselves as elected to cut back. It represented Federal expenditure, Federal employees, red tape, interference with individual rights and an unacceptable burden on industry. Garry Trudeau ran one of his celebrated cartoons pointing out that the word "environment" did not appear in the 167 pages of the "Contract With America".[7]

Bills were proposed to require the government to pay compensation where environmental protection reduced the value of property.[8] Legislation was introduced to require "risk assessment" and "cost-benefit analysis" before regulatory agencies could propose environmental legislation;[9] but this was not to apply to agency approval of, for example, new pesticides. Other legislation sought to cut the Environmental Protection Agency's budget by $1.5 billion, eliminating its role in protecting wetlands, regulating arsenic in drinking water and limiting enforcement of clean air regulations.[10]

Representative Don Young and Senator Frank Murkowski, both of Alaska, proposed to open up the 19 million acre Arctic National Wildlife Refuge for oil drilling. Representative Bud Shuster of Pennsylvania,

Chairman of the Transportation and Infrastructure Committee in the House of Representatives, sponsored what became known as the "Dirty Water Bill".[11] This would have relaxed federal water pollution control regulations, removed 80 per cent of wetlands from federal protection, subjected public health protections to cost-benefit analyses and required compensation for some wetlands protection. Representative Joel Hefley of Colorado proposed a bill requiring review of the national parks and proposals for eliminating those no longer required.[12] Senator Kay Bailey Hutchison of Texas moved an amendment to another bill to eliminate $1.5 million remaining in the budget of the Fish and Wildlife Service for "listing" endangered species.[13] The Republicans' Majority Whip in the House of Representatives, Tom DeLay of Texas, introduced a measure to repeal the Clean Air Act. The attack on environmental protection and the agencies that administered it was ferocious and comprehensive.

Some of the Republicans of the 104th Congress were given to extreme language when it came to the environment. Representative Don Young declared "I am proud to say that all environmentalists are my enemy . . . they are not Americans".[14] A Republican memorandum referred to "the environmental lobby and their extremist friends in the eco-terrorist underworld".[15] Even more moderate Republicans seemed in some way to be affected by the mood of the moment. Jack Kemp, Vice Presidential candidate in the 1996 election, referred in a debate with Vice President Gore to the Environmental Protection Agency's "reign of terror".

It is interesting to consider the extent to which the Republican freshmen of 1994 turned their backs on their own party's long record of environmental protection. It was, after all, Theodore Roosevelt who did much to strengthen the system of national parks and forests in America that would have been threatened by the legislation of the 104th Congress. The Environmental Protection Agency was set up by the Republican President Richard Nixon. President Nixon also signed the Clean Air Act of 1970, the National Environmental Policy Act of 1970 (which requires environmental impact statements to be prepared) and the Clean Water Act of 1972. Vice President George Bush, running against Massachusetts Governor Mike Dukakis, made a memorable campaign visit to Boston harbour, where he bobbed about in a boat complaining that it used to be only tea that was thrown into the harbour, but that under Mr Dukakis' governorship, it was "something else". President Bush's claim to be the "environmental President" was one way in which he chose to distance himself from President Reagan, and President Bush went on to sign the revised Clean Air Act of 1990.

ENVIRONMENTAL GROUPS' COUNTER-ATTACK

For environmental groups, the attacks launched by the 104th Congress were an electrifying call to arms. The League of Conservation Voters declared "Rather than simply contributing to worthy candidates (where we are constrained by federal spending limits) LCV plans to run hard-hitting political campaigns against the worst environmental offenders in key states and congressional districts".[16] John Adams, Executive Director of the Natural Resources Defense Council, promised that the NRDC would "fight like hell against the environmental threats from the 104th Congress".[17] The NRDC hired a new legislative team to work full time on reviewing the legislation and exposing its anti-environmental features.

In the Congressional elections of November 1996, the environmental groups took their revenge on some of their fiercest opponents. The Sierra Club and the League of Conservation Voters made a hit list of incumbents, and 16 of 19 defeated Republicans were on such a list.[18] Senator Larry Pressler lost his seat after the League ran 860 television advertisements against him and spent $138,000 because of his stance on safe drinking water.[19] Other Congressmen in Maine and North Carolina owed their defeat in large part to the advertisement campaigns directed against them by the League and other environmental groups.[20] By the end of 1996, John Adams of the Natural Resources Defense Fund said that "all of us who care about the environment can look back on what may be the single most significant victory in the history of the U.S. environmental movement. In the past two years, we have turned back an attack that the entire country thought was unstoppable."

DEMOCRATS AND REPUBLICANS: THE SHAPING OF AN ELECTION ISSUE

President Clinton is reported to have said to his Labor Secretary, Robert Reich, in January 1995 "You're right. . . . About the fights. We'll be defined by the fights we have. We've got to pick them carefully."[21]

It would seem that at about this time, or perhaps before it, President Clinton and the Democratic Party concluded that one of the fights they would take to the Republicans concerned the attacks of the 104th Congress on environmental protection. President Clinton was photographed drinking a glass of water beside a creek, vowing that he would not allow the Clean Water Act to be rolled back. The *New York Times* noted that, very sensibly, the water in the President's glass was out of a tap and not the creek in question.

In March 1995, Senator Bob Dole, who was to be President Clinton's Republican challenger in the 1996 Presidential election, was calling for support for his proposal to require a cost-benefit analysis before new environmental regulations were introduced. In an article in the *Washington Post* on 5 March 1995, Senator Dole wrote:

"The anti-reform fog machine is already clouding the air with claims that this effort will have dire effects on the health and safety of people and on the environment. Obviously, everyone wants to protect human health, safety and the environment. But the 'strongest' laws do not always mean the most costly laws. Is it too much to ask that we fulfil those responsibilities in a way that minimises costs to society?"

To require a cost and benefit analysis before introducing any environmental regulation would clearly slow down the process of making such regulations, and make it harder to introduce them at all where the benefits were difficult to quantify, or where the purpose of introducing them was precautionary rather than necessarily based on proven scientific necessity. One side of the arguments of what was to become the Presidential campaign was therefore beginning to form around ideas of limiting costs, complexity and burdens on business and taxpayers.

In a speech to the American Society of Newspaper Editors on 7 April 1995, President Clinton promised to veto legislation undermining the protection of clean water, clean air and toxic waste laws. He also threatened to veto legislation which would have required the compensation of private property owners where seashores, wetlands or open spaces needed protection, saying that the compensation would bankrupt local governments.

By the time President Clinton came to give his State of the Union address of 23 January 1996, the Democratic arguments on the environment could be seen to have been refined. There were promises to stand firm against congressional attacks on what were judged to be popular environmental laws, but there were also promises to find new ways to deliver cheaper, less prescriptive regulations for business. President Clinton said:

"Congress has voted to cut environmental enforcement by 25 percent. That means more toxic chemicals in our water, more smog in our air, more pesticides in our food. Lobbyists for polluters have been allowed to write their own loopholes into bills to weaken laws that protect the health and safety of our children . . . I challenge Congress to re-examine those policies and to reverse them."

But he added:

"To businesses this administration is saying: if you can find a cheaper, more efficient way than government regulations require to meet tough standards, do it . . . as long as you do it right."

He also promised to strengthen citizen right-to-know disclosure legislation.

This reference to businesses finding a cheaper more efficient way of delivering the same or better results was really a summary of Project XL, the administration's flagship policy for new and pragmatic "reinvented environmental regulation". Project XL is reviewed in more detail, somewhat critically, in Chapter 8 of this book, on pollution prevention.

By the time of the Presidential election campaign in the autumn of 1996, the environment had become one of the key issues for President Clinton as the Democratic candidate. In September 1996, perhaps combining business with pleasure, the President exasperated the solidly Republican Utah congressional delegation and delighted the environmental community by declaring the new Canyons of the Escalante-Staircase National Monument, covering 1.8 million acres of spectacular wilderness in Utah and, incidentally, underground reserves of perhaps seven billion tons of coal.[22]

In his stump speeches all around the country, President Clinton promised to "grow the economy and still protect Medicare, Medicaid, education and the environment". In many campaign stops, the President's account of achievements in the environmental area and of Democratic resistance to the assaults of the Republican Congress were accompanied by a speech from Vice President Gore on his matching efforts to "reinvent regulation", cut out waste in government and streamline its workings. In representative speeches, such as those in Springfield, Virginia, on 27 October 1996 or in Minneapolis-St Paul on 28 October 1996, President Clinton spoke of Democratic progress towards clean air, improved drinking water quality and protection of national parks against "their" assaults, and he promised to clean up 500 more toxic waste dumps.

In an article of post-election analysis in *Time Magazine*, modestly entitled "Why Our Game Plan Worked", the President's pollsters, Mark J. Penn and Douglas E. Schoen explained:[23]

"... our analysis suggested that the 1994 election was not a rejection of government per se; it was a rejection of big, intrusive government. The President emphasized a view endorsed by well over two-thirds of the American people: a fiscally prudent government can still provide decent medical care for senior citizens and children, a high-quality education system for young people and protection of the environment."

A *New York Times* editorial in 1997 underlined the same perception:[24]

"The voters did not want the Clean Water Act dismembered. They did not want Newt Gingrich [Republican Speaker of the House of Representatives] turning his conservative committee chairmen loose on the basic environmental laws. Whatever their reservations about Washington, they had no wish to transfer stewardship of America's natural resources to state, local and commercial interests."

The Democratic line on the environment in the 1996 Presidential election was not therefore an unqualified "green" policy. It recognised the "reservations about Washington" to which the *New York Times* editorial quoted above referred. Opinions about Washington in America are indeed often expressed more forcefully than as "reservations". The Republicans had tried to articulate this widespread American dislike of government in general, and big government in particular. In a telling exchange in one of the televised debates in the Presidential election campaign, Senator Dole had declared about President Clinton, "That's the difference between him and me. He trusts the government. I trust the people."

President Clinton has been accused of many things, but he is seldom accused of being less than astute as a politician. Democratic ideas for re-inventing environmental regulation were in part an attempt (which seemed to work for the purposes of the 1996 Presidential election) to borrow Republican ideas about limiting the size of government and the unnecessary complexity of laws.

THE NATURE OF THE DEBATE, AND LOBBYISTS V. THE PUBLIC

Many visitors to America are amazed at the horse-trading between Congress, Senate and the Presidency, but can be fairly reminded that this was what the founding fathers who wrote the Constitution envisaged. They did not want too many laws passed. They wanted the separation of powers to operate in such a way as to force compromise and consensus between the different arms of Government. The American system that requires a negotiated outcome to legislative proposals works that way because that is how it was always intended to work. In any event, there are superficial similarities between the way in which American Federal laws are negotiated and the way in which European Community directives and regulations are negotiated. One of the main differences is that in America the arguments take place within the parameters of a written constitution within a single state, whereas in Europe they are more open-ended, and no one can easily predict how far the parties to an argument may compromise their original positions.

In his book *Washington at Work, Back Rooms and Clean Air*, Richard E. Cohen describes the political events surrounding the passage of the Clean Air Act of 1990. He assesses the critical importance of President Bush's initial proposal for legislation and Presidential sponsorship, and then describes how the initial proposal became almost unrecognisable as the Senate and

Congress got to work on it. Cohen describes the struggles of Senator Mitchell of Maine to pass legislation, and the trench warfare of Senator Byrd of Virginia to defend the jobs and interests of miners. In the House of Representatives, Congressman Dingell fought to limit the Bill's effects on the Detroit automobile industry, while Congressman Waxman from California was equally dogged in his efforts to strengthen the Bill's provisions in order to tackle the problem of smog and air pollution in his home state. It took ten years of bitterly fought political debates before the Clean Air Act of 1990 was passed. Interestingly enough, in a scenario with which European legislators will be entirely familiar, the real haggling over the final stages of the Clean Air Act of 1990 was done in closed sessions and out of the public eye.

To a much greater extent than in Britain, a political party in America is less important than the furtherance of state and regional interests. Congressmen Dingell and Waxman fought their corners from within the same party, but it appears that there were times when you would not have known it. In Britain, by contrast, there are times when the party system is so tightly run that debate and discussion is excluded altogether. The Environment Act of 1995 was by no means as politically contentious as the American Clean Air Act of 1990, and political disputes took place only at the margins or on specific issues. There was cross-party support, for example, for the idea of setting up the Environment Agency and the Scottish Environment Protection Agency. But the way that committees are run in the United Kingdom Parliament requires the governing party to concede as few amendments to the Bill as possible, and to win all or nearly all of the committee votes. Several of the backbenchers on the government side in the committee stage of the Environment Bill were sufficiently disciplined about the timetable against which the Bill was being passed to make no interventions at all. It would be hard to imagine this happening in the American House of Representatives, and quite impossible for it to occur in the Senate.

But the American founding fathers might have been less familiar with the nature and extent of professional lobbying which now takes place within the American political system, and the amount of money involved. There are about 93,000 lobbyists and those who support them in Washington, D.C., 60,000 lawyers (many of whom are also lobbyists) and 15,000 journalists. One hundred and forty foreign embassies and the representative offices of countless other organisations from across America clamour for access and influence.

One lobbyist for a major corporation, addressing a seminar in February 1997,[25] reported receiving calls from federal politicians the day after the last elections, canvassing funds for the next one. He had apparently received requests from politicians for funds amounting to $250,000 in the previous month. His objective was "access enhancing", and for favourably disposed politicians from states containing his firm's major facilities, he would agree to "max out", or to pay the maximum allowable contributions. Although making financial contributions was only a part of his way of working, he advised on the spending of $250,000 in Political Action Campaign funds, $50,000 in personal contributions to individuals' campaigns, and more in "soft money" for more generally defined political purposes. All this for one company. Another lobbyist at the state legislature in Oregon, speaking in March 1997, remarked that he had probably given money to "most if not all" of the current legislators in that body on behalf of one or other of his clients.[26]

It is clear that once "big money" becomes a feature of political campaigns, it is exceedingly difficult to change the system. It is an unusual politician who wants to be the first to campaign without spending huge amounts on television advertising which may be available to his opponent, and an unusual corporation that wants to be the first of a number of competitors to break the cycle and to refuse to pay for access.

The fact that environmental laws in the United States are not a polluters' charter is evidence of strong countervailing influences at work in the political system. Legislation has been passed in both America and Britain to try to achieve clean air, clean water, to clean up contaminated land, to reduce waste and promote recycling, to control industrial emissions and to force the development of new technology and cleaner means of production. If money was the only thing that mattered, industrial concerns could have been expected to have used more of it, with greater success, to deny the progress that has been achieved in all of these areas.

One of the balances to the power of corporate money in the American political system is clearly the size and strength of environmental "non-governmental organisations" or NGOs. These have proliferated in numbers and grown in membership numbers and financial resources since the early 1970s and, as has been seen, they now play a direct and active role in American elections. The Natural Resources Defense Council, for example, a leading legal challenger in support of the environment to many administrative actions and inactions, grew from 18,000 members in 1975 to 175,000 members in 1995.[27] But the NRDC's revenues have grown even faster, from $1,810,436 in 1975 to $25,766,951 in 1995.[28]

CITIZENS IN ACTION

Active citizens' groups also have an enormous impact on the resolution of local issues, but, as in Britain, the challenge is to retain voter interest in the political process, and a sense that votes cast make a difference. The campaigning 104th Congress of 1994 was elected by only 27 per cent of the electorate,[29] a low turn-out that broke some records. A number of strategies are being attempted to raise the voting figures, such as Oregon's "vote by mail" system, thought by its proponents to provide a better match with current life-styles, such as households with two working parents.[30]

Ralph Nader, a celebrated consumer activist and environmentalist included on the 1996 Presidential ballot by a number of minor state parties, calls for "active citizen muscle" to combat what he sees as a drift of power into the hands of corporations.[31] The politically active but non-partisan League of Women Voters arrives at a similar conclusion by a less combative route. It issues a welter of publications explaining how best to understand and influence the legislative process, down to detailed advice on the best and most effective way to write letters to legislators.

In Colorado, the League of Women Voters' pamphlets include the office and home telephone numbers of all members of the state Senate and House of Representatives.[32] The League has now been co-opted to the Monitoring Council set up by the state governor in 1987 to oversee the clean up at the former nuclear weapons plant at Rocky Flats near Denver.[33] The way in which it uses existing legislation in the performance of this task is a measure of how far America has gone to open its legislative and decision-making processes to citizens active enough to take the opportunities given them to participate.

The National Environmental Policy Act, "NEPA", requires that for all federal actions that significantly affect the environment an environmental assessment or environmental impact assessment should be prepared. In both cases, opportunities arise for public comment. At Rocky Flats four environmental assessments and a site-wide environmental impact statement have provided a total of five such opportunities.

The Comprehensive Environmental Response, Compensation and Liability Act, also "CERCLA" or "Superfund" regulates clean-up of some of the worst hazardous sites. It provides for regular information to be given to the public and public comment to be sought. At Rocky Flats there are four information repositories, and even a public Reading Room. Importantly, CERCLA also allows for qualifying citizen groups to receive technical assistance grants to hire technical advisors to help evaluate technical information about a site's clean-up.[34] Such grants have been awarded at Rocky Flats to the Rocky Flats Cleanup Commission.

The Resource Conservation and Recovery Act, "RCRA", a further statute governing clean-up at the site, provides for public participation during the permitting process, when the permit is modified and when a final plan is amended.

The Federal Facilities Compliance Act, "FFCA", requires an inventory of federal facilities' wastes with provision for public comment on the final site treatment plan. And the Freedom of Information Act, "FOIA", makes extensive categories of information open to formal requests.

Of course, some of this machinery is open to citizens in Britain, but in most cases America has gone further to ensure that the workings of government are kept open by appropriate statutory measures. It is true that environmental impact assessments are now required by legislation implementing the European Directive to that effect of 1985.[35] The European Community is experimenting with making information on legislation implementing this Directive available on CD-Roms and on the Internet.[36] The Community also passed a short Directive in 1990 on freedom of access to information on the environment.[37] But no equivalent exists in Britain of the technical assistance grants given to qualifying citizen groups under American Superfund legislation: the complaint is most often heard in complex planning inquiries in Britain, where objectors to proposed developments can be "outgunned" not only in terms of time and resources but also in their ability to conduct thorough examination of technical information and arguments.

The Environmental Information Regulations[38] of 1992 again give effect in Britain to an equivalent European Community directive ensuring access to environmental information on request. While some environmental groups and a few solicitors' firms have become adept at using these regulations to telling effect, for several years no firm policy was made by government as to whether they should even apply to so basic a category of sources as privately owned utilities performing public functions, such as supplying water or electricity.[39] The government has said that this point may be addressed in its proposed freedom of information legislation. Many British environmental statutes provide for registers of public information[40] and place requirements on applicant for permits and licences to advertise the fact, with opportunities for public comment.[41] Freedom of information legislation is now in prospect for the United Kingdom, and the country is a signatory to an important new international convention on public access to information about the environment,[42] so it may be that British habits of secrecy are at last in decline.

APPOINTMENTS AND ENFORCEMENT

Just as the influence of politics is decisive in the way that environmental laws are passed, it is politicians who generally make the appointments of those who head the principal agencies charged with carrying out the laws. These appointees can make a critical difference to the whole outlook and policy of their agencies within a very short time of their being appointed. They can in many cases set the tone for the whole way in which environmental laws are enforced.

President Nixon appointed William D. Ruckelshaus as the first administrator of the Environmental Protection Agency in America. Ruckelshaus
promptly filed violation notices on three cities, Atlanta, Cleveland and
Detroit, for failing to build wastewater treatment plant.[43] Shortly afterwards
he and the Agency took action against the Jones and Laughlin Steel
Company and other major industrial concerns. President Reagan in 1981
appointed Anne Gorsuch as Administrator of the EPA. She made huge cuts
in the personnel and budget at the agency, and was seen as entirely hostile to
its previously vigorous enforcement policy.[44] Limited enforcement of the
Superfund legislation, and Gorsuch's arguments with Congress over her
refusal to hand over to the legislature internal documents relating to it, were
central to her resignation in March 1983. William Ruckelshaus was recalled
to be Administrator of the Agency, and his return was compared by one of
its senior staffers to the liberation of Paris.[45]

When the National Rivers Authority was set up in Britain by the Water
Act of 1989 under the chairmanship of Lord Crickhowell, a former Secretary
of State for Wales, one of its earliest actions was to prosecute Shell for a
major oil spill in the River Mersey, a case which led to a fine of £1 million on
the company. The effect was immediate. All companies were on notice from
that point that the Authority was capable of taking them on, and that under
its current leadership it might do so if their polluting activities were to war-
rant it. All appointments to positions of leadership of environmental regulatory agencies are a serious responsibility for the politicians who make them,
as the early signals sent about the agencies' likely enforcement policy are
extremely important.

DELEGATION AND DEVOLUTION

A significant debate in environmental law in America concerns the possible
delegation to the states from the federal government of responsibility for
enforcement of a number of environmental law programmes. The trend is
certainly towards wide delegation to the states, and there is even some argument about whether any Federal responsibility should be retained. Some academic commentators have gone so far as to call for the virtual abolition of
the Environmental Protection Agency as a costly, bureaucratic and unnecessary federal agency producing mountains of appallingly complex rules.[46] On
the other hand, those in the Environmental Crimes Unit of the Department
of Justice,[47] and in the Office of Criminal Enforcement at the Environmental
Protection Agency[48] can name states which will tend not to enforce environmental laws against particular corporations.

If the experience of the Environmental Protection Agency and the Department of Justice is correct, it implies support for retention of a significant Federal capability to enforce environmental laws where states will not. As Britain moves towards a more devolved and decentralised system of government, with more power going to the regions, assemblies in Wales and Northern Ireland and a Parliament in Scotland, it may encounter and need to resolve similar debates, and to seek the balance between excessive central control and the need for consistency and fairness in the enforcement and application of environmental laws.

One of the arguments for having an office of the Director for Public Prosecutions in England and Wales, as the forerunner of the existing Crown Prosecution Service, was always that the DPP would be able to apply a nationally consistent prosecution policy, including where local interests were at stake. The Environment Agency for England and Wales, set up by the Environment Act 1995, is committed to a strong regional structure, with local representation and participation in its advisory committees and decision-making. But at the same time it needs a credible and coherent enforcement and prosecution policy, applied evenly in Cornwall and Carlisle.

Where confrontation and polarisation have reached American levels, no trust remains that enforcement of the law can be left to the other side. Richard Cohen attributes much of the difference in length between the 1970 Clean Air Act in America (47 pages) and the 1990 Clean Air Act (314 pages) to Congressional mistrust at leaving enforcement discretion to agencies. The later legislation was filled with detailed and prescriptive formulae and enforcement mandates that had not been considered necessary before.

CONCLUSIONS

Senator Dole lost the Presidential elections in 1996, but the American electorate returned another Republican majority in Congress, albeit one with a smaller majority. Some Republicans such as Senator McCain of Arizona and Representative Sherwood Boehlert of New York called for revised party policies on the environment. Some of their colleagues, such as the Congressional delegation from Alaska, disagreed. The debate continues. But it is clear from the results of the Congressional elections of 1996 that something of the American public's firmly expressed distaste for big government remained, alongside that public's decisive rejection of all out attacks on environmental protection.

Perhaps this suggests that in America there is every chance that programmes of enforcement of environmental laws that can be shown to have worked, and worked well, will continue to be funded and supported. But also that the Federal and state agencies charged with enforcing environmental laws must vigorously explore and try to make sense of the various initiatives for targeting their enforcement effort more precisely towards perceived "bad actors", and allowing the genuinely compliant businesses and those making real efforts to reduce pollution and waste some tangible incentives for their good behaviour.

There will always be issues—it is suggested that global warming is one of them—where it is sensible to adopt the "precautionary principle". We would do well to take action before scientific proof is entirely conclusive where the consequences of failure to do so may be catastrophic, and where action delayed until the science is conclusive will come far too late.

But recent American political experience also suggests that where environmental laws and regulations go beyond what is necessary to protect the environment, there is a "margin" of political risk. A means is provided to opponents of all environmental regulations to attack laws as unnecessary, too burdensome and too expensive. The attacks may go much further than the "margin" of what is strictly unnecessary, and seek to remove what is really essential to environmental protection. The proposal to repeal America's Clean Air Act is one such example.

The challenge to both environmentalists and those in government concerned with environmental protection is to show either that the "precautionary principle" should be applied, or that the protection conferred by particular laws is indeed necessary. The Democratic party in America realised this in 1996, and President Clinton's strong defence of environmental laws came with a promise of "reinvented" and more streamlined regulations. For environmentalists, in the long term, it may be worthwhile considering how to answer Senator Dole's question about whether it is too much to ask that we fulfil responsibilities to human health, safety and the environment in ways which minimise costs to society.

REFERENCES

1. Examples of the sceptical genre exist on both sides of the Atlantic. Robert Hahn, in "Towards a New Environmental Paradigm", an essay in book called *Environmental Gore* (Pacific Research Institute for Public Policy, San Francisco, Cal., 1994) criticising Al Gore's *Earth in the Balance*, declared: "global warming is the ultimate example of media alarmism". For a British example of the genre, see the journalist, Matt Ridley (*Daily Telegraph*, 1 Dec. 1997): "global warming is one big fib".

    For me, the question whether there was any truth in the suggestion that global warming brought about by human activity was observable and under way was resolved by a visit to the Director of the Global Environment

Monitoring Service at the United Nations Environment Programme in Nairobi, Kenya in 1991. The Director confirmed that a measurable warming was in fact already under way, and the real debate was about how much further it would go.

2. For a commentary on the official U.S. government view of this evidence, see e.g. Ch. 12 of *Environmental Quality*, the 25th Anniversary Report of the Council on Environmental Quality, Executive Office of the President (the CEQ's report for the years 1994 and 1995).

3. In *Earth in the Balance—Forging a New Common Purpose* (Earthscan, London,1992), Senator Al Gore wrote (at 365):

   "as we send increasing quantities of greenhouse gases into the atmosphere, it will become more and more difficult to believe that the only consequence is the well-understood phenomenon of warming. 'Avalanches' of change in climate patterns are certain to occur and persist if we keep making this sandpile steeper and larger; moreover, the combination of several significant changes occurring almost simultaneously increases the risk of catastrophe significantly."

   Newspapers on 3 Dec. 1997 reported Vice President Gore as being prepared "to walk away" from a global climate change agreement at Kyoto if it was unsatisfactory to America (see e.g. *Financial Times* report, "Climate change talks hit stumbling block", Wednesday, 3 Dec. 1997, 6).

   That said, such comparisons are a bit of a cheap shot. All politicians answer to their constituencies, and ought not to be criticised for doing so in a book recommending more and not less public participation in environmental laws. And it is very hard to read *Earth in the Balance* without at the very least being convinced that these are Al Gore's deeply held personal beliefs.

4. First reactions of American legislators to the news of the Treaty were anything but encouraging. Senator Chuck Hagel (Rep. Nebraska) declared "There is no way, if the President signs this, that the vote in the Senate will even be close. We will kill this bill" (*Daily Telegraph*, 12 Dec. 1997). Senator John Kerry (Dem. Massachusetts) added "What we have here is not ratifiable" (*The Times,* 12 Dec. 1997).

5. Kyoto Protocol to the United Nations Framework Convention on Climate Change, Conference of the Parties, Third Session, Kyoto, 1–10 Dec. 1997—see e.g. Art. 24 on entry into force.

6. "Climate Trends": Ch. 12, *Environmental Quality*, 25th Anniversary Report, The Council on Environmental Quality, n. 2 above, 211.

7. Reprinted in *Wild Oregon*, Mar. 1996, Vol 23, No 2, and doubtless elsewhere. To an outsider, one of the very best things about the Republican Contract with America was the names of the bills that were promised for introduction within 100 days. They were:
   1. The Fiscal Responsibility Act
   2. The Taking Back Our Streets Act
   3. The Personal Responsibility Act

4. The Family Reinforcement Act
5. The American Dream Restoration Act
6. The National Security Restoration Act
7. The Senior Citizens Fairness Act
8. The Job Creation and Hope Enhancement Act
9. The Common Sense Legal Reform Act
10. The Citizen Legislature Act

At this point, in the matter of punchy titles to its laws, the Parliament of the United Kingdom and Northern Ireland must concede game, set and match to the United States Congress.

8. H.R. 925.
9. H.R. 1022.
10. H.R. 2099, the Fiscal 1996 Veterans Administration—Housing & Urban Development (VA-HUD)—Independent Agencies Appropriations Bill.
11. H.R. 961.
12. H.R. 260.
13. H.R. 889 (the Defense Supplementary Appropriations/Rescissions Bill). Fierce arguments continued throughout 1998 over a variety of Congressional proposals and counter proposals on the "re-authorisation" of the Endangered Species Act.
14. Jessica Mathews, "Prognosis for the Environment", *Washington Post*, 13 Jan. 1997.
15. *Ibid.*
16. League of Conservation Voters, Message from the President, Deb Callahan, Feb. 1996.
17. *Amicus Journal*, Winter 1997, Message from the Director.
18. Jessica Mathews, "Earth First at the Polls", *Washington Post*, 11 Nov. 1997.
19. "Environmentalists put some in Congress on extinct list", *San Antonio Express-News*, 10 Nov. 1996.
20. *Ibid.*
21. "Locked in the Cabinet", Washington Diary by Robert B. Reich, former Secretary of Labor, *New Yorker*, 21 Apr. 1997, referring to a conversation with President Clinton at Galesburg, Ill., 10 Jan. 1995.
22. *Oregonian*, Tuesday, 17 Sept. 1996.
23. *Time Magazine* extra, "The Election of 1996", Fall 1996.
24. "More G.O.P. Environmental Wars", *New York Times*, 26 May 1997.
25. Harkness Fellowships seminar in American politics, Brookings Institute, Washington, D.C. 5–7 Feb. 1997.
26. Visit to Oregon State Capitol, Salem, Ore., 19 Mar. 1997.
27. *Natural Resources Defense Council Annual Report 1995* (NRDC, Washington, D.C., 1995).
28. *Ibid.*
29. Meeting with Anne Richardson, office of Congresswoman Elizabeth Furse, Portland, Ore., 24 Sept. 1996.

30. Meeting with Oregon Secretary of State Phil Keisling, Salem, Ore., 19 Mar. 1997.
31. See e.g. "Excerpts from Ralph Nader's speech to the California Greens", 12 June 1996.
32. "Send A Message", *1997 Colorado Directory of National & State Officials* (League of Women Voters, Denver, Colo., 1997).
33. League of Women Voters of Colorado Education Fund, *Your Role at Rocky Flats—A Guide to Public Participation Opportunities at Rocky Flats Environmental Technology Site* (League of Women Voters of Colorado, Denver, Colo., 1997)
34. See the Comprehensive Environmental Response, Compensation and Liability Act of 1990, "CERCLA", ("Superfund"), sect. 9617.
35. Council Dir. 85/337/EEC of 27 June 1985 on the assessment of the effects of certain public and private projects on the environment [1985] O.J. L175/40.
36. For a European Community trial run at publishing the text, commentary and cases on environmental legislation on-line, see the Internet website concerning the Environmental Impact Assessment Dir.: http://www-penelope.et.ic.ac.uk
37. Council Dir. 90/313/EEC of 7 June 1990 on the freedom of access to information on the environment [1990] O.J. L158/56.
38. S.I. 1992/3240, (HMSO, London, 1992).
39. The case of *Griffin* v. *South West Water Services Ltd* [1995] IRLR 15 established that a privately owned company could nevertheless carry out a public service "under the control of the state" for purposes of E.C. legislation.
40. See Environmental Agency for England and Wales, *A Guide to Information Available to the Public* (Environment Agency, Bristol, 1996).
41. See e.g. s. 64 of the Environmental Protection Act 1990; or ss. 189–191 of the Water Resources Act 1991.
42. United Nations Economic and Social Council, *Convention on Access to Information, Public Participation in Decision-Making and Access to Justice in Environmental Matters* (UNECE, Geneva, 1 Apr. 1998), signed at Aarhus, Denmark, 23 June 1998.
43. Phyllis Myers, "The Road We've Travelled", *EPA Journal,* Sept./Oct. 1990, special edn.: "EPA: The First Twenty Years".
44. See e.g. Joel A. Mintz, *Enforcement at the EPA* (Univ. of Texas Press, Austin, Tex., 1995), ch. 4: "Destruction, Confusion, Confrontation and Disarray— EPA Enforcement and Congressional Oversight in the Gorsuch Era".
45. N. 43 above.
46. David Schoenbrod, Professor of Law, New York Law School, in "Why States, Not EPA, should set Pollution Standards", Regulation, 1996, No.4 of *The Cato Review of Business and Government.*
47. Meeting with Nancy Firestone, Deputy Assistant Attorney General, Environment and Natural Resources Div., U.S. Department of Justice, 3 Feb. 1997.
48. Meeting with Earl Devaney, Director, Office of Criminal Enforcement, U.S. Environmental Protection Agency, 4 Feb. 1997.

3

The Consent of the Governed I—Making the Laws

"Governments are instituted among Men, deriving their just Powers from the Consent of the Governed, that whenever any form of government becomes destructive of these Ends, it is the Right of the People to alter or abolish it . . . ".

American Declaration of Independence, 4 July 1776

"The principles of a free constitution are irrevocably lost, when the legislative power is nominated by the executive."

Edward Gibbon, The History of the Decline and Fall of the Roman Empire

THE LAWMAKING PROCESS IN THE UNITED KINGDOM

In 1777 Thomas Jefferson sat down to re-write most of the laws of Virginia, including the whole body of criminal laws inherited from the British legislature. He was not overly impressed by what he found, writing that:[1]

"I thought it would be useful, also in all new draughts, to reform the style of the later British statutes, and of our own acts of Assembly; which from their verbosity, their endless tautologies, their involutions of case within case, and parenthesis within parenthesis, and their multiplied efforts at certainty, by *saids* and *aforesaids*, by *ors* and *ands*, and to make them more plain, are really rendered more perplexed and incomprehensible, not only to common readers, but to the lawyers themselves."

It would be interesting, and perhaps uncomfortable, to know what Jefferson would have made of modern legislative drafting on either side of the Atlantic. There are three main ways in which environmental and other laws are presently made for the United Kingdom. First, the Westminster Parliament passes primary legislation. Secondly, officials in government departments draft, and ministers sign, Statutory Instruments or secondary legislation. Thirdly, officials, and at a later stage, ministers negotiate and agree European Directives and Regulations. European Regulations are automatically law in all Member States of the European Community. Directives are required to be transposed into national law. In each case it is possible to see a widening gap between the circle of people making the laws and the knowledge and involvement of the public.

The party system in the Parliament at Westminster is dominant. There are only ever a tiny number of Members of Parliament elected as independents. Elections to the House of Commons reflect the tight control of the political process exercised by the parties. The British electorate appears to have grown used to voting for a party candidate rather than one who is necessarily from their area or especially representative of their way of life. Elections are decided on voters' overall views of the public programmes and manifestos, often on the basis of only two or three fundamental questions—"will I be better off with this party?", "am I tired of that party?" and so on. General election campaigns in Britain can take as little as six weeks, and then the government changes for up to five years.

Once in office, the winning party generally gives primacy in its legislative programme to the policies from its election manifesto. Beyond that it has wide latitude to determine its legislative priorities, as long as it can maintain the internal party discipline necessary to win all the votes in the House of Commons, including, where necessary, confidence votes.

There has traditionally been relatively little scope under the Westminster system of government for the electorate to express a clear view on one individual issue at a time, unless it is a major issue in the election manifestos on which the main parties disagree. The system works so as to require the inclusion of a large number of items in party manifestos, but the electorate cannot pick some and reject others.

Environmental protection is by no means as politically charged an idea in Britain as it is in America. An example of this is the joint declaration in support of the importance of countryside protection signed in 1996 by the leaders of all three main parties in Britain.[2] Where they want something done about the environment, the British have tended to involve themselves in an issue-specific environmental organisation. Membership numbers of environmental organisations in Britain tell part of this story. The following is a table showing membership of selected voluntary environmental organisations in 1971, 1981, 1990 and 1995:[3]

Table 3.1 Membership numbers: thousand

	1971	1981	1990	1995
National Trust	278	1,046	2,032	2,293
National Trust for Scotland	37	110	218	230
Royal Society for the Protection of Birds	98	441	844	890
Greenpeace UK	–	30	372	380
Civic Trust	214	–	222	301
Royal Society for Nature Conservation/ Wildlife Trusts	64	142	250	260
World Wide Fund for Nature	12	60	247	219
Friends of the Earth	1	18	110	110
Ramblers Association	22	37	81	109
Woodland Trust	–	20	66	150
Council for the Preservation of Rural England	21	29	44	45

There are more members of the National Trust (supporting the preservation of historic houses, countryside and coastline) in Britain than there are members of all political parties combined.

In addition to legislation based on the manifesto, governments also respond to what they perceive as a widely held public feeling that "something must be done" about an issue, sometimes with a rushed legislative effort that is later found to be hard to apply. Otherwise the government's legislative programme is filled out with the successful departmental "bids" for Bills. There are always many more "bids" than there is Parliamentary time to deal with them, and pressure to include more topics in Bills once time is secured for them is intense. New legislation is one marker of a department's place in the Whitehall pecking order. More is generally regarded as better.

Since May 1997, referendums have been held in Scotland and Wales about the devolution of power to their assemblies. A referendum was held in London in May 1998 about the election of a mayor, and a majority of the low turn out of voters who participated favoured the idea. Northern Ireland held a simultaneous referendum with the Republic of Ireland in May 1998 to vote on the outcome of the peace process there. And the whole United Kingdom has been promised a referendum if a decision is made to recommend joining a single European currency. This represents a significant increase in efforts to seek a mandate for fundamental change on "issue-specific" proposals. But Britain still lacks the means for the public to choose, for example, one party's environmental policies and another party's economic management.

THE AMERICAN BALLOT MEASURE PROCESS

In the United States, by contrast, voters in some states, particularly in the West, have the mechanism of the ballot measure. By this means, once a given number of voters in a particular state express a wish for it by signing a petition, a measure must be put on the ballot for the next election and, if it is passed, it becomes the law of that state. Opinions vary as to how worthwhile this procedure is. Some people complain that wealthy individuals are always in a position to pay enough money to ensure that their pet projects are placed on the ballot measure, by paying for campaigns to collect the necessary signatures. Others see the ballot measure process as an essential freedom. Certainly it is easier to finance the inclusion of a measure on a state ballot than to ensure that a majority of voters support it.

One example of such an initiative was Ballot Measure 38 on the 1996 Oregon ballot, which concerned a proposal to ban livestock grazing alongside many streams, thereby limiting "non-point source" pollution and temperature pollution and erosion, to the benefit of spawning fish. Non-point source pollution is pollution from a variety of different sources such as cattle or sheep in fields along a river, rather than one clearly identifiable "point" source, such as a factory. In the run up to the election the voters had all the arguments rehearsed by the protagonists at every opportunity through the media and direct campaigning. The Oregon Cattleman's Association attorney embarked on a "campaign" sweep through Eastern Oregon drumming up opposition to the measure.[4] The General Counsel for the Oregon Farm Bureau manned the Farm Bureau's stand at the Salem State Fair in August 1996, distributing literature hostile to the ballot measure.[5] The backers of the measure at the Oregon Natural Desert Association in Bend in Eastern Oregon were equally energetic.[6] All were campaigning hard. In the process of that campaign, it was inevitable that the public should become better informed about the subject.

The formal voter's pamphlet sent to every Oregon voter contained the full text of the ballot measure.[7] It set out an explanatory statement about its effect, required by Oregon law to provide an impartial explanation of the measure, with representatives from each side of the debate. There were printed messages and arguments from those supporting the measure (such as fishing associations and Indian tribes) and those opposing it (such as farmers' organisations). Having considered all this in greater or lesser depth, Oregonians voted "no" on Measure 38. Oregon's Democratic Governor, John Kitzhaber, opposed the passage of Measure 38, which was also hampered by the arrest, shortly before the vote, of one of its sponsors on charges of shooting cows which had strayed onto his land. Nevertheless, the debates on the Measure shifted the centre of the argument, and lent force to Governor Kitzhaber's effort to achieve voluntary agreement by farmers to seek ways to limit "non-point source" pollution from cattle in streams. The Measure was therefore a politically significant event though it was not passed by the voters.

In some ways, the voter in the ballot measure process was treated almost as a juror, and faced with the competing arguments of sets of opposing advocates. By means of this process the Oregon voter could express a decided opinion about one issue, independently of his or her political views on the programmes of the two main political parties. Oregon supported the Democratic candidate for President in the 1996 election, but returned a Republican as Senator in the race held at the same time.

Another example of the debates on an environmental ballot measure proposal concerned Oregon's Bottle Bill. Ballot Measure 37 on the November 1996 ballot[8] would have extended Oregon's recycling laws to containers of non-carbonated drinks and other categories of drink containers. In a public debate,[9] a proposer from the Oregon State Public Interest Research Group, "OSPIRG", argued that 100 million containers a year were sent to litter or landfill, and it was time to extend the reach of the 1971 Oregon Bottle Bill, which had led to an 80 per cent reduction of litter on roads. His opponent, representing "Oregonians Against Measure 37" argued that recycling was already growing rapidly, that the measure would result in anomalies and muddle, and that many of the original legislators who had advocated and passed the original Bottle Bill were against the measure. So, incidentally, were many of the firms and grocery retailers who supported the organisation "Oregonians Against Measure 37".

The debate was one way of drawing out a single issue on which Oregonian voters would ultimately have their say. It was also a reminder that in America, perhaps too often, opinion on environmental issues tends to polarise, with little dialogue between the very articulate advocates of different views. There was probably a very good case for extending Oregon's Bottle Bill, but Measure 37 itself could have resulted in some difficult problems of interpretation. But both speakers in the debate seemed to find the idea of exploring any middle ground between them rather odd, and the prospects of their hammering out a compromise on the issue seemed remote.[10] In the event, the measure was not accepted by the electorate, and the Bottle Bill was not extended as had been proposed.

Oregon's Secretary of State, Phil Keisling, who is responsible for the state's election laws and processes, regards the ballot measure process as valuable, but in need of reform.[11] He favours rules revisions to raise the number of signatures required to propose a ballot measure, with lower numbers of signatures for measures which the state legislators could amend, and a higher number for measures which would alter the state's constitution. He has referred to the two volumes of ballot measures on the 1996 ballot as "like War and Peace", and he would also like to see a ban on the paid collection of signatures for ballot measures.

This ballot measure process may require amendment, but it forces both state and federal politicians to take a stance on issues that are ultimately chosen by the voters in their state. As one ballot measure protagonist put it,[12] the significance of the system in terms of educating the public and encouraging its participation in the political process was incalculable. He had earlier supported legislation in the state legislature on an environmental question, where the issues were known to perhaps half a dozen people: with the ballot measure that he was sponsoring, every newspaper in the state had an editorial on it.

America, of course, elects many more of its officials than Britain, such as its judges, sheriffs and school boards. This is one reason for the apparent responsiveness of officials to the demands and expectations of the public. Sometimes the difference can be seen in the simple matter of the provision of relevant papers.

For example, at a meeting of the Oregon Environmental Quality Commission, the board to which the state's Department of Environmental Quality reports, rule amendments and proposed Commission rulings, and appeal hearings on civil penalty assessments are held in public and on the record. Officials discuss and explain proposals to change the Department of Environmental Quality's rules in public meetings. The public is provided with copies of the Commission's agenda and all agenda items on a large table outside the room in which the meeting takes place.[13]

This may be contrasted with the experience of a member of the public visiting the United Kingdom Parliament at Westminster. First he must queue to go through the elaborate security procedures, a necessary chore in most Western democracies. Then he will be directed by superior Palace of Westminster staff in white tie and tails, with large metal coats of arms round their necks, to wait in line at the side of corridors, before being admitted at last to the public gallery, an uncomfortable attic space with hard benches from which he can peer down at his legislators.[14]

A visitor to the Westminster Parliament during the second reading debate on a Bill, where speeches are made on the Bill's general policy, or at question time, when specific questions are put to ministers, may be able to follow pretty well what is being discussed. But those attending the committee hearings of a Bill, either in Commons committee or before the whole House of Lords, have to listen to Parliamentarians working through long lists of amendments by number. To follow this at all coherently, it is necessary to be able to refer to the latest text of the Bill and the day's "marshalled list" of amendments. But no one thinks to provide any of this material to visiting members of the public, although there are plenty of unused copies kept aside for Members of Parliament. The suspicion is strong, therefore, that the physical presence of some members of the public is tolerated at these proceedings, but nothing is done to make that experience meaningful. There seem to be low expectations on both sides.

Despite some Westminster carelessness about the real involvement of the public in the lawmaking process, and its echo in Whitehall attitudes, the lawmaking procedures at Westminster are sufficiently well understood that, when they feel the need to do so, members of the public can still become involved. A "Countryside March" in London on 1 March 1998 brought over a quarter of a million people to the streets of the capital, most of them protesting against a proposed ban on fox hunting contained in a "Private Member's Bill" sponsored by an individual Member of Parliament. Parties of constituents lobbying their MPs are a common sight. MPs' constituency surgeries, where they handle numerous problems and concerns for their constituents, are well attended, and MPs' mail bags full. The system could well use some reform of its procedures, but the passage of controversial legislation still attracts a lively public interest and participation in the margins. The same can hardly be said about the passage of secondary legislation.

SECONDARY LEGISLATION IN ENGLAND

Each year, the departments of government in Britain draft literally thousands of statutory instruments. Powers to make such regulations are taken with ever greater frequency in primary legislation.

Here is an example. Section 87 of the Environment Act 1995 is the regulation-making power in Part IV of the Act, which concerns air quality. It provides:

"(1) Regulations may make provision—
  (a) for, or in connection with implementing the [National Air Quality] strategy[15];
  (b) for, or in connection with, implementing-
    (i) obligations of the United Kingdom under the Community Treaties, or
    (ii) international obligations to which the United Kingdom is for the time being a party,
    so far as relating to the quality of air; or
  (c) otherwise with respect to the assessment or management of the quality of air."

There follow three pages of particular matters which such regulations may contain. It may be worth identifying the elements for which section 87 provides statutory authority, because it is fairly typical of many hundreds of such provisions in the statute book. Section 87(1)(a) means that once the Government has formulated a National Air Quality Strategy, as it is required to do, it has the means and legislative authority to put it into effect by making binding regulations. This will be backed up as necessary by the power to create and enforce criminal offences.

The effect of section 87(1)(b) is that wherever the United Kingdom, through the negotiations of its officials and the agreement of its ministers takes on or is subject to a European Community commitment, or signs an international treaty, relating to air quality, it has the means to deliver compliance by making binding regulations in national law.

Section 87(1)(c) is a catch-all, to ensure that there are no gaps in the legislative authority to make regulations "with respect to the assessment or management of the quality of air". Potentially, the management of air quality is a very wide area indeed. It is, on the whole, unlikely that a future Secretary of State would seek to close all factories in Britain, or ban all cars from its roads in regulations made under this provision. But it can be seen that in order to make effective regulations in an area of great concern to the public, large inroads are made on the freedom of individuals to do as they please. The tendency of such provisions is to shift power from Parliament to the executive, from public debate to bureaucratic discretion.

The total volume of statutory instruments is almost as remarkable as the number of powers which enable them to be made. For example, in the month of December 1997 19 statutory instruments were made covering housing, the environment and local government within the Department of the Environment, Transport and the Regions (only one of the main Whitehall departments, albeit one with a very wide range of responsibilities):

The Housing Grants Construction and Regeneration Act (Commencement No. 3) Order 1997

The Relocation Grants (Form of Application) Regulations 1997

The Local Government Act 1988 (Defined Activities) (Exemption) (Stevenage Borough Council and Three Rivers District Council) Order 1997

The Local Government Act 1988 (Defined Activities) (Exemption) (Easington District Council, Epping Forest District Council and London Borough of Merton) Order 1997

The Local Government Act 1988 (Defined Activities) (Exemption) (Bath and North East Somerset District Council) Order 1997

The Local Government Changes for England (Valuation Tribunals) Regulations 1997

The London Docklands Development Corporation (Planning Functions) Order 1997

The Long Residential Tenancies (Principal Forms) Regulations 1997

The Air Quality Regulations 1997

The Environment Act 1995 (Commencement No. 10) Order 1997

The Rent Assessment Committee (England and Wales) (Amendment) Regulations 1997

The Long Residential Tenancies (Supplemental Forms) Regulations 1997

The Non-Domestic Rating (Chargeable Amounts) (Amendment) (No. 2) Regulations 1997

The Smoke Control Areas (Exempted Fireplaces) Order 1997

The Town and Country Planning General (Amendment) Regulations 1997

The Non-Domestic Rating Contributions (England) (Amendment) Regulations 1997

The Secretary of State for the Environment, Transport and the Regions Order 1997

The Conservation (Natural Habitats, &c.) (Amendment) Regulations 1997

The Local Authority (Contracts) Regulations 1997.

For particularly significant regulations, Parliament may require that they be put before both Houses for debate by means of "affirmative resolution", whereby there must actually be a vote approving the regulations. Regulations subject to affirmative resolution cannot be amended, but must either be accepted in full, or rejected, which hardly ever happens. For the great majority of regulations "negative resolution" procedure is deemed sufficient. The regulations are "made", and take effect when signed by the required number of Ministers, but there is a period, usually 40 days, in which objection can be taken to them in either House of Parliament. Again, such objections are rare.[16]

It is unrealistic to suppose that individual MPs or peers have time to read, let alone dissect, the drifts of regulations being produced. Instead they have appointed a joint committee of both Houses to do the job for them. The Joint Committee on Statutory Instruments or "JCSI" performs the rather heroic task of trying to read almost everything. It scrutinises regulations to ensure that they do not go beyond the powers conferred by Parliament. It also casts a critical eye over the drafting, and its report can make uncomfortable reading within departments, where those who have been working on a set of regulations may find them reported to Parliament for "defective drafting". The Joint Committee can call for memoranda to explain and resolve ambiguities. In all this, the Committee performs a very necessary task. However unwelcome its advice may be to the draftsmen of regulations, all such scrutiny must result in more carefully drafted law.

What the Joint Committee on Statutory Instruments does not do, it not being within its terms of reference, is to pass any direct judgement on the political aspects of the regulations passing its doors. For all but the most contentious regulations, therefore, Parliament has stepped back from detailed political scrutiny and consideration of their impacts. Various other mechanisms have been attempted in an effort to replace political scrutiny, such as requiring drafts of regulations to be accompanied by a "compliance cost assessment" and by a "regulatory appraisal". Usually little more political attention is directed to these documents than it is to the regulations themselves.

It is also clear that no fully effective means of public consultation has been developed which directly informs members of the public of the laws coming their way, let alone canvassing their opinions on those laws. It is true that industry groups, trade associations, environmental groups and so on are quite often consulted on drafts and proposals for regulations in areas of direct concern to them. "Consultation" in these cases may consist of stuffing a few dozen envelopes with a draft, sending it to a list of interested organisations and having an official summarise the replies, calling for amendments where they seem to be necessary in response to major concerns. It is not a very precise science.

This "envelope stuffing" form of consultation was referred to in a debate in the House of Lords on the Beef Bones Regulations 1997,[17] a contentious measure banning the sale of beef on the bone, based on scientific advice of a remote risk of contracting New Variant Creuzfeldt Jakob Disease from any beef on the bone infected by Bovine Spongiform Encephalopathy ("BSE" or mad cow disease). Leaving aside the arguments, which were intense, over whether this ban was necessary or scientifically justifiable, the remarks of the debate's sponsor, Lord Willoughby de Broke, on the consultation procedures for the regulations are worth considering. He said:[18]

> "Your Lordships may be interested to learn that the consultees on the matter of the Beef Bones Regulations included some of the following: the British Fur Trade Association; the National Association of Tripe Processors; the European Documentation Centre; the Al Hasaniya Moroccan Womens' Centre; the Goat Advisory Bureau; the Association of Masters of Harriers and Beagles; the British Ceramics Confederation—are we at risk from eating off bone china? Perhaps we should be told. The consultees also included the West Indian Standing Conference and finally, and crucially, the Association of Circus Proprietors. But the list did not include any of the beef herd book societies or breeders associations, such as the Aberdeen Angus, Hereford or any of the other principal suppliers of animals to farms."

There is scarcely ever any kind of public meeting in Britain to explain or discuss draft regulations. Government offices in the regions, which could be used to issue bulletins or hold meetings about batches of forth-coming regulations (and European Directives in negotiation) are not used for that purpose. It is scarcely ever a part of a British civil servant's job to travel round his own country explaining the effect of forthcoming regula-tions to town meetings of citizens affected by them. Many American offi-cials would find that idea and responsibility much less surprising. Officials working for departments of individual American states talk with confi-dence about every corner of those states, because they tend to have been there. But some Whitehall officials might work for years without visiting areas of their country much beyond Greater London. But the same British civil servants may travel repeatedly to Brussels to negotiate regulations and directives of even wider effect with their counterparts from other Member States of the European Community. Some regulations are suffi-ciently obscure that members of the public would be highly unlikely to want to spend their days or evenings discussing them. But it is also true that many regulations are of huge impact on the daily lives and businesses of members of the public.

It would not be overwhelmingly difficult, or prohibitively expensive, to require that drafts in progress of all regulations be released on the Internet. One effect of such a step would be to break out of the circle of semi-professional consultees, the trade associations and groups, to which effective consultation is now confined. Government policies, however obscure, would be more widely publicised. The speed of consultation could be increased. Opportunities to head off problems, where the disadvantages had not been properly understood within Whitehall, would be enhanced. The problems identified, and thus perhaps averted, could be political or technical.

Placing draft regulations on the Internet would give opportunities for greatly enhanced international co-operation. For example, with only a very little organisation, it would be possible to arrange for comments from the relevant parts of environmental ministries and agencies in other European Community Member States and elsewhere, thus building the network of exchange of information which seems indispensable to negotiated European lawmaking.

There are already examples of major improvements in the ways that recently made law is made available to the public. House of Lords judgments that used only to be available days or weeks after being given while tran-scripts were made are now released within hours and generally available on the Internet. Commencement orders, which bring statutory provisions into force used to be notoriously difficult to keep up with, even for academics and law firms with extensive libraries. In theory, and occasionally in practice, it is possible for a department to bring provisions of primary legislation into force the day after a minister signs the commencement order. Now these orders, and other statutory instruments that have been made, are available on the Internet very rapidly. This is real progress.

But finding the means to tell the public about laws as soon as they are made, while welcome and necessary, is not the same as finding effective ways to involve the public in making the laws. If they are not actively involved in business groups and trade associations or other groups with the time and resources to keep them informed, the first that many people know about regulations is often when a local government or other official tells them that they can no longer do something, or that some activity is now compulsory or forbidden. Such a process can only add to the sense of powerlessness felt by the governed, who are told so little about the agendas of the governors.

Many regulations are made in order to put into effect European requirements. In these cases, public consultation of the sort suggested above would serve only a limited purpose, as the making of the regulations is itself a legal requirement. The time for useful consultation about the main principles (as opposed to the manner of their implementation) has already been and gone. It is absolutely standard for a provision in new legislation to contain procedures for various forms of consultation before a particular step is taken, but for exceptions to be provided where it is necessary to implement a Community or other international obligation. It is therefore worth considering the means of involving the public in the making of European laws.

NEGOTIATING EUROPEAN COMMUNITY LAW

European Community law is made partly by regulations, which are directly binding upon all Member States of the Community and citizens of the Union, but mainly by directives agreed upon by the Member States, which are then required to be "transposed" into national legislation in each State. Failure to transpose such directives within an agreed timetable, or to observe and apply them once transposed, is policed by the European Commission, which has the right to refer the Member State concerned to the European Court of Justice for a ruling that it is in breach of Community law.[19] This can now be accompanied by a fine levied against the Member State by the Court.[20] Such fines, which the Commission has promised to levy with increasing frequency, can be anything but a minor matter for Member States. In one recent case brought against Germany alleging continuing failure to implement the Drinking Water Directive, the Commission proposed a fine based upon a proportion of Germany's Gross Domestic Product.[21]

There are now rather more than 200 pieces of European Community legislation governing most aspects of the natural environment—water, waste, integrated pollution control, air pollution, radioactive substances (governed by the Euratom Treaty[22]), hazardous substances and so on. It is impossible to make national legislation without ensuring its consistency with European Community environmental law, and very often the purpose of national legislation is precisely to give effect in national law to a particular European Community directive.

The way in which European Community environmental laws are made therefore becomes critically important to the way in which they will ultimately be received and applied by the people to whom they are directed. With the increased application to environmental issues of "qualified majority voting" among Member States of the European Union on environmental issues[23] one country cannot veto a bargain struck by a majority of other member states. Legislation in the area is therefore made by international negotiation, bargaining and consensus. What emerges at the end of this process is a political compromise and not necessarily a coherent legal text, and this often seems to obscure the fact that it is actually legislation, just as the way that the amending treaties are worded can obscure the fact that they are actually constitutional amendments. The United Kingdom cannot on its own decide the legislative programme that the European Community will adopt. However, if it is to avoid being towed along by events and by the priorities of other Member States, it will have to put more effort into influencing the strategic planning of that programme, working with other Member States and with the European Commission.

There is also little doubt that the United Kingdom does itself few favours by failing, even after 25 years of membership of the European Community, to allocate the same resources to the negotiation of directives that it affords to the passage of national legislation. For all legislation before the Westminster Parliament, a "Bill team" is formed on which policy administrators and lawyers from the government department sponsoring the legislation work together. The Parliamentary branch of the sponsoring department handles the circulation each morning to each relevant official of all the amendments tabled for that day, and there is a well established system for drafting a government response and a speaking note for each amendment, cleared by those responsible for both the policy and the legal drafting. Any amendments tabled by the government or which it is likely to accept are cleared with Parliamentary Counsel, specialist legal draftsmen who seek to ensure internal consistency in the legislation.

Even today, no equivalent to this system is applied to European Community legislation. Directives, despite their legal status and effects, are routinely negotiated by policy officials with no United Kingdom government lawyers present, with far fewer resources and much less administrative back-up to ensure the prompt circulation of drafts and texts to other interested parties. This is no more sensible than excluding policy-makers from the making of policy, and inevitably results in a greater number of textual problems and misunderstandings than is actually necessary, even with a negotiated lawmaking process. Many opportunities to correct drafting mistakes, to clear up ambiguities, to resolve problems and to avoid impossible or unreasonable obligations are thrown away at the early stage of negotiations, when discussions take place at official level before Ministers are involved. Legal problems, and a variety of unexpected results in the wording, are routinely discovered when the directives come to be implemented into national law. With some environmental directives costing billions of pounds to implement, unforseen results and interpretations to a directive's text can be very expensive, and the comparative costs of providing proper resources for their negotiation are trivial.

For better law to emerge from this process, the different disciplines necessary to negotiate a directive would have to be better co-ordinated at an earlier stage, and have sufficient resources, in terms of time and manpower, to continue to co-ordinate their efforts throughout the passage of a directive's negotiation. There are precedents for this kind of administrative reform. Before the institution of the Fraud Investigation Group at the Director of Public Prosecutions' Department in England and Wales, and the Serious Fraud Office, cases of fraud used to be subject to separate investigation by a number of agencies, with very little co-ordination of their efforts. Inspectors appointed by the Department of Trade and Industry might investigate a company's affairs for a couple of years, and conclude that all was not well. Then a police investigation would begin to go over much of the same ground. Eventually this would conclude, and a great weight of documentary evidence would be delivered to lawyers at the Director of Public Prosecutions' Department, who would work slowly through what had already been done, and would frequently complain that gaps in the evidence required further investigation, or that much of the documentary evidence was less than relevant or useful (rather as lawyers implementing directives often complain that provisions do not make sense, are ambiguous or have a different meaning from that intended by the directive's negotiators). By the time this fraud investigation process had concluded, any resulting prosecution was years after the event of the fraud, and many of the perpetrators had opted for warmer climates and a comfortable retirement. One conclusion of the fraud investigation reforms in England and Wales, initiated by a report from the Appeal Court judge Lord Justice Roskill, was that all disciplines should work together. Lawyers, accountants and police began to co-ordinate their efforts from the outset of inquiries, and, not surprisingly, results began to improve. The same kind of process needs to happen with the negotiation of directives.

Directives start with a proposal from the European Commission. This is a public document, widely available and discussed in both national parliaments and generally. Often there are extensive efforts to achieve wide public consultation on proposals, including those made by the European Commission. Once the Presidency for the time being of the Community decides to take up and work on a proposal, however, the shutters come down on public involvement.

The proposal is given to the Working Group of the Council of Ministers. This is a meeting of national delegations from each Member State. Typically, those attending are the attachés from each country's Permanent Mission, or Embassy, to the European Community, with as many national officials or technical experts as the proposal merits and the Member State can afford to send. Council Working Group meetings are chaired by officials from the Member State holding the Presidency of the Community. They are also attended by officials from the Commission and by the Secretariat to the Council of Ministers. Delegates speak in their own language, and simultaneous translation is provided into all other Community languages. Meetings of this group can agree amendments to a proposal which may change it out of all recognition, but all such meetings are closed to the public. No public record is made of the proceedings of Council Working Groups, and even formal amendments to the text of a proposal are not made public.

When the Council Working Group has got as far as it can on negotiation of a draft directive, the text is referred to a mysterious committee known as COREPER. This is a meeting of senior officials from Member States' Permanent Missions to the Community. National experts are excluded from meetings of COREPER, while the diplomats negotiate further political compromises in order to try to achieve a text with which all Member States can live. Meetings of COREPER are not open to the public or reported.

From here, the draft directive moves to consideration in meetings of the Council of Ministers. Environment ministers from the Member States meet to consider draft environmental directives. They may, and often do, agree further political compromises to the text of the draft directive. By the time the draft reaches the Council of Ministers, points taken on it tend to be major political ones rather than drafting points. Meetings of the Council of Ministers are not open to the public.

Only then does the much-changed draft directive emerge from behind closed doors, with its referral to the European Parliament for its opinion. With the implementation of the Treaty of Amsterdam, a "co-decision" procedure will give the Parliament a role alongside the Council of Ministers in determining the final shape of a directive, with more brokering of deals, amendments and negotiations.

What is quite clear is that many of the critically important decisions about the shape of the law are made within the Council Working Groups, the COREPER committee and the Council of Ministers, none of which meets in public. Some of these mechanisms for achieving political compromise may be necessary to get 15 Member States with some very different national interests working together. It is remarkable that the system works at all, let alone that it should work well enough to have produced over 200 pieces of environmental legislation. This extraordinary procedure may be called many things, but fully democratic is surely not one of them. Somewhere, the balance seems to have been lost between political effectiveness and public accountability.

It will be interesting to see whether the United Nations Convention on Access to Information, Public Participation in Decision-Making and Access to Justice in Environmental Matters,[24] opened for signature at Aarhus in Denmark on 23 June 1998, will help to promote more open lawmaking within the European Community. The institutions of the Community are included as "public authorities" to which the provisions of the Convention will apply. Article 8 of the Convention commits parties to "strive to promote effective public participation at an appropriate stage, and while options are still open, during the preparation by public authorities of executive regulations and other generally applicable legally binding rules that may have a significant effect on the environment". If that is the case, should Council Working Groups, the meetings of COREPER and meetings of the Council of Ministers be taking place in future behind closed doors as they negotiate environmental directives?

The pace of negotiation of an individual directive varies largely, depending on the priorities of the country that holds the Presidency of the European Community at the time. Like the Speaker of the House of Representatives in America, the Presidency of the Community has a certain control over what is tabled for debate and how fast or slowly it progresses. When it is a priority of the Presidency the process can be hectic, with working groups of official delegations from each of the 15 Member States of the European Community meeting every week or so, discussing articles and texts with simultaneous translation from Finnish, Greek, Italian, English, French, German, Spanish, Dutch, Flemish, Swedish, Danish and Portuguese, and producing numerous amendments and textual proposals for discussion.

As has been noted, the European Parliament is formally consulted on the outcome of all the drafting sessions. But as everyone knows who has tried to influence or alter legislation of any sort, the later in the process an intervention is made, the harder it is to have any effect. For democracy to catch up with the way that these laws are made, there would have to be far more openness about all stages of a directive's passage, with negotiations in public and machinery for the release to the public of all drafts and proposed amendments. The Internet provides a system that would make this possible as and when the political will exists to bring it about. A website could be maintained for each directive under negotiation, with all formal amendments to a Commission proposal required to be posted on it. To make public consultation meaningful, national delegations would have to have the resources to take public comment and interventions into account. The way in which these laws are made today can only contribute to the sense of powerlessness and alienation felt by ordinary citizens from the lawmaking process, and perhaps also from the end result, as another set of concrete, and expensive, obligations emerges from the fog of a faraway negotiation.

BETTER LAW FROM EUROPE?

Written evidence from the Department of the Environment to the House of Lords European Communities Environment Sub-Committee given in 1991[25] conceded that negotiation and compromise within the European Community had in the past sometimes produced unclear legislation which was difficult to implement. This evidence concluded:

"It seems to us to be more important to have good legislation that works, rather than to strive constantly to add more to the statute book, without worrying too much about its quality and effectiveness."

In 1996 the European Commission, which drafts all legislative proposals for the European Union issued new legislative guidelines.[26] These contained a number of admirable objectives:

"Better law-making. That is the key slogan of this policy. . . . The aim is to ensure that legislative texts are of the proper quality and consistency, that the drafting process is open, planned and coordinated and that monitoring and evaluation are more thorough."[27]

The Commission's Memorandum cited the involvement of outsiders in the lawmaking process under the heading "Wider External Consultations".[28] It referred to the publication of the Commission's annual work programme in the Official Journal and the fact that the programme is debated in the European Parliament. It mentioned hearings and information seminars organised by the Commission, advice received from advisory committees or groups of independent national experts, and other notices in the Official Journal. That said, the Commission warned darkly that:

"Openness must not . . . create such an administrative burden that it is doomed to end in failure . . . the Commission's powers of initiative must be safeguarded."

The Memorandum went on to reaffirm the policy adopted by the Commission in 1992 "whereby the widest possible external consultation should be held on all new Commission initiatives", which of course includes all legislative proposals brought forward by the Commission.

This is all very well, but perhaps not many members of the public in Europe find time to read the Official Journal of the European Communities, or such scanty coverage as their national press provides of the proceedings of the European Parliament. The policy of wide consultation of external interests covers policy initiatives or proposals, but not negotiations in progress on directives, which is where the law is really being made.

THE NATIONAL PARLIAMENT AND EUROPEAN COMMUNITY LEGISLATION

There might be less of a separation between lawmakers and public if the national Parliament had stepped in to fill the information gap, or to debate and scrutinise European Community legislation with the care that is merited by the extent of its effects. But an inter-departmental review conducted within Government in 1993[29] expressed doubts on this score. It quoted a report by the Hansard Society Commission on the Legislative Process[30] and remarks by one of its members, Mr Vernon Bogdanor:

"Europe was seen as a discrete and separate issue which could be tacked onto Parliament's traditional business as a kind of optional extra. It was seen as something extraneous, as a separate and insulated political system whose points of contact with the UK Parliament would be very few. This attempt, to continue as before, as if Europe could remain a self-contained system, seems doomed to failure"

The same Report concluded that:

"Parliament and the Government must abandon the 'head in the sand' approach that is sadly characteristic of too many Members and adjust their response to European Community legislation so that consideration is given to it in ways that are more effective than those at present employed."

The 1993 inter-departmental review added:[31]

"We were told that as soon as an EC Commission proposal is tabled the Netherlands Parliament receives a brief which sets out the purpose of the Directive, the type of legislative changes and problems which might be expected. The whole Parliament has the opportunity to comment and thereby influence negotiating strategies. By contrast, in the UK Explanatory Memoranda (EMs) are placed in the Library of the House and scrutiny is delegated to the Parliamentary Scrutiny Committee and its various sub-committees. Only a minority of proposals are recommended for debate by the whole House and only in exceptional circumstances do the committees call ministers for examination."

These criticisms have force. The United Kingdom Parliament has failed so far to carry out a root and branch review of its procedures and to catch up with the way that Community legislation is actually made. As a result, its contribution to the review and improvement of Community legislation is far less than it could be. The House of Commons and the House of Lords each has a Scrutiny Committee to review European Community legislation. These committees are supplied with explanatory memoranda on proposed directives, and they can and do call in ministers, officials and outside witnesses to give opinions and answer questions about the implications of the proposals, although this is a very mild mannered inquisition compared to an American Congressional committee. Very importantly, successive governments have given an undertaking embodied in a resolution of the House of Commons (but which applies to both Houses) that no minister will give agreement to Community legislation in the European Council of Ministers, which is still the subject of scrutiny by the Committees.[32] This gives the opportunity to the Committees to conduct their inquiries and produce their reports.

The initial reports of the Scrutiny Committees, particularly those of the House of Lords, can be valuable, carefully considered, well researched and thoughtful responses, which carry much weight within government. Where a proposed directive is proceeding quite slowly, and there is time for government ministers and officials to read the quite lengthy reports that the Committees produce with enough care, they are of real benefit. Certainly they perform a useful purpose in providing better analysis of Community proposals for the wider public.

But where the system breaks down is in response to the fast moving timetable for negotiations of a directive that is being given priority—by definition the most important directives at that time. Each time a formal revision is made to a Commission proposal, a revised explanatory memorandum is sent to the Scrutiny Committees, but they receive no report and play no real part in the negotiations that take place in between, and so often it is here that the real essence of a directive is decided and political choices made. The stately pace of the Westminster Parliament does not correspond to the hectic pace of negotiations. And by and large, the officials negotiating directives are not looking over their shoulders and wondering how they will explain their actions to the Scrutiny Committees. At a debate in April 1998 by the House of Commons Scrutiny Committee on the proposed Water Framework Directive, only one Article of the Directive was specifically referred to. "Scrutiny" at that level of generality makes little political difference.

In some respects, the European Parliament is better placed to influence legislation by the treaty provisions which require it to be consulted at the end of the negotiation process, but before a directive is finally agreed. The

European Parliament has also been given effective powers to veto or amend more legislation, so that some account has to be taken of it by negotiators. That is probably a more influential role than giving an opinion on a proposal at the outset of a negotiating process, and then losing track of subsequent developments.

As the national Parliament leaves the field of European lawmaking, its place is taken by the British and European executive, the nomenklatura. Where laws were once debated by elected representatives, they are now proposed by an unelected Commission, and negotiated by unelected officials and finally agreed by elected ministers. The result is that laws are made not by debate, but by negotiation, and the national executive has made efforts to equip itself for its new legislative responsibilities. The Department of the Environment even issued to its civil servants copies of a manual on negotiation written by one of its staff who had served at the office of the UK Permanent Representative to the European Communities.[33]

The legislative procedures that are now required by the Maastricht Treaty,[34] which amended the Treaty of Rome, have to be read and re-read before they can be fully understood by those working with them every day. How many members of the public know the difference between the "co-operation procedure"[35] and the "co-decision" procedure? Consideration of these procedures makes it clear that democratic accountability and involvement in this legislative process, such as it is, comes from the enhanced powers and role of the European Parliament, together with such accountability as may or may not be provided by elected ministers attending meetings of the Council of Ministers. Arguments continue within national Parliaments as to whether the European Parliament can or will ever provide democratic oversight of European institutions, and a counterweight to the Council of Ministers, in the way that many national Parliaments and assemblies seek to do for their national and regional governments. A number of factors make it difficult for the European Parliament to assume that role. Its members are elected from huge constituencies of half a million voters or more. Its deliberations take place in another country, and are reported inadequately by a disinterested national press.

Explaining to members of the public what is going on, let alone seeking their meaningful participation in this lawmaking process, will require a major change in attitudes among ministers and officials in European Union Member States and at the European Commission. Raymond Barre, a former Prime Minister of France and European Commissioner, is reported to have remarked to the Aspen Institute that he never did understand why public opinion mattered. But such ineffable confidence in government by elites is surely only justified when elites get 100 per cent of the questions right 100 per cent of the time, for which the precedents are not extensive.

THE "COPY OUT" DEBATE

Once a directive has been agreed upon by the European Union, it becomes the responsibility of each Member State to give effect to it within the agreed timetable. It does this by implementing, or "transposing" the directive into its national law. The way in which this is done has been the subject of a fierce debate within Whitehall. This "copy out" debate sounds rather like obscure theology, but in fact says a great deal about the way that European legislation is made.

On one view, the directive being implemented should be re-written or translated as necessary, so that the English draftsman can assure himself that each element of the directive is properly reflected in the national law. This approach also seeks to satisfy the common law aim of enabling anyone to know what the law is, without recourse to the courts for interpretation.

The other view is that those implementing European legislation should simply "copy out" the main provisions of directives, and import them into English common law "as is", whatever they mean. This is in many cases a very practical approach. Increasingly the English courts have made clear their willingness to look beyond national legislation which is based on European directives, and to construe any ambiguities in it by reference to the original requirements of the directive. It is in any event a requirement of European Community law that implementing legislation should be construed in the light of the directive on which it is based. Those concerned about excessive burdens and "over-implementation" sometimes argue that it is better simply to rely on the original wording of the directives rather than trying to elaborate on them.[36] Others worry that seeking to interpret or translate directives only invites challenges by the European Commission under Article 169 of the Treaty of Rome or adverse rulings from the European Court of Justice if the directives' provisions are not read correctly.

Thus practicality struggles with principle. For directives with a high level of technical content, which may be well understood by the particular scientific community in each Member State, there may indeed be little to be gained from re-interpretation by national lawyers. But the "copy out" technique is also used in response to ambiguities in directives which those transposing them cannot resolve. Directives represent political compromises and trade-offs. The nature of negotiation is such that it is not possible to take every point, to go on insisting on clarity at every stage of every line, if that priority is not shared by sufficient of the other Member State delegations. Despite the best intentions of all concerned, it would be surprising if this system did not result in the inclusion of a fair number of ambiguities and unclear terms and phrases in directives. At this point the proponents of "copy out" appear at their least heroic. Their argument is that ambiguities, no matter what their implications, should be imported onto the national statute book. They say, in effect, "I do not know what it means, let us leave it to the courts to puzzle out". This is a counsel of despair. To an individual member of the public it says that, having had no part in the making of a law, he is not even to be told what his own government thinks that it means.

One part of the problem here can only be resolved at the European level. It consists of the difference between the way that European Community laws are made and the way that they are enforced. The laws—the directives and regulations—are also political agreements negotiated by national officials and ministers. But they are interpreted and enforced by the European Commission and the European Court of Justice as "black letter law", to be implemented and applied in every particular, every line and every detail. European Union law has not yet provided the Commission and the Court with the means to interpret directives and regulations, and the various implementing national legislation, in the light of the way that they are actually made.

CONCLUSIONS

In each of the lawmaking fora considered in this chapter, Westminster, Government departments and Brussels, lawmakers seem to be wrapped up in their own procedures, often to the exclusion of an uninformed public. It is ultimately destructive of the rule of law to allow the distance between lawmakers and the governed to grow and grow. There must be a revival of valid public consultation before laws are made. Public support, particularly for environmental laws, is absolutely necessary to their long term survival.

Whether or not Britain ever adopts a ballot measure process on the American model to permit the public to set some part of the agenda, there is much that can be done immediately to provide the public with better information and more opportunities to participate in the making of laws. Release of all draft regulations and details of directives in negotiation onto the Internet would be a first step in re-establishing contact between lawmakers and the governed.

Meanwhile, there are many ways in which the United Kingdom could achieve its objective of better drafted environmental laws in the European Community. It could start by re-examining the resources which it allocates to the negotiation of directives, and the strategy which it adopts for influencing the legislative programme within the Community. The influence of the Westminster Parliament on this process is much less than it could be, and the quality of its oversight and scrutiny once negotiations are under way is poor, mainly because it has failed to adapt to the way that directives are negotiated, and because individual Members of the House of Commons spend little time mastering the detail of directives.[37]

REFERENCES

1. Thomas Jefferson, *Autobiography*, in *The Life and Selected Writings of Thomas Jefferson* (ed. Adrienne Koch and William Peden, Random House, New York, 1993), 45.

2. On 9 Feb. 1996, prompted by the Council for the Protection of Rural England, John Major (then Conservative Prime Minister), Tony Blair (then Labour Leader of the Opposition) and Paddy Ashdown, (leader of the Liberal Democrats) jointly signed a letter to *The Times*. It echoed a similar letter from 1929 signed by their predecessors Stanley Baldwin, Ramsay MacDonald and David Lloyd George, and declared "During the next few months we shall differ on so many problems of public importance that we gladly take the opportunity of showing that on one subject we speak with a united voice namely, in advocating the protection of our countryside in its rich personality and character".

3. Table 16.4, 233, Department of the Environment, *The UK Environment* (HMSO, London, 1992) and Table 10.28, Department of the Environment, Transport and the Regions, *Digest of Environmental Statistics No. 19, 1997* (HMSO, London, 1997).

4. Telephone interview with Lindsey Slater, Counsel for the Oregon Cattleman's Association, Sept. 1996.

5. Meeting with Joseph H. Hobson Jr., General Counsel, Oregon Farm Bureau, Salem, Ore., 28 Aug. 1996.

6. Meeting with Bill Marlett, Oregon Natural Desert Association, Bend, Ore., October 1996.

7. State of Oregon Voter's Pamphlet, Vol. 1 of 2, State of Oregon General Election, 5 Nov. 1996, 115.

8. *Ibid.*, 107.

9. Debate on Measure 37—the Bottle Bill, Northwestern School of Law of Lewis and Clark College, Portland, Ore., 17 Sept. 1996.

10. Daniel Kemmis, former minority leader and speaker of the House of Representatives of Montana, and mayor of Missoula, Mont., has written an interesting account of ways in which to promote dialogue in communities rather than the "headlock" between opposing interests not listening to each other, which he sees as partly the result of American constitutional tradition: Daniel Kemmis, *Community and the Politics of Place* (University of Oklahoma Press, Norman, Okla., 1990.

11. Meeting with Oregon Secretary of State Phil Keisling, State Capitol, Salem, Ore., 19 Mar. 97.

12. Meeting with Bill Marlett, n. 6 above.

13. Meeting of Oregon Environmental Quality Commission, Portland, Ore., 10 Jan. 1996. An outline of the layout of this meeting is included in Ch. 7, Table 7.1.

14. A member of the public watching the Committee Stage hearings on the Environment Bill in the House of Lords late one night was observed by a colleague from the Department of the Environment to lean back at one point in a long speech to rest her back. She was abruptly told by an attendant to "sit up or get out", an attitude which does not speak of public ownership of a representative assembly!

15. A national air quality strategy is required to be prepared by s. 80 of the Environment Act 1995. The first such strategy was issued on 26 Aug. 1996.

16. Having said that, there was in 1998 a Conservative party opposition tactic in the Westminster Parliament of "praying against", or objecting to, *all* regulations made by the Labour government. This could have resulted in numerous committee debates on obscure Statutory Instruments, which in turn would clutter up the government's legislative timetable.

17. S.I. 1997/2959.

18. H.L. Official Report, Vol. 585, No. 92, Col. 1106, Tuesday, 27 Jan. 1998.

19. Art. 169 Treaty of Rome: to become Art. 226 Treaty of Rome (as amended by the Treaty of Amsterdam).

20. Art. 171 Treaty of Rome (as amended by Art. G(51) Treaty of Maastricht): to become Art. 228 Treaty of Rome (as amended by Treaty of Amsterdam). See also the leading European Community law Cases C–6/90 and C–9/90, *Francovitch and Bonifaci* v. *Italian Republic*, [1991] E.C.R. I–5357, [1993] 2 C.M.L.R. 66.

21. Cases C–121 and 122/97, *Commission* v. *Germany,* alleging non-implementation of the Drinking Water Directive, and proposing a fine based on a proportion of Germany's GDP brought by the European Commission under Art. 171(2) of the Treaty of Rome for failing to implement judgments of the Court.

22. Treaty Establishing the European Atomic Energy Community (signed at Brussels, 17 Apr. 1957), "the Euratom Treaty": as amended by Title IV (Art. I(1) to (29)), Treaty of Maastricht.

23. See Title XVI Treaty of Maastricht, Title XIX Treaty of Rome as amended by Treaty of Amsterdam.

24. U.N. Economic and Social Council, "UNECE", 1 Apr. 1998: Committee on Environmental Policy, Fourth Ministerial Conference, "Environment for Europe", Aarhus, Denmark, 23–25 June 1998.

25. H.L. European Communities Committee, Sub-Committee F (Environment): Enquiry on Implementation and Enforcement of EC Environmental Legislation. Written evidence submitted by the Department of the Environment in response to questions posed by the sub-committee, Oct. 1991.

26. General Guidelines for Legislative Policy, Memorandum from the President, European Commission. See also the resolution by the European Council of Ministers, Council Resolution of 7 Oct. 1997 on the drafting, implementation and enforcement of Community environmental law [1997] O.J. C321/1.

27. *Ibid.,* 2.

28. *Ibid.*, 6.
29. Geraldine Alliston *et al.*, *Review of the Implementation and Enforcement of EC Law in the UK—Scrutiny Report* (Department of Trade and Industry, London, July 1993).
30. Lord Ripon of Hexham, *Making the Law: the Report of the Hansard Society Commission on the Legislative Process* (Hansard Society for Parliamentary Government, London, 1993).
31. *Ibid.*, 37, para. 3.20.
32. H.C. Resolution, 30 Oct. 1980, updated on 24 Oct. 1990.
33. James Humphreys, *Negotiating in the European Union: How to Make the Brussels Machine Work for You* (Century, London, 1997)
34. Treaty on European Union (signed in Maastricht on 7 Feb. 1992). This Treaty amends the Treaty establishing the European Community (signed in Rome on 25 Mar. 1957) ("the Treaty of Rome"), and insofar as the Maastricht Treaty mainly consists of amendments to other texts, it is not a masterpiece of the draftsman's art or an easy read.
35. The Treaty of Amsterdam of 1997 extended the "co-decision" procedure to a number of areas, including environmental proposals with a legal base of Art. 130(s)(1) of the Treaty of Rome. The effects of the Treaty of Amsterdam are set out in a written Memorandum by the Foreign and Commonwealth Office, recorded in the Minutes of Evidence taken before the H.C. Foreign Affairs Committee on Tuesday, 4 Nov. 1997.
36. See e.g. paras. 4.17–4.19 of the Review, n. 29 above above.

4

The Consent of the Governed I—The Public and Science

"Rule 1. Accept and Involve the Public as a Legitimate Partner"

U.S. Environmental Protection Agency's Cardinal Rules of Risk Communication[1]

Members of the public live with risks every day. They cross roads, drive cars, live and go to work in cities with high crime rates or where terrorism is a daily fact of life, and they take their chances with avoiding ill health. It seems quite possible that public understanding and acceptance of risk is much higher than officialdom supposes, but it depends on good information and a relationship of trust. Where either is absent, a public reaction—officials would say "overreaction"—is only to be expected.

In the case of risks from scientific advances, the public is often required to take the risks without knowing about them. Retention of most of the information, where it exists, by a small number of experts, often employed in industries promoting the technologies in question, seems guaranteed to promote public anxiety and possible hostility to scientific interventions.

This chapter briefly considers the issue of the public and science from several different angles: risk assessment, dioxins, pesticides, transgenic plants, food safety and public access to information about the environment. The argument is not that public concerns should always prevail. The public is not necessarily the best judge of which risks are most serious. When the U.S. Environmental Protection Agency conducted its survey, "Unfinished Business", in 1986, for example, the Agency rated health risks from radon as a high priority, while the public did not.[2] It seems likely that the Agency was the better informed of the parties in that instance. In Britain, for example, it has been reported that as many as one in 20 lung cancer deaths (1,800 people per year) may be attributable to radon in homes.[3] Rather, the argument of this chapter is that public concerns should be recognised and addressed. Not all new science is bad—it can obviously bring huge benefits to society—but its risks should be properly explored and fairly explained. There is, sometimes, another point of view than that of scientific experts.

SCIENCE AND PUBLIC OPINION

Science is a vital component of successful environmental laws. Good science ensures that the real problems of the environment are identified and addressed. Without the painstaking and authoritative work of the British Antarctic Survey in identifying the hole in the ozone layer above Antarctica, it is unlikely that Prime Minister Margaret Thatcher, herself a chemist, would have been persuaded that this was a problem that mattered, and that international agreement to tackle it must be made a priority.

In some areas, public distrust of science and scientific research is almost total. When Dr Seed of Chicago announced in January 1998 that he was proposing to undertake cloning of human beings, with a series of interviews in which he briskly dismissed any doubts about the desirability of such research, he showed just how far science can go beyond public acceptance and support. The President of the United States had already responded to the announcement of the successful cloning of a sheep (called Dolly) in Scotland by announcing an urgent inquiry, and subsequently a prohibition on the use of any Federal funds or facilities to support research that would have resulted in human cloning. But apparently this did not represent a sufficient indication to the likes of Dr Seed of what was acceptable.

There are practical implications for science which is carried out against a background of public distrust. A public backlash can bring about legislation to limit poorly explained research or to cut off sources of funding for it. On this level alone, it might be thought to be worthwhile scientists taking the time to take the public with them in endorsing their research. When this is done successfully, the results in terms of public participation and endorsement can be spectacular. NASA's Pathfinder mission to Mars in July 1997 had pictures sent back from the Sojourner space vehicle as it travelled over the surface of the planet released live onto the Internet. By August 1997 over 600 million "hits" had been made on Internet websites carrying these pictures, sometimes over 60 million "hits" per day, a number equivalent to the total population of the United Kingdom. Surely this suggests that the public at large does not have an unreasoning fear of science and scientific progress as a whole.

PROBLEMS WITH RISK ASSESSMENT

Very many products and processes are not risk free. This often leaves regulators, policy-makers and governments with difficult choices about the levels of protection from risk that may be necessary or desirable, and the likely cost of bans or regulatory controls. Increasingly, these choices are informed by complex "risk assessments" and "cost and benefit analyses". These seek to use mathematics and economics to quantify risk and to set rules for the levels of risk that, broadly, the public or its governments can live with. It is clearly easier for governments to make choices by following a set of rules than by considering first principles in each case. But this preference can lead people to regard risk assessment and cost and benefit analysis as more authoritative, and more scientific, than they actually are.

In 1989, the Council on Environmental Quality in America, part of the Executive Office of the President, brought out an important guide to the principles of risk assessment.[4] This guide considered that risk assessment techniques were a useful means of framing and considering questions of risk to human health or the environment. But it warned against relying too much on these techniques, saying that:

> ". . . they may convey a level of precision that does not satisfactorily reflect the tentative nature of the underlying assumptions and the large uncertainties that typically characterise risk assessment."

Risk assessment techniques, then, according to the Council on Environmental Quality, are useful as far as they go. But no one should claim that risk assessment alone can endow what are really political choices with some kind of unanswerable scientific authority. William Ruckelshaus, a former Administrator at the U.S. Environmental Protection Agency, has compared the data from risk assessment to a captured spy: "if you torture it long enough, it will tell you anything you want to know".[5] This remark reflects the fact that risk assessments are sometimes used to justify a decision that has already been taken, instead·of being objective assessments of different choices.

John Adams' book *Risk*[6] gives a telling account of how cost and benefit analysis only works if no one is allowed to enter the number "infinity". The analysis breaks down if, for example, someone insists that there is no monetary compensation that would make up for his having a motorway through his garden, or that there is no price that she would put on the value of the life of a member of her family. Faced with this dilemma, cost and benefit analysts change the questions. Adams explains how the Royal Society's 1992 report on risk came to the conclusion that the "value of statistical life to be used in the cost-benefit of risk changes would be £2–£3 million".[7] Perhaps the response to this should be to require the cost and benefit analysts to apply their tests to named members of their own families.

Like risk assessment, cost and benefit analysis also needs to be seen in perspective. It may be useful to know that a particular course of action would only result in marginal benefits but would definitely result in huge costs. It may be worthwhile requiring policymakers to stop and think about that. But it is not sensible to let the process of cost and benefit analysis dictate policy rather than inform it. It is usually much harder to assess environmental benefits than costs.

Many decisions have come to be based very heavily on assessments of "acceptable" risk. In the United Kingdom, the Health and Safety Executive has published guidelines entitled *The Tolerability of Risk from Nuclear Power Stations* (revised in 1992).[8] This document attempts to distinguish "tolerability" from "acceptability". It argues that "acceptability" implies a willingness to accept the risk, while to "tolerate" a risk is apparently to keep it under review and to reduce it further when this is possible. This is a very fine distinction which may elude many people. One might have thought that to tolerate a risk one would have had to decide to live with it.

The Health and Safety Executive document sets out three tests:

"(a) whether a risk is so great or the outcome so unacceptable that it must be refused altogether; or

(b) whether the risk is, or has been made, so small that no further precaution is necessary; or

(c) if a risk falls between these two states, that it has been reduced to the lowest level practicable, bearing in mind the benefits following from its acceptance and taking into account the costs of any further reduction."[9]

These tests, and especially the third test, carry a number of very subjective assumptions within them about what is "practicable" and the real value of costs and benefits. Is it right to set a maximum tolerable risk of death at around one in 1,000 for nuclear workers? Is it sensible to assume that a one in a million *per annum* risk of contracting cancer or a serious hereditary defect as a result of exposure to radiation is "tolerable", and therefore that no further improvements should be sought if these entail cost? What is a hereditary defect that results from exposure to radiation which ought not to be regarded as serious?

It would be possible to receive as many answers to these questions as members of the public to whom they are addressed. The Health and Safety Executive makes considerable efforts to achieve effective public consultation on its proposals, for example by placing its consultation drafts of regulations on the Internet. But the language of laws and regulations in this area can be enormously discouraging to sensible public participation.

For example, the European Community Directive on basic safety standards for ionising radiation[10] contains the following definition of an "Effective Dose":

"*Effective dose* (E): the sum of the weighted equivalent doses in all the tissues and organs of the body specified in Annex II from internal and external irradiation. It is defined by the expression:

$$E = \sum_T w_T H_T = \sum_T w_T \sum_R w_R D_{T,R}$$

where

—$D_{T,R}$ is the absorbed dose averaged over tissue or organ T, due to radiation R,
—w_R is the radiation weighting factor and
—w_T is the tissue weighting factor for tissue or organ T.
The appropriate w_T and w_R values are specified in Annex II. The unit for effective dose is the sievert."

This all concerns how much radiation human beings can absorb without suffering damage to their health. It is couched in language that only technical experts can understand. This leaves the experts in control of the application of the law, applying risk assessment and cost-benefit analysis to decide what is tolerable, what is acceptable and what precautions must be judged to be unreasonably expensive.

DIOXINS

The techniques of risk assessment seem to be at their most threadbare when dealing with acutely toxic chemicals where there is no apparent "safe level" to fall back on and where adverse effects could arise from very small concentrations. One such category of chemicals is the dioxins.

A dioxin known as "TCDD", or 2,3,7,8–tetrachlorodibenzo–p–dioxin is produced at paper mills during the manufacturing process. It can be produced from the reactions of wood preservatives, from certain pesticides sprayed on trees, from the use of chlorine gas to bleach wood pulp, and from the discharge of dissolved lignin and other materials, which, as the U.S. Council on Environmental Quality report on risk analysis points out "are routinely released by paper mills into local waterways as wastes, which typically contain dioxins."

The Council's guide states that risk analysts can study paper mill processes, chemical reactions and raw materials used, and "construct models that estimate dioxin emissions and concentrations in the air, water and land. Where knowledge gaps exist, assumptions are made that may lead to substantial uncertainties in the estimates".[11]

The problem is that any such uncertainties, let alone substantial uncertainties, are not very good news when TCDD is, in the words of the guide "one of the most acutely toxic man-made compounds known".[12] In April 1997 the U.S. Environmental Protection Agency brought out a draft priority chemical list[13] ranking 800 chemicals by their persistence, bioaccumulative properties and toxicity to humans and the environment. TCDD was equal first on this list, in such company as Aldrin, Dieldrin and DDT. In the United

Kingdom, the toxicity of many other dioxins, furans and PCBs is measured by reference to the equivalent effect of TCDD.[14]

Four years after the Council on Environmental Quality brought out its guide to risk assessment, the case of *Dioxin/Organochlorine Center* v. *EPA*[15] was brought. The environmentalists who brought the case lost the battle in court but appear to have won the argument outside it.

Under the provisions of Section 303 of the Clean Water Act,[16] the U.S. Environmental Protection Agency was required to review state water quality standards, and, where necessary, to impose effluent limitations. Where these would not be enough to bring water into compliance with quality standards, Total Maximum Daily Loads, "TMDLs" were to be calculated. TMDLs in effect, therefore, are the maximum amount of a pollutant that can be introduced into water without violating water quality standards, with an allowance for seasonal variations and a margin of safety. The Agency used a water quality standard of 0.013 parts per quadrillion for 2,3,7,8–tetrachlorodibenzo–p–dioxin, when calculating the TMDL for the Columbia River Basin.

Two environmental groups challenged the Agency's establishment of a TMDL. In setting the water quality standard, the Agency had considered the national average consumption of freshwater and estuarine fish, that is, 6.5 grammes per day. The Agency had assumed that if the affected community consumed fish with the maximum level of dioxin in ambient water, and allowing for the effects of dioxin levels becoming concentrated further up the food chain (bioaccumulation), it would do so at the level of the national average. But the plaintiffs argued that even on the Agency's own estimates, Native Americans, Asian Americans and other low-income populations along the Columbia consumed an average of between 100 and 150 grammes of fish per day over a year, using the river for traditional and subsistence fishing.

The court upheld the Environmental Protection Agency's TMDL. It deferred to the Agency's technical determinations, and concluded that it had reasonably estimated that the actual consumption of dioxin, even based on levels of consumption of 150 grammes of fish per day, would be less than the amount allowed by the water quality standard, since not all fish in the Columbia carried the maximum amount of dioxin. Anyway, the court remarked, a 23 in a million risk of cancer from eating 150 grammes of "maximum residue fish" was acceptable.

Professor Gerald Torres of the University of Texas, on whose analysis of the case these paragraphs are based, has remarked,[17] "EPA's victory in this case can be attributed more to its conservative risk analysis than to its sensitivity to the varying dietary habits of affected minority communities. . . . The fact is that in ignoring the differences of culture, class and race, the dioxin

TMDL for the Columbia River resulted in a disproportionate distribution of risk of cancer for minority residents along the Columbia River."

It seems no coincidence that Professor Torres, a year later, when helping to draft the President's Executive Order on Environmental Justice,[18] included specific requirements for Federal agencies to incorporate environmental justice considerations in risk assessments, and to take into account subsistence hunting and fishing. These issues are now part of the Environmental Protection Agency's strategy for implementing the Executive Order. What was lost in court was won shortly afterwards in the political arena.

The *Dioxin/Organochlorine Center* case showed a need for risk assessment to move out of the laboratory and into the real world. The case, or rather its aftermath, showed the way in which questions of "environmental justice" or "environmental equity" in America are coming to affect the way that risk assessment is carried out. There is, increasingly, a requirement in America for clear and understandable language in risk assessments, for close attention to real local conditions, and for genuine public participation. And the case raised, but did not answer, the big issue of whether technology had yet provided sufficiently sophisticated monitoring techniques to regulate "safe levels" of such dangerous substances.

Michael Deland, Chair of the U.S. Council on Environmental Quality from 1989 to 1993, has said:[19]

> "We are now confronting, because of our industrialized society, an entirely different variety and much more insidious and complex form of pollution, namely toxics. We measure pollutants now, not in tons, but in parts per million, trillion or quadrillion. The challenge that we've not yet been able to meet adequately is the causal relationship between a part per million, trillion, quadrillion, of a given pollutant, and its effect on our health and that of our kids. That is where a good deal of our research needs to be."

Who won the argument about the dangers of the 2,3,7,8 dioxins? In Canada, under the Toxic Substances Management Policy, the government has published scientific chapter and verse justifying the "virtual elimination from the environment" of this substance as one of the most toxic or "Track 1" substances: persistent, bioaccumulative and resulting primarily from human activity.[20] In Britain and in America by contrast, regulators persist in attempting, or purporting to be able, to regulate emissions of a deadly substance which some of the best scientists consider can scarcely be measured with the necessary precision. It may be possible on paper to set requirements to measure parts per quadrillion, but the water quality monitoring technology necessary to carry out this task has been described as at the stage of "schoolboy science."[21]

There are a number of paper mills along the Columbia River in Oregon and Washington states. They are colossal factories, taking in cords of timber floated down the river by tugs and barges. On a cold day in winter, steam and vapour rise in clouds from the mill stacks, and from the effluent which runs along canals leading from the plant into settling ponds and lagoons next to the river itself. The paper mill in Camas, Washington, on the north bank of the Columbia can be smelled several miles across the valley in Oregon. It would require a high level of optimism from regulators and the public to suppose that at plant such as these it is always possible to measure pollutants in terms of parts per quadrillion in such a consistent and carefully calibrated way that allowable amounts were never exceeded. Yet that is the basis of the system of "total maximum daily loads". Perhaps it implies that the existing system of dioxin regulation in America and Britain promises the public more, in terms of scientific certainty and safety, than it can deliver.

In May 1997, the U.S. Environmental Protection Agency announced a new policy on paper mill emissions which will significantly reduce, but not eliminate, dioxin emissions. Requiring paper mill operators to cease using chlorine bleaching processes altogether was judged to be unreasonably expensive. Dioxins seem likely to continue to be a major issue in Britain, as incineration of municipal waste continues, and the issue of the incineration of sewage sludge becomes more pressing with the promised end to dumping at sea in 1998. Dioxin levels in milk are being reduced, but dioxins have been found at elevated levels around some industrial installations in Britain.[22] The public is sometimes said to have an irrational fear of dioxins, but it seems that many of its questions are worth asking.

PESTICIDES

In America it is reported that pesticide use reached an all-time high of more than 1.2 billion pounds in 1995.[23] This is over twice as many pounds of chemicals as were used when Rachel Carson published *Silent Spring* (540 million pounds on 1964).[24] A U.S. General Accounting Office report in 1993 stated that over 50,000 pesticide products have been registered since the relevant legislation (known as FIFRA)[25] was enacted in 1947. The General Accounting Office report points out that "most of these pesticides were registered before their long-term health and environmental effects were fully understood".[26] In 1972, and again in 1988, Congress required the Environmental Protection Agency to undertake re-registration of pesticides. But as at July 1992, the Environmental Protection Agency had reached final decisions on only two out of 17,000 products subject to re-registration. By March 1997 only 148 of the 604 active ingredients requiring re-registration had completed the process, which the Agency estimated would take until the year 2002.[27]

In the United States, the Port Import Export Reporting Service (PIERS) of the *Journal of Commerce* transcribes records of shipments from US ports. Companies can apply to the US Treasury Department to have their names withheld from PIERS transcriptions. This results in the term "Order" being noted as the shipper. The specific chemical names of the pesticides are also omitted from the shipping records. This makes it impossible to identify as many as two thirds of the pesticide products exported from American ports. The Foundation for Advancements in Science and Education has researched this topic [28] and reports total US pesticide exports as follows:

1992	490,113,733 pounds	76% product unidentified
1993	486,138,116 pounds	74% product unidentified
1994	526,172,740 pounds	73% product unidentified
1995	630,040,438 pounds	–
1996	687,601,508 pounds	–

The same reports went on to name the companies which were granted the right to have their names blocked from shipping record transcriptions between 1992 and 1994. Between 1992 and 1996 over two billion pounds of pesticides left American ports with their specific chemical names omitted, often being described simply as "pesticide" or "weed killing compound".

One attraction of exporting pesticides, whether openly or concealed under descriptions such as "Order", is that exports are frequently to less regulated markets, where there is not so much fuss about enforcement of environmental laws, and perhaps less time is taken to establish safe methods of application. Many people would find it surprising that it appears that as much as 300 tons of DDT was exported from the United States, mainly to Peru, in 1992.[29]

Between 1992 and 1994 the USA exported nearly 109 million pounds of pesticides to Latin America, where farm workers are 13 times more likely to suffer pesticide poisoning than US farm workers.[30] Despite all this, it appears that *per capita* food production in Latin America may actually be falling.[31]

Between 1989 and 1990 in the United Kingdom, the total tonnage of pesticide active ingredient used decreased by 20 per cent, while the area treated increased by about 9 per cent.[32] Nevertheless, the United Kingdom government has accepted, in national litigation brought by Friends of the Earth,[33] that pesticides residues in excess of European standards have occurred and are continuing to occur in a number of samples of UK drinking water, while arguing that these fall far below the levels of any discernible or adverse effects on human health. The argument in the Friends of the Earth drinking water litigation was over whether the UK Government was discharging its obligation in European Community law to achieve compliance with the standards of the Drinking Water Directive as quickly as possible. National courts concluded that no evidence had been produced to the contrary.

In the United Kingdom, the Working Party on Pesticides Residues carried out a study between 1991 and 1993 for the Ministry of Agriculture, Fisheries and Food of pesticides residues in a number of foodstuffs.[34] This reported that in the samples taken, "no pesticide residues" were found in 77 per cent of bread, 54 per cent of milk and 62 per cent of potatoes. Allowing for the occasional statistical inaccuracy,[35] the reader of this report is left to puzzle out that nearly half of the milk sampled contained traces of organochlorine pesticides, while a third of the bread sampled and over a third of potatoes sampled also contained pesticide residues.

The Working Party report is soothing in tone:

> . . . "the presence of OP [Organophosphorous] residues in bread is not unexpected as these pesticides are used as grain protectants, i.e. they are applied after harvest."

This may be so, but the reasons for the report's complacency about the presence of these products in staple foods is not entirely clear when the U.S. Environmental Protection Agency is conducting a wholesale review which may result in their removal from the American market.

The same picture is reflected in other foodstuffs sampled. Residues of Organophosphorous grain protectants were found in 21 per cent of the 29 samples taken by the study of infant rusks. The study even found that 53 per cent of the samples of farmed salmon taken in 1991 contained DDT. It is right to point out that many of these samples will reflect the very low levels of detection now available in chemical sampling. However, legislation is proposed for the United Kingdom to set up a new Food Standards Agency, and it remains to be seen whether that Agency will take the view that having a quarter of infant rusks containing Organophosphorous pesticide residues is acceptable.

In Russia in 1989, it was reported by an environmental adviser to President Yeltsin[36] that 30 per cent of foodstuffs contained DDT, and 32 per cent chloroflors over recommended health levels. 72 per cent of butter, and 42 per cent of childrens' milk contained pesticides at dangerous levels. It was also noted that, as pesticide use declined as a result of the recession in recent years, the harvest had actually increased. Imported pesticides, probably organo-phosphorous, have been implicated in the outbreak of an entirely new disease in Russia in 1989, polyneuropathy or "flat foot". The symptoms are inability to control foot movement due to die-back in the long nerve to the foot. Thirty students helping with the potato harvest in the Urals were the first victims, and there have been a further 200 cases recorded between 1989 and 1992.[37]

The Chinese National Statistical Bureau reported 48,377 pesticide poisoning cases in 27 provinces in 1995, but its number of 3,204 fatalities is still startling. Highly toxic organophosphate insecticides caused many of the poisonings. Meanwhile the Chinese Ministry of Chemical Industry set an annual target for pesticide production of 230,000 tonnes.[38]

But public concern about pesticide effects has not gone away, and is not without its effects. In 1996, the City of San Francisco introduced a sweeping new ordinance requiring all City departments to eliminate or minimise the use of pesticides and to develop integrated pest management policies.[39] Use of all the most toxic pesticides was banned outright. Use of all other pesticides was required to be reduced by 50 per cent of the amount used in 1996 by 1 January 1998, with a target of a 100 percent reduction by the year 2000. Other requirements of the ordinance concern the posting of warning signs and information about pesticide applications.

FOOD SAFETY AND THE DELANEY CLAUSE

The safety of most food in America was until recently protected by the "Delaney clause" of the Food, Drug and Cosmetic Act. This required that no substance "found to cause cancer" should be added to the food supply; it did not apply to fresh fruit and vegetables. The Council on Environment Quality's guide to risk analysis referred to the difficulties faced by the Food and Drug Administration in implementing this clause as the "classic case" showing "zero risk goals have proven difficult, if not impossible, to achieve".[40] If a pesticide that caused cancer in man or laboratory animals concentrated in processed food at a level greater than the tolerance of the raw agricultural commodity, the effect of the Delaney clause was to ban the setting of a tolerance for the substance. As some alternative pesticides had potentially higher, non-cancer, risks to human health, the Environmental Protection Agency itself referred to this as the "Delaney paradox".[41]

To some environmentalists, the Delaney clause was an important means of safeguarding public health.[42] They regard its replacement with a requirement for health-based risk assessment as likely to underestimate such factors as lifetime exposures, cumulative exposures to a variety of substances, effects on children and effects on breast cancer rates in women, from such toxic chemicals as pesticides.

For the pesticide production industry, however, the demise of the Delaney clause was a cause for celebration. Passage of the Food Quality Protection Act of 1996 was described by the President of the American Crop Protection Association (representing the U.S. pesticide industry) as "a particularly gratifying victory".[43]

But if the Delaney clause was hard for the Food and Drug Administration to apply, it is difficult to feel anything but sympathy for the Environmental Protection Agency in having to apply its replacement provisions in the 1996 legislation.

There is to be a single health-based risk assessment standard for all pesticide residues in food, whether the food is fresh or processed. The Environmental Protection Agency must make a finding that a pesticide residue is "safe" for it to be allowed. To be "safe", there must be "a reasonable certainty that no harm will result from aggregate exposure to the pesticide", which in terms of legislative precedent means no more than a one in a million lifetime risk of cancer. The Environmental Protection Agency must even make a specific finding that pesticide residues are safe for infants and children.

Rachel Carson wrote about tolerances in the chapter of *Silent Spring* entitled "Beyond the Dreams of the Borgias":[44]

"In effect, then, to establish tolerances is to authorize contamination of public food supplies with poisonous chemicals in order that the farmer and the processor may enjoy the benefit of cheaper production—then to penalize the consumer by taxing him to maintain a policing agency to make certain that he shall not get a lethal dose. But to do the policing job properly would cost money beyond any legislator's courage to appropriate, given the present volume and toxicity of agricultural chemicals. So in the end the luckless consumer pays his taxes but gets his poisons regardless."

As so often, one is left wondering how much we have learned since Rachel Carson's warnings were published.

The Food Quality Protection Act of 1996 requires the Environmental Protection Agency to re-assess 9,700 tolerances within ten years of the law's passage on 3 August 1996. The Agency has started with a review of organophosphate and carbamate insecticides, which make up nearly 85 per cent of the insecticides applied to crops in the United States.[45] Where, as often, data are incomplete for the cumulative effects upon children, the Agency has been trying to apply an extra margin of safety of ten times the limits set for cumulative exposures. These margins could well result in the removal from sale of large numbers of products.[46] In the United Kingdom, on the other hand, as has been seen, we seem content to find traces of these products in a third to half of our foods, including infant foods.

Political pressures upon the Agency have been immediate, intense and, it must be said, entirely predictable. For example, the House of Representatives Agriculture Committee has written to the Agency urging it to base its re-assessment decisions on "sound scientific data", and to avoid "unnecessary loss of products or product uses critical to our farmers, ranchers, residential and non-residential users".[47] The agricultural and agrochemical industries have warned of the problems in removal of existing products, and in slowing down the registration of new products.[48] Environmentalists, on the other hand, have complained that some of the relatively few tolerances actually set may not be "safe",[49] and that the whole approach to setting tolerances is both incomplete, and routinely by-passed by procedures such as emergency registration.

To put a regulator in the position of making a positive finding that a pesticide is "safe" is to place a very heavy burden upon it. The Environmental Protection Agency seems to have been left in the middle of a political shooting gallery. It cannot try out the pesticides on classes of primary schoolchildren, so it sets wide margins of safety about which industry then complains. What is an acceptable risk of harm? How much is really known about individual pesticides, let alone the interaction between a number of different chemicals? The book *Our Stolen Future*[50] by Theo Colborn and others concerns the possible effects of endocrine disruptors, and serves as an important reminder of three things. First, while most health standards address possible risks of cancer, there are other risks, such as those of reproductive effects, which may arise from chemicals in the environment.[51] Secondly, not a great deal is known about the effects of the interactions in the environment of more than one chemical. Thirdly, the amounts of chemicals which may have significant adverse effects may be much smaller than was earlier understood. It is not surprising that for regulators on both sides of the Atlantic, but especially in America, further study of the effects of endocrine disruptors has become a top priority.[52] The U.S. Environmental Protection Agency has been prompted to screen up to 15,000 chemicals produced in quantities of over 10,000 pounds a year for endocrine-disrupting effects, following a report from one of its advisory committees.[53]

It is a curious stage at which to relax the health and safety testing requirements for pesticide use on "minor use" crops[54] including many fruits and vegetables. We have, after all, been here before. In 1925 authorities in Britain rejected shipments of American fruit bearing arsenic residues exceeding British standards. An apple grower from Oregon, Llewelyn Banks, found the resulting legislation governing legal tolerances so outrageous that it sued the U.S. Bureau of Chemistry, later the Food and Drug Administration, alleging "conspiracy, persecution and malicious interference with the normal trend of business".[55] In 1997, citing organophosphate levels on imported fruit, parents in Britain were warned by the government to ensure that their children peeled fruit before eating it.

GENETICALLY ENGINEERED CROPS

It is interesting that Monsanto, one of the largest manufacturers of chemicals in the United States with annual chemical sales of $3 billion, has announced its intention to spin off its chemical business altogether. Apparently Monsanto sees the future in genetically engineered products such as disease resistant crops, and is investing heavily in this technology. The benefits of some forms of disease resistance may be readily appreciated. They could include reduced dependence on the use of pesticides, but it is not clear that this is how the new gene technology will be applied in practice. Monsanto is producing strains of crops resistant to its own pesticide Roundup. Farmers will therefore be able to pay Monsanto for Roundup with which to spray before and after planting, and pay them again for plant crops resistant to the Roundup, which sounds wonderful for Monsanto, but perhaps less so for the farmers, and least of all for the environment and sustainable forms of agriculture.

The Chief Executive Officer of Monsanto has complained that the public does not always seem to appreciate scientific advances in the field of genetic engineering. "What used to be an anti-nuclear group is now an anti-biotech group", he is quoted as telling *Forbes* magazine,[56] "People are worried that we are tinkering with fundamental forces that are more powerful than we are."[57]

If the public has a few worries on this score, it appears that some at least of them are shared by distinguished scientists from the Massachusetts Institute of Technology. Jane Rissler and Margaret Mellon, in *The Ecological Risk of Engineered Crops*[58] have identified the main risks of this technology. Transgenic crops may become weeds. Novel genes may flow from the transgenic crops to wild relations and create more weeds. Virus resistant transgenic crops could produce new viruses and alter the host range of existing viruses. The widespread monocultures of crop plants, which modern biotechnology takes as a given, are particularly vulnerable to any disease strain that breaks through the resistance barrier.[59] New forms of resistance tend to be found in wild cultivars and, where these have been lost through interbreeding with transgenic strains, entire crops could be lost.

Clearly the scientists in this field are having an exciting time. Apart from cloning sheep, they have produced potatoes with genes from chickens, silk moths and viruses; tomatoes with genes from winter flounder (for their antifreeze properties), viruses and bacteria; tobacco with genes from Chinese hamsters; and melons, cucumbers and squash with extra virus genes.

Rissler and Mellon concede that some products of biotechnology will be positive and beneficial. But they also state:

... "not all applications will prove beneficial, and society need not regard technology as a sort of train that cannot be stopped once it gets on track. We can and must learn to evaluate technologies and, where appropriate, to say no."

TOXIC SUBSTANCES, AND PUBLIC ACCESS TO INFORMATION

The U.S. Environment Protection Agency publishes an annual Toxics Release Inventory under the Emergency Planning and Community Right-to-Know Act of 1986. This law was expanded by the Pollution Prevention Act of 1990, and requires that each year manufacturing facilities meeting certain thresholds must report their estimated releases and transfers of listed toxic chemicals for inclusion on the public register.

The public can derive invaluable information from the data on toxic releases. For example, the 1994 EPA Toxics Release Inventory[60] reported that a total of 2,260,210,725 pounds of toxic chemicals were released in the USA for that year by all TRI facilities. In a later table[61] the same Toxics Release Inventory shows the "Top 10 TRI Parent Companies with the Largest Total Releases, 1994". This table shows the total emissions to air, surface water, underground injection and land reported for the facilities governed by the ten reported parent companies. In other words, in 1994 and again in 1995, about a quarter of all releases of toxic chemicals in the United States were the responsibility of as few as ten parent companies. In the 1994, some 732,337,742 pounds of toxic chemical releases, or about a third of the total for the whole United States, derived from the "Top 50 TRI Facilities". An example of the figures given for the years 1994 and 1995 is as in Table 4.1.

The development of the Toxics Release Inventory has been critical both to the reduction of toxic chemical releases and to the inclusion of an articulate, informed and questioning public as part of the environmental decision-making process in America. But reporting of emissions by facility has also obliged industrial companies to start taking more account of local residents' and communities' concerns. The passage of the Emergency Planning and Community Right-to-Know Act of 1986 led to huge efforts by industry to burnish the public image affected by publication of the release data. On the eve of the reporting deadline, Monsanto's then Chief Executive Officer declared his intention to reduce his firm's air emission by 90 per cent by 1992.[62] In Silicon Valley, electronics industry facilities report reducing toxic emissions by a full 89 per cent since the Toxics Release Inventory was introduced. Firms such as IBM promised to eliminate the chemical freon from all its processes within three years after heading the list of the "dirty dozen" in local newspaper reports based on Toxics Release Inventory data.[63]

Table 4.1 Top 10 TRI parent companies with the largest total releases

1994		1995	
Company Name	Total Releases in pounds	Company Name	Total Releases in pounds
Dupont	203,569,404	General Motors Corporation	152,817,158
ASARCO Inc	69,355,764	E. I. DuPont de Nemours & Co	152,234,807
Renco Group Ltd	66,084,321	ASARCO Inc	107,218,810
IMC Global Inc	47,746,806	Hoescht-Celanese Corp	78,245,705
International Paper Company	43,111,887	Renco Group Inc	72,677,969
General Motors Corporation	36,841,746	Shell Oil Co	56,592,993
Courtaulds United States Inc	34,521,923	Essex Group Inc	53,005,880
Monsanto Company	27,391,091	Johnson Controls Inc	52,029,954
Arcadian Partners LP	26,395,613	Exide Corp	51,305,826
Georgia-Pacific Corporation	26,209,076	Monsanto Co	48,779,344
Subtotal	581,227,631	**Subtotal**	824,908,446
Total Releases for all TRI facilities for the reporting year	2,260,210,725	**Total Releases for all TRI facilities for the reporting year**	2,208,749,411

Toxics Release Inventory data have been used creatively as the basis for some of the most successful initiatives to reduce pollution and emissions, such as the Environmental Protection Agency's "33/50" Programme, which measured and achieved 50 per cent reductions in emissions and transfers of 17 target chemicals within four years (see Chapter 8). It is an essential means for businesses as well as communities to measure progress or lack of it. It is also a means whereby both Federal and state regulators push facilities into dialogue with their surrounding host communities. Community "outreach", education and participation will be required of any company applying to have a Supplemental Environmental Project made part of its civil law settlement of regulatory violations, either under the Federal rules applied by the Environmental Protection Agency or by state rules in states such as Texas.

Yet the most enthusiastic proponents of the Inventory and right-to-know legislation admit that it has a long way to go before it gives a full picture of pollution in the United States. It has been said that only 5 per cent of toxic pollution in the USA is reported under the existing right-to-know laws.[64] Consideration of Toxics Release Inventory data on the level of individual facilities can be misleading. The inventory may refer, for example, to the reportable emissions of lead in slag produced by a copper mine in Arizona, but require no reporting of sulphuric acid use at the mine site.[65] Yet visitors to such a mine can see hundreds of thousands of tons of rock being shovelled out of the mountainside, put in open and often unlined pits, and sprayed continuously, 24 hours a day, with sulphuric acid, to wash out copper in solution. It is not hard to see that this process, which has not so far been caught by formal reporting requirements, may be far more damaging than some of those that are caught by the law. It is likely that this sort of issue will be dealt with in forthcoming reforms of the right-to-know laws. But the laws themselves are generally reckoned to have been an important success.

In August 1996 in Kalamazoo, Michigan,[66] President Clinton announced a proposal to expand community right-to-know laws, saying that:

> "In the decades since we've passed the first one, businesses have reported reducing toxic emission by 43 per cent. Right-to-know works. Don't be fooled about it. It makes a big difference."

Since this speech and apparently as a result of it, the U.S. Environmental Protection Agency has announced that it would open a new Center for Environmental Information and Statistics. This Center, which opened to the public on 1 January 1998,[67] will compile and issue integrated environmental statistics and trend data, and make electronic access by the public easier, pulling together many of the Environmental Protection Agency's current on-line information systems.

At the same time, the Agency announced a new Office of Children's Health, and to go with it "a Family Right-to-Know Initiative to expand access to vital information about children's health, so that families can make informed choices concerning environmental exposures to their children". In a formula with which many in Whitehall will be familiar, the press release added that "the Agency's restructuring will be carried out within existing budgetary constraints", so it remains to be seen what can be achieved by the Agency in these areas for the same amount of money. What is interesting is the heavy emphasis on public information and public participation.

The same is true of Environmental Protection Agency material on its initiatives in the field of environmental justice. The definition of environmental justice with which the Agency works refers not just to the *fair treatment* of all people regardless of race, ethnicity, culture, income or education level and so on, but to their *meaningful involvement* in the development, implementation and enforcement of environmental laws, regulations and policies. For example, the Agency's Environmental Justice Strategy, prepared in response to the President's Executive Order 12898,[68] declares:

> "Environmental justice begins and ends in our communities. EPA will work with communities through communication, partnership, research, and the public participation process."

CONCLUSIONS

David Rejeski of the Council on Environmental Quality, in a paper on risk assessment, wrote that:[69]

> . . . "unlike earlier periods, when public opinion concerning risk was largely ignored, or seen as requiring correction, a dialogue with the public has become a basic tenet governing most institutional strategies for risk management. The first cardinal rule of risk communication developed by the Environmental Protection Agency states "Accept and involve the public as a legitimate partner".

It is often said that environmental laws should be based upon "sound science". There is also a place for the "precautionary principle". Some circumstances require that action is taken before the scientific hypothesis has been proved. But if "sound science" was to mean the best available scientific opinion, impartially given and properly explained, few would argue with the proposition that environmental laws should reflect it. That would be a gold standard of sound science, and real science can sometimes fall short of the ideal. Scientists have a duty to explain the limits of their certainties. The public at the receiving end of decisions based upon risk assessments, or the setting of tolerances, or the taking of inovative risks, needs to be told more about what is at stake and what the options are. The development of the Toxics Release Inventory in America is evidence of the very effective use which the public can make of generally available scientific information.

David V. Bates, a scientist and authority on air pollution and risk assessment, has said that:[70]

> . . . "we can at the very least, I suggest, stress the complexity of living processes. The public is surely right in believing that our entrepreneurial ingenuity in introducing new chemicals or new processes into our environment, and disseminating them widely, far outstrips our ability to assess them."

It is for these reasons that it is argued that the public's view of scientific issues deserves and needs to be heard. Scientists may set the tolerances and determine the "acceptable" levels of pesticides and chemicals, but we and our children drink the water and eat the food containing these substances.

REFERENCES

1. Environmental Protection Agency, *Rules and Guidelines for Effective Risk Communication* (Covello and Allen, Washington, D.C., 1988).
2. John J. Cohrssen and Vincent T. Covello, *Risk Analysis: A Guide to Principles and Methods for Analyzing Health and Environmental Risks* (Executive Office of the President, Council on Environmental Quality, Washington, D.C., 1989), 21: EPA Report, *Unfinished Business* (1989), part on "Risk Estimation, Risk Perception and Priority-setting".
3. *The Times*, 19 May 1998, "Radon blamed for 1 in 20 lung cancer deaths", citing *British Journal of Cancer* of the same date.
4. N. 2 above.
5. William D. Ruckelshaus, "Risk in a Free Society", 14 *Envtl. L Rep.* (Environmental Law Institute, Washington, D.C.) 10,190 (May 1984): quoted by Robert R. Kuehn in "The Environmental Justice Implications of Quantitative Risk Assessment", *University of Illinois LR* (1996), No.1.
6. John Adams, *Risk* (University College London Press, London, 1995).
7. A. Marin, *Risk: Analysis, Perception and Management*, Appendix on Cost and benefits of risk reduction (Royal Society, London, 1992).
8. See Stephen Tromans and James Fitzgerald, *The Law of Nuclear Installations and Radioactive Substances* (Sweet & Maxwell, London, 1997) "Tolerability of Risk", para. 2–17.
9. (HMSO, London, 1992).
10. Council Dir. 96/29/Euratom of 13 May 1996 laying down basic safety standards for the protection of the health of workers and the general public against the dangers arising from ionising radiation. This can be found in Health and Safety Commission, *Proposals for revised Ionising Radiation regulations and Approved Code of Practice*, Consultative Document, also to be found at the Health and Safety Executive web site on the Internet—www.open.gov.uk/hse/condocs/
11. *Ibid.*, 58: "Case Study: Dioxins and Source/Release Assessment".
12. *Ibid.*
13. U.S. EPA, Office of Solid Waste and Emergency Response, *The Prioritized Chemical List*, Apr. 1997 draft.
14. In the UK the toxicity of 17 other dioxins and furans and 8 PCBs is measured by a Toxicity Equivalency Factor, which is a number related to the number 1 given to the the most toxic dioxin 2, 3, 7, 8, TCDD.
15. No. C93–33 (W.D. Wash., 10 Aug. 1993): the case is analysed by Professor Gerald Torres in the article in (1993–4) xxi *Fordham Urban LJ*. The description

of the point at issue in this case draws on Professor Torres' account, for which I am most grateful.

16. Properly, the Federal Water Pollution Control Act, 33 U.S.C.A. (ss. 1251 to 1387).
17. *Ibid.*, 449.
18. Executive Order 12898 of 11 Feb. 1994, "Federal Actions to Address Environmental Justice in Minority Populations and Low-Income Populations", Federal Register Vol. 59, No. 32, Wednesday, 16 Feb. 1994.
19. "Reflections on 25 Years", quoted at p. 33 of *"Environmental Quality", 25th Anniversary Report*, The Council on Environmental Quality, Executive Office of the President of the United States, containing the CEQ's report for the years 1994 and 1995.
20. Extract Canada Gazette, Part 1, 22 Mar. 1997, Department of the Environment, "Notice Concerning the Assessment of Aldrin etc. . . . . Against Track 1 Criteria of the Toxic Substances Management Policy".
21. Meetings at the Executive Office of the President, Office of Science and Technology Policy, Washington, DC, 4 Feb. 1997.
22. Report in *ENDS Report*, Issue 276, London, Jan. 1998, citing Ministry of Agriculture, Fisheries and Food, "Dioxins and PCBs in Retail Cow's Milk in England" (1988) Food Surveillance Sheet 136, MAFF, London, and Environmental Agency, "Environmental Monitoring of Dioxins and Furans in Air Deposition and Herbage around the Coalite Works, Bolsover, Derbyshire" (Environment Agency, Bristol, 1998).
23. U.S. EPA Office of Prevention, Pesticides and Toxic Substances, *Pesticides Industry Sales and Usage, 1994* and *1995 Market Estimates* (U.S. EPA. Washington, D.C., Aug. 1997). The trend in decline in the amount of active ingredient used in the U.K. seems to be continuing: see Department of the Environment, *Indicators of Sustainable Development 1996* (HMSO, London, 1996), Table, "Pesticide Usage", 137.
24. Natural Resources Defense Council (NRDC) and US Public Interest Research Group (USPIRG) press release, 28 May 1996. Rachel Carson (*Silent Spring*, Hamish Hamilton, London, 1968, 14) stated that 124,259,000 lbs of synthetic pesticides were *produced* in the USA in 1947, compared to 637,660,000 lbs produced in 1960.
25. Federal Insecticide, Fungicide and Rodenticide Act, Public Law 92–516.
26. U.S. GAO, "Pesticides: registration delays jeopardize status of proposed policy reforms", GAO /T–RCED–94–98, 1993.
27. 1996 Food Quality Protection Act: Implementation Plan, U.S. Environmental Protection Agency, Office of Prevention, Pesticides and Toxic Substances 1997 (Washington, D.C., Mar. 1997), quoted in article by Caroline Cox, "Pesticide Registration—No Guarantee of Safety", *Journal of Pesticide Reform*, Summer 1997, Vol. 17, No. 2.
28. FASE Research Report "Exporting Risk: Pesticide Exports from U.S. Ports 1992–1994", Carl Smith, FASE, 4801 Wilshire Blvd, Los Angeles CA 90037. For the same report for 1995–6, see Internet website http://www.fasenet.org/pest 95–96 html

29. *Ibid.*

30. R. T. Tansey, M. R. Hyman, R. S. Jacobs and L. Merrill, "Eradicating the Pesticide Problem in Latin America" (1995) *Business and Society Review*, 55–9, quoted in Carl Smith, "Exporting Risk—Pesticide Exports from US Ports 1992–1994", *Global Pesticide Campaigner*, June 1996, Vol. 6, No 2.

31. H. Holl, G. Daily, F. R. Erlich, "Integrated Pest Management in Latin America" (1990) 17(4) *Environmental Conservation*, quoted in Carl Smith's article cited in n. 30 above.

32. Department of the Environment, *The UK Environment, 1992* (HMSO, London, 1992), 213, Fig. 15.4. For updated U.K. figures, see also n. 23 above.

33. *R v. Secretary of State for the Environment, ex parte Friends of the Earth Limited*, Schiemann J. Mar. 1994, [1994] 1 Env L.Rep. 11: *R. v. Secretary of State for the Environment, ex parte Friends of the Earth and another*, C.A. (Civil Div.) 25 May 1995, *Independent*, 7 June 1995, *The Times*, 8 June 1995.

34. "Surveillance and Estimation of Dietary Exposure to Pesticides, Report of the Working Party on Pesticide Residues: 1991–93", the 50th report of the Steering Group on Chemical Aspects of Food Surveillance (MAFF, London, 1996).

35. *Ibid.*, para. 34 states that no pesticide residues were detected in 62% of potato samples: para. 41 of the report states that pesticide residues *were* detected in 48% of samples, which appears to give a total of 110%.

36. "Russia—An Environment in Crisis:, lecture at Royal Geographical Society, London, Apr. 1995 by Professor Aleksei Yablokov, Chairman of the Inter-Agency Commission on Ecological Security of Russia's National Security Council, adviser on environment to President Yeltsin.

37. B. Revich, quoted in Olga Bridges and Jim Bridges, *Losing Hope: The Environment and Health in Russia* (Avebury Studies in Green Research, Aldershot, 1996), 221.

38. *Agrow*, 3 May, 19 Apr., 1 Feb. 1996; *Pesticides News*, June 1996; *Pesticide Action Network Updates* service, Issue No. 27, Aug. 1996.

39. San Francisco Board of Supervisors, File No. 97–96–52; San Francisco Administrative Code Ch. 39.1 to 39.7.

40. N. 2 above, 25.

41. *EPA Partners for Pesticide Environmental Stewardship*, EPA 733–N–97–001, Mar. 1997, PEST SMART Update # 5.

42. Meeting with Ellen Hickey, Co-ordinator of Information and Publications, Pesticide Action Network, San Francisco, Cal., 18th Oct. 1996.

43. Adam Kirshner, "New U.S. Food Quality Protection Act: Does it Protect Consumers?" *Global Pesticide Campaigner*, Sept. 1996.

44. *Silent Spring* was published in London by Hamish Hamilton in 1963.

45. *Agrow*, No. 297, 30 Jan. 1998.

46. See e.g. "Environmental Agency Under Fire on Safety Rules", *New York Times*, 29 Dec. 1997.

47. *Agrow*, No. 299, 27 Feb. 1998.

48. *Agrow*, No. 298, 13 Feb. 1998.

49. See e.g. remarks of Caroline Cox, n. 27 above, about the U.S. EPA's "safe" tol-

erance for the use of the herbicide oxyfluorfen on strawberries. See also U.S. EPA 1997 "Oxyfluorfen: Pesticide tolerance for emergency exemption" (1997) Fed. Reg. 62(80): 20104–11.

50. Theo Colborn, Dianne Dumanoski and John Peterson Myers, *Our Stolen Future—Are We Threatening Our Fertility, Intelligence and Survival? A Scientific Detective Story* (Penguin, New York, 1997).

51. For a thorough scientific review of the state of research on endocrine disruptors at the time of its publication, see Robert J. Kavlock *et al.*, "Research Needs for the Risk Assessment of Health and Environmental Effects of Endocrine Disruptors: A Report of the U.S. EPA-sponsored workshop", 104 *Environmental Health Perspectives*, Suppl. 4, Aug. 1996.

52. Environment Agency (for England and Wales), *Endocrine-disrupting substances in wildlife, and Endocrine-disrupting substances in the environment: What should be done?* Rio House, Aztec West, Almondsbury, Bristol BS12 4UD (1998).

53. *ENDS Report* 278, Mar. 1998 (Environmental Data Services Ltd.).

54. N. 43 above.

55. Thomas Dunlap, DDT, *Scientist, Citizens and Public Policy* (Princeton University Press, Princeton, N.J., 1981), 44, quoted in Robert F. Wasserstrom and Richard Wiles, "Field Duty—U.S. Farm workers and Pesticide Safety" World Resources Institute Study 3, July 1985. Though a few years old, the latter study is a useful review of the issue.

56. Robert Lenzner and Bruce Upbin, "*Monsanto v. Malthus*" *Forbes*, 10 Mar. 1997, quoting Monsanto CEO, Robert Shapiro.

57. He may have had in mind remarks such as those of the environmentalist Ralph Nader to the California Greens, who complained that with the patenting of genes, we are "40 year away from humanoids". It was therefore interesting that President Clinton responded to the news from Britain of the first successful cloning of a sheep by calling for an immediate report, and then in June 1997 banning the use of any federal facilities for similar experiments with human beings, also proposing legislation to make this ban effective in regulating all such research outside.

58. (Massachusetts Institute of Technology and Union of Concerned Scientists, Boston, Mass. 1996).

59. A similar point is made by Edward Tenner in *Why Things Bite Back: Technology and the Revenge of Unintended Consequences* (Knopf, New York 1996) 110: "monoculture and drenching with the same herbicide seems likely to result in herbicide resistant weeds."

60. At 38.

61. *Ibid.*, at 41.

62. Malcolm K. Sparrow, *Imposing Duties—Government's Changing Approach to Compliance* (Praeger, Westport, Conn., 1994),95, quoting Susan Rosegrant "The Toxics Release Inventory: Sharing Government Information with the Public", John F. Kennedy School of Government, Harvard University, Cambridge, Mass.

63. Meeting with Lawrence E. Cowles, Environmental Health and Safety Manager, Read-Rite Corporation: Chair, Environmental Committee, Silicon Valley Manufacturing Group, Fremont, Cal., 6 May 1997.
64. Carolyn Hartman, US Public Interest Research Group, presentation at National Pollution Prevention Roundtable Spring Conference, Denver, Colo., 2 Apr. 1997.
65. Visits to Asarco Inc, Ray complex, Hayden, Ariz. 18 Feb. 1997 and Cyprus Miami Mining Corporation, Claypool, Ariz., 19 Feb. 1997.
66. Remarks by the President to the People of Kalamazoo, 28 Aug. 1996, copy obtained from the White House Office of Speechwriting.
67. U.S. EPA Press Release Environmental News, Thursday, 27 Feb. 1997 "Browner announces new EPA Offices to support children's health, regulatory reinvention and Right-to-Know".
68. U.S. EPA 222–R–95–002, Apr. 1995, EPA Environmental Justice Strategy: Executive Order 12898, Office of Environmental Justice.
69. David Rejeski: "GIS and Risk: A Three-Culture Problem", in Michael F. Goodchild, Bradley O. Parks, Louis T. Steyaert, *Environmental Modelling with GIS* (Oxford University Press, 1993).
70. David V. Bates, *Environmental Health Risks and Public Policy: Decision Making in Free Societies* (University of Washington Press, Seattle, Wash. 1994).

5

Common Problems, Common Themes?

There is a trend towards specialism within the field of environmental law. The number and complexity of the statutes and regulations within each field make it increasingly difficult, even for a lawyer working almost exclusively on environmental law, to master all of its aspects. It is difficult to be equally authoritative about the laws on waste, radioactive substances, contaminated land, water and air pollution, land use planning, wildlife and countryside protection and so on. Environmental lawyers tend to specialise, either by choice or simply by virtue of the work they take on.

It is therefore sometimes difficult to identify common trends across a number of environmental issues that may be important to the wider question of how to make environmental laws work better. This chapter takes several widely differing environmental issues and looks for common themes. It considers three well known issues: environmental degradation in Russia, the environmental justice movement in America and water pollution in the Mississippi River. And it speculates on whether any of the common themes to be drawn from these three issues may be relevant to three current environmental issues: the pressure of development in Britain and America, the growth in traffic volumes in both jurisdictions and the issue of global warming.

Clearly there are going to be limits to this process of looking for common themes to environmental problems. There is unlikely to be some kind of global "solution" or universal truth to be discovered just outside the margins of one's own specialism. But the pursuit of specialism in both environmental law and policy making carries some risk of missing the wood for the trees.

Environmental regulators are often urged to take an integrated approach to the protection of the environment. The Environment Agency for England and Wales was brought together for this express purpose in 1995, formed from the waste regulation arm of local authorities, the National Rivers Authority, which protected the water environment, and Her Majesty's Inspectorate of Pollution, which regulated industrial emissions.[1] However, it will be some time before each of that agency's pollution control staff is equipped to deal with pollution issues in all the different media. The U.S. Environmental Protection Agency too has attempted a variety of initiatives to break down the barriers between the fiefdoms of its different "Offices", to try to get those who know about water to co-operate fully with the experts on underground storage tanks, or toxics, or indoor air pollution. In the European Community, the Directive on Integrated Pollution Prevention and Control[2] is supposed to have made major inroads on the process of integrating pollution control mechanisms.

The integration of environmental policy-making and an integrated approach to making environmental laws has not quite happened yet. The tendency is still to wrestle with the problems one medium at a time, and to have legislation specific to air, water and land. It is worth considering what we may be missing.

RUSSIA'S BELEAGUERED ENVIRONMENT

Professor Alexei Yablokov, Chairman of the Inter-Agency Commission on Ecological Security of Russia's National Security Council, and adviser on the environment to President Yeltsin, has said that 75 per cent of surface water in Russia is undrinkable.[3] Considering for a moment the size of Russia, this statistic is remarkable. Groundwater in Russia is also massively contaminated.

Four nuclear reactors and 11,000 containers of solid nuclear waste have been dumped in the Kara Sea. In the city of Tomsk 2 in 1993 100 square kilometers was polluted by a nuclear explosion. There have been 115 underground nuclear explosions in the area of the former USSR, and some of that radioactivity is now reaching the surface. There are 50 to 60 radioactivity incidents in Moscow every year. The storage dump for spent nuclear fuel rods from the Russian Pacific Fleet is piled up in the open and protected only by barbed wire.

The wastage of natural resources entailed by Russia's disregard of the environment is spectacular. An estimated 1.2 per cent of Russia's total oil production is lost through spillage. There are several hundred big spills *per annum*, about two a day. A further 10 per cent to 20 per cent or more is probably lost in transit through the pipeline system.[4] One of the brightest lights observable on Earth from space is the gas being flared to waste in Northern Siberia. Eleven million hectares (24.2 million acres) of forest have been clear cut in Siberia. Partly as a result, Siberia now has 40 per cent less ozone over it than the previous average. As much as 1.6 million hectares (3.52 million acres) of land was despoiled by mining and the extraction of peat and building materials between 1976 and 1991.[5] Some 49,760 hectares of land (109,472 acres) is contaminated with Cs–137 (Curie) radiation.[6]

The effects of Russia's failed environmental policies, and those of the former Soviet Union, are national, regional and global. Over 100,000 square kilometers of land have been submerged by the rising levels of the Caspian Sea, while the Aral Sea is disappearing as the rivers that feed it have been diverted, leaving a fishing fleet stranded in a growing desert of contaminated dust.

Human Consequences

The state of the environment in Russia should be seen first and foremost as a human tragedy. Between 1980 and 1992, there was an 8.4 per cent increase in stillborn babies.[7] One of the many health effects of the state of the environment on Russian children has been the appearance of "yellow children", especially in the Altai region, brightly pigmented and with damaged brains, livers, blood, central nervous systems, kidneys and adrenal glands and retarded physical development[8]: half of those that survive are chronic invalids. Currently the most favoured explanation for this phenomenon is exposure to spent rocket fuel[9] and its products in the environment. Pictures of congenital birth defects from pollution "hotspots" like Chernobyl and Chelyabinsk, once seen, are not easily forgotten.

The human effects of Russia's environment can be found recorded in its statistics for life expectancy. Life expectancy in Russia fell between 1992 and 1995. It is now on average 58 years for men, compared to 76 years in the West. In grossly polluted areas like Magnetogorsk and Chelyabinsk it is nearer 50 years. In Dzerzhinsk, 235 miles East of Moscow, it is reported to be 42 years for men and 47 years for women.[10]

A Difference of Kind, or a Difference of Degree?

Commentators on the Russian environment sometimes imply that the country's problems are wholly different in kind from anything found in the West, as if none of that could ever happen here. It is doubtful whether this view stands up to close examination.

Valery Gnusarkov, a retired factory worker from Dzerzhinsk, was quoted in an article in the *Daily Telegraph* in 1997 as describing the air pollution in his area in these terms:[11]

> "The kids used to play hide and seek in orange fog a few years ago. . . . The smell was horrible, but you got used to it. The sky was always multi-coloured—green, yellow and grey. On the week-ends it was especially nasty."

But the description of the air in Dzerzhinsk in 1997 is not so very different from Claude Monet's description of the air in London in 1901 (Monet being more enthusiastic about the pollution because it was a challenge to paint):[12]

> "The fog in London assumes all sorts of colours: there are black, brown, yellow, green and purple fogs, and the interest in painting is to get the objects as seen through all the fogs."

Many people in Britain and elsewhere profess to be shocked by Russia's dumping of canisters of nuclear waste in the Kara Sea. Perhaps they tend to overlook the similar canisters dumped by Britain and other nations in the deep oceans in the 1950s and 1960s, and the long lines of upturned drums stored today at some of Britain's nuclear establishments, drums that would all have been dumped at sea but for the moratorium on marine dumping introduced in 1993 under the London Dumping Convention.[13] Issue by issue, it seems that the difference between the Russian environment and the environment in Western countries is not different in kind, but different in degree, in that Russia's environment is markedly worse. Similar problems have either been encountered in Western environments in the forgotten recent past, or they exist in Western countries today, albeit in a less extreme form.

International Pollution

Apart from its terrible human and economic consequences, the scale of environmental degradation in Russia is an immediate reminder of the international aspect of pollution and environmental issues. For Americans, only 50 miles separate Russian and Alaskan islands. The Northern provinces of Norway are only a few dozen miles from the port of Murmansk and the gross radioactive pollution of the military installations of the Kola peninsula. For several Welsh farmers still under semi-permanent restrictions on lamb sales because of radioactive contamination of their land from the Chernobyl radiation cloud, Russia is presumably quite close enough. It is easy to understand the lively interest that Europeans have in the current state of nuclear reactors made to the same design as that in Chernobyl, in Armenia and at Kozloduy in Bulgaria.

But forms of pollution other than nuclear pollution cross boundaries and confuse regulatory responses. High chimney stacks at American power stations put out the sulphur dioxide emissions that make acid rain in Canada, just as the high stacks in Britain help make acid rain in Scandinavia. Radioactive discharges into the Irish Sea from British Nuclear Fuels' plant at Sellafield on the west coast of England affect lobsters and seaweed off the coast of Norway and cause concern to the people of Ireland, while illegal drift nets based in Ireland decimate returning runs of migratory Atlantic salmon bound for the rivers of Britain. What goes up in the industrial Ruhr in Germany has a tendency, because of prevailing wind directions, to come down in South East England. The government of the state of Texas showed little interest in helping Mexico tackle the pollution problems just across its border, until its own environmental regulator pointed out that more than 50 per cent of the pollution generated by maquiladora industries in Mexico lands back in America.[14] It is increasingly clear that we need not only our own environmental laws to work, but those of other nations as well. As environmental law has developed as a subject, the study of comparative environmental laws, and how to make them work effectively together, has received less attention than its practical importance would justify.

No Lack of Science: What Went Wrong?

It is perfectly clear that any country with the scientific expertise to build an orbiting space station, even one like Mir, has the necessary skills to operate effective pollution treatment at most, if not all, of its factories. Nor is Russia a country with no history of the development of environmental laws and standards. The Russian scientist Dobroslavin wrote in 1874 that "water should be clear, colourless, should not have a sediment if left standing and should not have any taste or smell",[15] a prescription that would probably be recognised by the Drinking Water Inspectorate in Britain today. Dobroslavin introduced the concept of maximum permissible levels for individual substances in drinking water as part of quality assessment, in a textbook published in 1903, which puts the European Union's most recent revision of its 1980 Drinking Water Directive into some perspective. How, then did Russia come to such a state of wreckage of its environment?

Given that Russia is perfectly capable of passing environmental laws, and perfectly capable of basing them upon the most sophisticated science available, a large part of the blame for the failure of its environmental laws must lie in the failure to develop the means and the will to enforce them. Professor Yablokov has spoken about an area of Russia the size of France with only seven environmental inspectors in it, which tells its own story. But the problem goes wider than mere numbers and resources of enforcement personnel, vital as that is, and cannot be entirely separated from wider issues of the rule of law.

It is quite clear that under the regimes of Stalin and Brezhnev, no single aspect of the environment (with the possible exception of the Politburo's hunting reserves) ever took priority over the goals of military superiority, economic development and the demands of production. In a police state, expressions of concern about the environment could always be represented as a minority and bourgeois interest, which is ironic, because no one suffers more from the effects of pollution in Russia than its workforce and proletariat. Brezhnev-era officials, and latter-day business folk have always been able to get into their limousines and drive away.

The state of the environment in Russia, then, is direct evidence of the corruption of the political process and the complete absence of functioning democracy for such an extended period of time. The environment is one of the political issues just below political and economic survival that concerns everyone when it becomes bad enough. There is no mystery about its being, with crime, near the top of Russians' concerns in most opinion polls. Everyone has to breathe the air, drink the water, eat the pesticides and suffer the consequences.

Russia is a country of prodigiously talented people that is testimony to the fact that the worst environmental outcomes are achieved in countries where public opinion is ignored or suppressed, where corruption is allowed to flourish and where information on the true state of the environment is denied to its people. There is no Western democracy that is entirely comparable to Russia. But if the thesis is accepted that many of the real differences between its environment and that in the West are differences of degree and not differences of kind, Russia may provide us with a series of reminders.

CLOSER TO HOME: THE ISSUE OF ENVIRONMENTAL JUSTICE IN AMERICA

The concept of environmental justice, as discussed in America, concerns the disproportionate impact of some environmental policies on poor and minority communities. In America this has led both to attempts to develop legal concepts and rights, and to a political and social movement to promote environmental "justice" or "fairness", and to combat what is sometimes called environmental "racism". Environmental justice is seen by many in America as critical to the health and welfare of the poor and minorities in that country.

There were a number of landmarks on the way to the present high state of awareness of this issue in America. The implications of environmental policies for minorities were considered in a number of reports in the 1970s.[16] In 1983, prompted by Congressman Fauntroy, the U.S. General Accounting Office brought out a report to the effect that three out of four hazardous waste facilities in Region 4 (the South) of the U.S. Environmental Protection Agency were sited in African American communities.[17]

In 1987, the United Church of Christ produced its most notable report on environmental justice, entitled *Toxic Wastes and Race in the United States*.[18]

In 1990, Robert Bullard brought out his book *Dumping in Dixie*,[19] which became one of the first textbooks on environmental justice. By 1992, the U.S. Environmental Protection Agency had established an Office of Environmental Justice. And in 1994, President Clinton issued Executive Order 12898 requiring 11 Federal agencies to make the achievement of environmental justice part of their mission.

In Louisiana, the state's Department of Environmental Quality has set up its own Environmental Justice Programme, pointing out that:[20]

> . . . "with a population of over 4,200,000, Louisiana is home to over 800 chemical and petrochemical manufacturing facilities, oil refineries, paper mills, grain elevators and hazardous waste facilities. Many of these facilities are located along the 120 river miles which separate Baton Rouge from New Orleans. . . . In addition to being heavily industrialized, this area contains many rural, unincorporated, poor, predominantly African-American communities. These communities are some of the poorest in the United States. In fact, this area (part of the Lower Mississippi Delta Region) has been certified by the United States Congress as being the poorest in the nation".

In fact 24 per cent of Louisiana's population lives in poverty,[20] which is remarkable considering the variety and wealth of the corporations and industries operating in the state, by whose emissions their health is affected.

Several of the notable academic authorities on this topic in America have concluded that legal remedies for the problems of environmental justice may be difficult to pursue. Professor Robert Kuehn of Tulane University Law School in New Orleans has written about the unequal enforcement of environmental laws in different communities.[22] He reviewed the evidence of unequal penalties and unequal clean-up of waste sites, and noted that a number of cases had been brought alleging that these amounted to a breach of the civil rights of those affected, but that these cases had failed to establish an intent to discriminate on the part of the enforcement agencies. Professor Kuehn concluded:

> "The observation that most community environmental struggles are not won solely through the hands of lawyers is profoundly accurate. If equal enforcement of environmental laws is to be achieved, then all aspects of the enforcement process need to be opened up to the residents of the affected communities—their participation in making enforcement decisions must be sought out, their opinions and desires respected and addressed, and their ability to protect their own communities and police the facilities in those communities enhanced."[23]

Professor Kuehn accepts that some legal mechanisms offer some hope of achieving more even enforcement of environmental laws. He gives as an example the increased use in civil penalty assessments made by regulatory agencies of Supplemental Environmental Projects. These projects, which are considered in more detail in Chapter 7, often require specific actions to be taken to benefit the local environment and to provide better information to local communities, instead of simply fining the person or firm who has violated environmental statutes. But he is equally ready to point to political and social pressures as the way to achieve results. In Louisiana, he has noted the effectiveness of right-to-know legislation in raising levels of public awareness; the use of advisory groups with technical support funded by permit applicants, as in Superfund Technical Assistance Grant Programmes, allowing local communities to hire their own experts to investigate a proposal; and better public notice of proposals.[24]

Professor Gerald Torres of the University of Texas Law School was formerly Counsel to the Attorney General, and one of the authors of the President's Executive Order on Environmental Justice. He has analysed two lines of cases in America where plaintiffs have sought to advance the idea as a legal concept. The first group was based on constitutional civil rights, arguing that for identifiable communities to be disadvantaged by carrying greater environmental burdens than other communities offended constitutional principles of equality as found in the civil rights statutes.[25] Professor Torres noted that these cases were largely ineffective. The second line of cases tried to address the equality question and the maldistribution of burdens by tackling environmental statutes and the regulations used to implement them. Professor Torres has said that these cases "have had a mixed bag of successes and failures". He identified the really important change as being one in the regulatory culture.

Professor Torres has argued that:[26]

> ... "litigation, while at times useful and even necessary, may not be the most productive forum for people of color to address the environmental hazards imposed upon their communities. The doctrinal constraints of the equal protection clause, statutory limitations of substantive environmental laws and regulations, as well as practical and political considerations, all counsel that the battle for environmental justice may be better fought in the political, rather than judicial, forum."

THE PRESIDENT'S EXECUTIVE ORDER ON ENVIRONMENTAL JUSTICE OF 1994

A Presidential Executive Order on environmental justice signed in 1994 has been one of the most important ways in which the executive in America has sought to reform the way it addresses the question. The Order[27] requires that:

> ... "to the greatest extent practicable and permitted by law ... each Federal agency shall make achieving environmental justice part of its mission by identify-

ing and addressing, as appropriate, disproportionately high and adverse human health or environmental effects of its programs, policies and activities on minority populations or low-income populations."

An inter-agency working group was established, each agency or Federal department involved was required to develop a strategy to implement the order, key changes were made to widen the scope of risk assessment to include, for example, populations' dependence on subsistence consumption of fish and wildlife, and there was heavy emphasis on public participation and access to clear public information. Professor Torres, who helped to draft the Executive Order, has expressed the hope that it would become "naturalized into the DNA" of the agencies,[28] becoming part of their decision-making process in the same way as the National Environmental Policy Act of 1969[29] requirements for environmental impact statements.

White House briefing on the Executive Order emphasised the element of public participation and information:[30]

"Each Federal Agency shall provide opportunities for community input in the NEPA process, including identifying potential effects and mitigation measures in consultation with affected communities and improving the accessibility of meetings, crucial documents and notices."

The influence of the Executive Order can be seen to have worked down and out through the branches and regional offices of federal government agencies. For example, from general guidance on the elements of the Order,[31] the U.S. Environmental Protection Agency has gone on to develop strategies in each region for its implementation.[32]

The Environmental Protection Agency has now developed an Agency-wide strategy for implementing the Executive Order.[33] The expressed goals of this strategy are:

"* No segment of the population, regardless of race, color, national origin, or income, as a result of EPA's policies, programs and activities, suffers disproportionately from adverse human health or environmental effects, and all people live in clean, healthy and sustainable communities.
* Those who live with environmental decisions—community residents, State, Tribal and local governments, environmental groups, businesses—must have every opportunity for public participation in the making of those decisions. An informed and involved community is a necessary and integral part of the process to protect the environment."

The Environmental Protection Agency's strategy promises that future legislation will incorporate techniques to improve public participation, and will "be responsive to environmental justice health research and data needs". In other words, concepts of environmental justice will increasingly play a part in all sorts of aspects of environmental laws in America: how risks are assessed, how laws are written, how they are enforced and how the public is involved. The environmental justice issue in America underlines that it is critical not only that environmental laws should work and be effective, but that they should do so consistently and fairly across all sections of society.

THEMES OF THE ENVIRONMENTAL JUSTICE MOVEMENT

The history of the environmental justice movement in America suggests that environmental laws by themselves can go only so far in addressing environmental problems. Without the vigorous and active participation of the communities affected, the legal means to address their problems were relatively ineffective. The political aspect of environmental lawmaking was explored in Chapter 2 of this book, but is clearly evidenced in many countries and at all levels. In Russia, while the majority of the people had no means of political expression or involvement in environmental issues, the state of the environment went into precipitate decline. In America's poorest communities, the real improvements began when the issue became important politically.

Executive action to address environmental problems can be effective, but depends upon there being an effective machinery of government in place to deliver results. The American President signs Executive Orders and the Russian President signs decrees, but there is quite a difference in the institutional capacity of America and Russia to make things happen as a result.

The environmental justice movement has also emphasised the critical importance of effective enforcement of environmental laws, and the need for this enforcement to be evenly and fairly applied.

DRINKING THE MISSISSIPPI

The great Mississippi River starts its long journey in Lake Itasca in Minnesota. From the farmland of Minnesota and Tennessee it collects its first loading of pesticides and herbicides, the run-off from urban areas and the sewerage from the towns and cities along its banks. It is estimated that 100,000 metric tons of pesticides and more than 6.3 million tons of nitrogen fertiliser were applied to cropland in the Mississippi basin in 1991.[34] For decades past the hundreds of industries along the Mississippi have dumped their wastes, often untreated, into the river. Garbage dumps and landfills, waste oil, chemicals, fertiliser wastes, dioxins from paper mills, nuclear material from the Department of Energy processing facility at Paduka, Kentucky have all joined the stream. A sign at the entrance to Times Beach, just outside St Louis, in 1986 read as follows:

"CAUTION
HAZARDOUS WASTE SITE
DIOXIN CONTAMINATION
* stay in your car
* minimize travel
* keep windows closed
* stay on pavement
* drive slowly".[35]

In Centreville, Mississippi, waste flowing into the Buffalo river, a tributary of the main river, is known locally as "the Valley of the Blobs", and by the Environmental Protection Agency as "Rubber Glaciers".[36] Waste rubber from Exxon Chemical's plant in Baton Rouge and DuPont's facility in Laplace, Louisiana, was dumped there by a commercial hazardous waste facility operating 45 miles south of Baton Rouge. Just north of Baton Rouge is Devil's Swamp, a 52-acre site where thousands of barrels of toxic and hazardous waste were dumped between 1965 and 1980. The swamp is also grossly contaminated by the "Petro" site. Twice a year it floods, and the contamination carries on down the river.

Below Baton Rouge is the River Road which runs along the Mississippi levees, and which is home to so many of the great chemical manufacturing plant in America, like the huge Agrico fertiliser factories. Pipes lead across the road above the cars, taking water in to the plant and discharging effluent back into the river.

And downstream of all this lies the city of New Orleans. In Britain in 1995 the Severn Trent water company was prosecuted for the criminal offence of supplying water unfit for human consumption to the city of Worcester.[37] Chemical contamination passed through a sewage treatment plant, also run by the Severn Trent company at Wem in Shropshire, flowed 70 miles downstream and passed undetected through the drinking water treatment plant in Worcester and several other places. Water in supply in the city was found to taste and smell foul, although strenuous efforts which resulted in an accurate analysis of the chemical involved, several days later, indicated no evidence of other adverse health effects. The incident should serve as a "wake up call" for all companies and facilities drawing water directly from a heavily used river source, without the benefit of bankside storage, which allows a little more time for analysis before water is piped to households.

The city of New Orleans draws its drinking water directly from the Mississippi River, at the elderly Carrollton water treatment works. It would be surprising if this state of affairs did not result, sooner or later, in a serious chemical contamination incident affecting the city's drinking water supply. As it is, some 15 years ago fly ash particles passed into New Orleans' drinking water. In 1981, the Georgia Pacific Chemical company released 42 tons of waste from a sludge pit near Baton Rouge. The phenols in the waste caused New Orleans drinking water to taste like oil. With the addition of chlorine disinfectant, the oily taste could still be detected in concentrations of parts per billion.[38] This is the river of which Thomas Jefferson wrote in 1784:[39]

> "This river yields turtle of a peculiar kind, perch, trout, gar, pike, mullets, her-rings, carp, spatula-fish of fifty pounds weight, cat-fish of one hundred pounds weight, buffalo fish, and sturgeon. Alligators or crocodiles have been seen as high up as the Acansas, It also abounds in herons, cranes, ducks, brant, geese and swans."

When the Mississippi River flooded in 1993, the authorities warned against direct skin contact with sandbags used to control the floods, because of the levels of pesticides, industrial waste and sewerage that they con-tained.[40] Yet this is the source of New Orleans' drinking water. In all, 1.5 mil-lion people in Louisiana drink water supplied from 22 treatment plants on the main Mississippi river, and five more on the Bayou Laforche.[41]

LESSONS OF THE MISSISSIPPI

The idea of drinking the Mississippi brings home a number of points about environmental laws. Their efficacy is an international matter, but it is more than that. It affects minorities and the underprivileged, but it affects every-one else too. It is a matter of legitimate concern to everyone who drinks water in New Orleans, white or black, rich or poor, that environmental laws are observed over the long term and over a wide area. Pollution may be of recent origin, or the "bio-accumulative" legacy of production methods using polychlorinated biphenols, "PCBs", dioxins, furans or DDT. The laws which govern the use of pesticides on farmland in Minnesota, the emissions of PCBs in Kentucky, the release of dioxins from paper mills in Louisiana or the disposal of oily wastes in Mississippi state, matter to the water drinkers of Louisiana.

THREE ISSUES FOR THE FUTURE:
DEVELOPMENT, TRAFFIC AND GLOBAL WARMING

Three issues on the current environmental agenda in both America and Britain—the pressures of development, the likely rise in traffic volume and the effects of global warming—are also worth considering in terms of the demands that they may place upon future environmental legislators, and the level of understanding and co-operation that may exist between those legislators and those for whom they pass laws.

Wherever environmental laws and laws for the protection and conservation of the countryside hold the line, the pressure to wear them down and find chinks in the armour is relentless. Nowhere is this more true than in the field of development, a phenomenon which affects America just as much as it does Britain. The outskirts of Portland, Oregon, for example, have witnessed some of the fastest growth and development anywhere in America. This is fuelled in part by the booming economy along America's west coast, and the extension of a computer and electronics industry "corridor" up from Silicon Valley in California and down from Seattle in Washington state. Just outside Portland is the spectacular Columbia River Gorge, where a National Scenic Area Act protects a large area against unbridled development. Laurie Annan, Executive Director of the "Friends of the Columbia Gorge", has identified the pressures of population growth and development as the toughest threat that the area faces, and gives the following statistics.[42] Between 1986 and 1994, population growth in the areas of Clark County, Gresham and Troutdale, the areas adjoining Portland, was 33 per cent, 75 per cent and 48 per cent respectively. The last ten years have seen a doubling of commuting from the Gorge area. Seven hundred thousand people are expected to move into the area in the next ten years.

While not quite as dramatic as growth in other cities of the American west, such as Phoenix, Arizona, which is growing at the rate of an acre an hour, Portland, Oregon, even with its careful town planning, green belt policies, promotion of greater density and discouragement of urban sprawl, is showing signs of the problems of success. Computer and high tech industries gobble up greenfield sites on its boundaries, where groves of hazel nut trees and vineyards can be seen giving way to construction sites. For many of them, the assumption of Superfund liabilities for any site they take on is a further factor in encouraging development on virgin farmland rather than re-use of "brownfield" sites.[43] Ironically, the farmland itself can prove to be affected by decades of pesticide use.

In Britain, too, new development seems certain to be one of the key factors with which environmental laws will have to contend in the next few decades. Household numbers in the U.K. are expected to grow much faster than the growth in population, partly as a result of factors such as the rising divorce rate, falling rates of remarriage, an increase of single-person households and more elderly people living alone. Current estimates are of a growth in household numbers of 4.4 million in England between 1991 and 2016, an increase of 23 per cent.[44] These figures, which were obscure and relatively uncontroversial as recently as 1996 are now hotly disputed and very politically contentious as major planning decisions come to be taken based in part on the figures. Even if the Government achieved the target of building 60 per cent of these new households on previously used land, it would still leave 1.76 million new homes to be built on greenfield sites. Every town and village could be different as a result, and many areas of countryside will change forever as they are slated for new developments or even new towns.

An increase in population of 20 per cent (2.6 million) is expected within the next 30 years in the parts of the Chesapeake watershed in Maryland, Pennsylvania, and Virginia.[45] In fact the close similarity between this category of environmental problems in Britain and America suggests that comparisons between the various solutions being worked on in both countries could usefully be more regular and systematic.

It is ironic that there seems to be a kind of inverse law affecting development. Where unbridled development has taken place such as that in some western cities of America, with few constraints on developers, the potential is stored up for many more regulatory interventions in the future. One inevitable result of urban sprawl is the generation of more traffic and air pollution. And legislation to combat air pollution can be highly interventionist, prescriptive and bossy. This can be seen from American plans to spend an estimated $6 billion to $9 billion on the implementation of proposed new standards for ozone and particulates in air, or the wide new powers taken in Britain in the Environment Act 1995[46] to implement the National Air Quality Strategy.

The issue of development is driving the evolution of policy and law, in both America and Britain. With the one will come the other. It matters greatly that the correct balance is struck between what is necessary as regulation and the infringement of personal freedoms. The well established land use planning legislation in both jurisdictions is going to be severely tested by development on the scale presently envisaged. For smaller decisions, the land use planning system in both countries has clear policies and practices for public consultation and public participation. But for the largest planning issues in Britain, planning inquiries such as those concerning Terminal 5 of London's Heathrow Airport or the construction of the Sizewell B nuclear power station in Suffolk seem to go on for ever. If the pressures of development are such that applications are made to build whole new towns, better means may have to be found to ensure proper public participation and the ability to challenge a developer's case effectively, without resulting in planning paralysis.

TRANSPORT AND TRAFFIC

In 1989, the Department of Transport in England published forecasts of probable traffic growth in Britain between 1988 and 2025. Two levels were used, based on different projections of economic growth. The high forecast was of a 142 per cent increase, and the low forecast was of an 83 per cent increase. In other words, it was expected that traffic in Britain will more or less double by 2025 on current trends.[47] The number of cars on the road has increased from 2.5 million in 1951 to about 20 million in 1990,[48] and is set to increase further.

The Royal Commission on Environmental Pollution, in its Eighteenth Report, on Transport and the Environment, commented on these projections:

> "There is general recognition that further growth in road traffic on anything like the scale shown in the 1989 forecasts would have enormous repercussions for the environment, and widespread doubt about whether it would be practicable to accommodate such growth."[49]

The description of increasing volumes of traffic in the Chesapeake Bay area of America could equally well fit Britain:[50]

> . . . "gains made in cleaning up individual cars are likely to be offset or even out-stripped by growth in vehicle miles travelled".

What regulations will be necessary, what laws will result from an increase in traffic on anything like the scale of the forecasts of the then Department of Transport? Quite clearly traffic increases of this magnitude have all sorts of implications for road building, for the use of aggregates, for air pollution, for traffic regulation. Once again, the development of effective environmental laws, generally supported by the majority of those affected by them, will be a critically important part of government's response to the traffic issue.

Since May 1997 Britain's Labour government has merged the Department of the Environment with the Department of Transport. It has used Britain's Presidency of the European Union in 1998 to hold joint meetings of the Council of Ministers between both environment and transport ministers from the Member States of the Union. And it has promised to promote its Integrated Transport Policy in 1998 as the cornerstone of its efforts to tackle the issues comprehensively.

CLIMATE CHANGE

"Global warming" declares Robert Hahn in a book critical of the views of Vice President Al Gore "is the ultimate example of media alarmism".[51] This view is not shared by the Global Environmental Monitoring Service of the United Nations Environment Programme in Nairobi, Kenya, nor by the group of scientists assembled by the United Kingdom government to provide advice on the likely effects of global warming on Britain.

The U.K. contributes 2.7 per cent of the world's carbon dioxide,[52] 1.2 per cent of its methane[53] and its share of other contributors to the climate changes currently under way and observed by the Intergovernmental Panel on Climate Change (IPCC). About 2.8 tonnes of carbon *per capita* per year are emitted in the U.K., as compared with about five tonnes *per capita* per year in the United States and 0.2 tonnes per year for many developing countries.[54]

In 1996 the U.K. Climate Change Impacts Review Group, mainly composed of distinguished academics, proposed a "scenario" for the United Kingdom for the decades of the 2020s and 2050s, assuming that no major global policies of reducing greenhouse gas emissions were enacted.[55]

This group expects the climate in Britain to be about 0.9 degrees Centigrade warmer (than the 1961–1990 average) by the 2020s, and about 1.6 degrees Centigrade warmer by the 2050s. The exact effects of such a temperature rise are hard to predict overall, let alone in their specific regional effects. But they are expected to include a five-centimetre rise in sea levels per decade, exacerbated by the fact that South and East England is sinking slightly, while the North of Britain is rising. Therefore, the North of Britain is expected to become wetter, the South drier, with a shift in climate northward by 200 kilometres and upward by 200 feet for every one degree Centigrade rise in temperature. This is bad news for Alpine plants in the Cairngorms, and many of the nature reserves in the South of England may prove to be in the wrong place for the new trends. More extreme weather events are predicted, and threats of flooding in parts of East Anglia, Lancashire, Yorkshire, Lincolnshire, Essex, Somerset, Sussex, the Thames estuary, North Wales, the Clyde and Forth estuaries and Belfast Lough.

Vice-President Gore has put the question of global warming in these terms:[56]

"What will global warming produce—a new worldwide bureaucracy to manage the unimaginable problems caused by massive social and political upheavals, mass migration, and the continuing damage to the global environment by civilisation itself? Is that what we want? Wouldn't it be better to prevent the chaos instead of scrambling to cope with it after it occurs?"

Whatever the answer to these questions, whether society chooses to try to prevent the "chaos" of global warming or to "scramble to cope with it after it occurs", the use of environmental laws will be part of the response. The lawmaking process needs to be put in good repair, the compact between lawmakers and the governed re-defined and re-made if any impact is to be made successfully on problems of such a global scale.

CONCLUSIONS

Perhaps after all some common themes have emerged from this chapter's exercise in lateral thinking. The international element to many of our environmental problems, and to any effective solution to them, can be seen in Russia's environment, and in the response to global warming. If the Kyoto Protocol is ratified, future environmental laws may be required specifically to deal with emissions trading, for example between America and Russia.

The need for effective public participation, and the importance of active political support for environmental protection, emerged from most of the issues described in this chapter. The greater the problem, the greater the need for effective steps to ensure public understanding and support for what may be prescriptive measures.

The value of an integrated approach to environmental issues, rather than one dealing only with one environmental medium at a time, can be seen in the question of the Mississippi, which may be polluted on a farm or factory in Kentucky but drunk in Louisiana.

Finally, the chapter touched on the central importance of fair, consistent and effective enforcement of environmental laws, an issue important to Russians and Americans, and to the rest of us. The next two chapters of this book consider in more detail aspects of the criminal and civil enforcement of environmental laws in America that may be of particular significance to the United Kingdom.

REFERENCES

1. Environment Act 1995, Pt. I.
2. Council Dir. (96/61/EC) of 24 Sept. 1996 concerning Integrated Pollution Prevention and Control [1996] O.J. L257. Primary legislation to implement this Dir. may be introduced into the Westminster Parliament in autumn 1998.
3. Prof. Alexei Yablokov, lecture "Russia—An Environment in Crisis" at the Royal Geographical Society, London, Apr. 1995. Except where stated, the statistics given in this section are drawn from this lecture.
4. Olga Bridges and Jim Bridges, *Losing Hope: The Environment and Health in Russia* (Avebury Studies in Green Research, Aldershot, 1996), 102, also recommended as an overview of environmental pollution and its health effects in Russia.
5. *Ibid.*, 94.

6. *Ibid.*, 110.

7. *Ibid.*, 179, Table 5.3.

8. *Ibid.*, 221.

9. Apparently Asymmetrical Dimethyl Hydrazine.

10. Nanette van der Laan, "Struggle for life in Russia's poison city", *Daily Telegraph*, 2 May 1997.

11. *Ibid.*

12. Quoted by David V. Bates, *Environmental Health Risks and Public Policy: Decision Making in Free Societies* (University of Washington Press, Seattle, Wash., 1994).

13. London Dumping Convention 1972: the 26th Meeting of parties in Nov. 1993 banned the dumping of all radioactive wastes in the open sea (Resolution LC.51(16), amending Annex I and II of the Convention). See Stephen Tromans and James Fitzgerald, *The Law of Nuclear Installations and Radioactive Substances* (Sweet & Maxwell, London 1997), on international rules on sea disposal.

14. Meeting at Texas Natural Resources Conservation Commission, Austin, Tex., 5 Nov. 1996.

15. N. 4 above, 56.

16. Council on Environmental Quality, *Council on Environmental Quality, Annual Report 1971* (CEQ, Washington, D.C., 1971) acknowledging that racial discrimination adversely affected the urban poor and the quality of their environment; see also U.S. Commission on Civil Rights, the Federal Civil Rights Enforcement Effort—1974 (1975) criticising the U.S. Environmental Protection Agency for failing to take into account the implications of its policies for minorities and the poor.

17. U.S. General Accounting Office, *Siting of Hazardous Waste Landfills and their Correlation with Racial and Economic Status of Surrounding Communities* (U.S. GAO, Washington, D.C., 1983).

18. United Church of Christ, Commission for Racial Justice, *Toxic Wastes and Race in the United States: A National Report on the Racial and Socio-Economic Characteristics of Communities with Hazardous Waste Sites* (United Church of Christ, New York, 1987). This report was updated in 1994: *Toxic Waste and Race Revisited*.

19. *Dumping in Dixie: Race, Class and Environmental Quality* (Westview Press Inc., Boulder, Colo., 1994).

20. Janice F. Dickerson and Roger K. Ward, *Environmental Justice in Louisiana— The Louisiana Department of Environmental Quality's Environmental Justice Program* (Louisiana, D.E.Q., Baton Rouge, Lou., 1996).

21. Heather L. Gold and Kenneth E. Thorpe, *Louisiana Health Care Data Book*, prepared for the Institute of Health Services Research, Department of Health Systems Management, Tulane University Medical Center (Tulane, New Orleans, Lou., 1996).

22. Robert R. Kuehn, "Remedying the Unequal Enforcement of Environmental Laws" (1993–4) 9 *St. John's Journal of Legal Commentary*, 625.

23. *Ibid.*, 667.
24. Interview with Professor Kuehn, Tulane University Law School, 25 Oct. 1996.
25. Gerald Torres, "Keynote Address: Changing the Way Government Views Environmental Justice" (1993–4) 9 *St. John's Journal of Legal Commentary* 543, at 545: see also 541–2.
26. Gerald Torres, "Environmental Burdens and Democratic Justice" (1993–4) xxi *Fordham Urban Law Journal*, 431, at 436).
27. Federal Register, Vol. 59, No. 32, Wednesday, 16 Feb. 1994. President's Executive Order 12898 of 11 Feb. 1994, "Federal Actions to Address Environmental Justice in Minority Populations and Low-Income Populations".
28. Interview with Professor Torres, Austin, Tex., 5 Nov. 1996.
29. 42 U.S.C. § 4321 *et seq.*
30. The White House, Office of the Press Secretary, 11 Feb. 1994, Memorandum for the Heads of All Departments and Agencies, Subject: Executive Order on Federal Actions to Address Environmental Justice in Minority Populations and Low-Income Populations.
31. EPA InSight Policy Paper, Mar. 1994, EPA–175–N–94–001 Executive Order 12898 on Environmental Justice.
32. See e.g. Memorandum dated 30 Sept. 1994, "Region 10 Vision of Environmental Justice," promising for the Agency's Region 10, based in Seattle, "EJ training for all employees" and a "variety of community outreach activities".
33. EPA Environmental Justice Strategy: Executive Order 12898, EPA/200–R–95–002, Apr. 1995.
34. U.S. Department of Agriculture and U.S. Environmental Protection Agency estimates, quoted in Dennis Demcheck, "Water Quality in the Mississippi River: Reputation and Reality", *U.S. Geological Survey*, Envirodecision, Vol. 2. No. 3.
35. Michael H. Brown, "The National Swill—Poisoning Old Man River" *Science Digest*, June 1986.
36. Letter from William Fontenot, Louisiana Department of Justice, Public Protection Division, 15 May 1997.
37. Contrary to s. 70 of the Water Resources Act 1991.
38. Discussions by telephone with William Fontenot, Lousiana Department of Justice, May 1997.
39. Notes on Virginia, Query II.
40. Chris Offutt, "Troubles as the Water Drops", *New York Times*, 1 Sept. 1993, A19, quoted in Edward Tenner, *Why Things Bite Back, Technology and the Revenge of Unintended Consequences* (Knopf, New York, 1996).
41. Dugan S. Sabins, *Louisiana's Water Quality Strategy for the Mississippi River* (Louisiana Department of Environmental Quality, Office of Water Resources, Baton Rouge, Lou.).
42. Lecture at Northwestern School of Law of Lewis and Clark College, Portland, Ore., Sept. 1996.

43. A point made during a visit to the WaferTech semiconductor plant construction site, Camas-Washougal, Wash., with Bill Renfroe, Environmental Affairs Manager, 13 May 1997.

44. Government Green Paper "Household Growth: Where Shall we Live?" Cm 3471 (Department of Environment/HMSO, London, 1996).

45. Tom Horton and William M. Eichbaum, *Turning the Tide: Saving the Chesapeake Bay* (Island Press, Washington, D.C., 1991).

46. See e.g. s. 87 and Sched. 11.

47. Royal Commission on Environmental Pollution, Eighteenth Report, *Transport and the Environment*, Cm 2674 (HMSO, London, 1994), 19.

48. *The UK Environment 1992* (Department of Environment/HMSO, London, 1992), 219, para 15.62.

49. N. 46 above,19, para. 2.31.

50. N. 44 above.

51. Robert W. Hahn, "Toward a New-Environmental Paradigm", in John A. Baden *et al.*, *Environmental Gore—A Constructive Response to Earth in the Balance* (Pacific Research Institute for Public Policy, San Francisco Cal., 1994).

52. N. 48 above, 30, para 3.11.

53. *Ibid.*, 32, para. 3.16.

54. *Ibid.*, 30, para 3.11.

55. United Kingdom Climate Change Impacts Review Group, Second Report, *Review of the Potential Effects of Climate Change in the United Kingdom* (Department of the Environment/HMSO, London, Mar. 1996), p.i.

56. Senator Albert Gore, *Earth in the Balance: Ecology and the Human Spirit*, 79.

6

Use of the Criminal Law

"You want to make criminal offences serious, or criminality becomes meaningless."

Nancy Firestone, Deputy Assistant Attorney General, U.S. Department of Justice

THE CASE FOR THE CRIMINAL LAW

The U.S. Environmental Protection Agency has estimated that about 44 per cent of the facilities that it inspected in the Fiscal Year 1995 violated at least one environmental statute, and nearly 20 per cent violated three or more such statutes.[1] Some of these violations may have been trivial, or even inevitable. Managers of complex industrial facilities have to comply with highly complex environmental statutes. When a team of inspectors from the Agency visits a plant such as an oil refinery, it would be surprising if they found "nothing to report", given the complexity and prescriptive detail of so many of the environmental regulations applying to it.

Nevertheless, the Environmental Protection Agency can make a case for its criminal enforcement effort by reference to the number of firms and individuals committing environmental crimes. Hitherto, the Agency has published an annual report known as its "Enforcement Accomplishments" report, full of statistics about the number of civil and criminal enforcement actions brought that year. Preparation of such statistics is always a necessary part of defence of enforcement budgets.[2] Uncertainty whether this approach alone is enough, and concern that more should be done to help firms to comply rather than just punish them when they do not, has resulted in this report being re-named the "Enforcement and Compliance Assurance Accomplishments Report".

The Environmental Protection Agency is therefore not entirely immune from the tendency to mix messages and confuse objectives that is always possible where regulators are responsible for policing laws and for ensuring more generally that they are effectively complied with. The Agency's report for fiscal year 1995 contains this throw-back to the traditional approach (amidst more "user-friendly" news about compliance assurance):[3]

"Incarceration is a key component of the criminal enforcement program because of its deterrent effect. Individuals are more likely to be deterred from criminal environmental misconduct because of the stigma associated with a criminal conviction, as well as potential imprisonment. Those who are convicted and sentenced to jail cannot pass the sentence on as another 'cost of doing business'; it must be served by the violator. Since 1990, individuals have received over 422 years of incarceration for committing environmental crimes."

It is almost impossible to measure the effectiveness of criminal enforcement simply by the collection of statistics such as that for "years of incarceration". An analogy would be with newspaper reports of drug seizures. When we hear that half a ton of cocaine has been seized at the docks, is that evidence of the stunning effectiveness of Customs and Excise operations, or of the growing confidence of drug smugglers in importing their product in such bulk, or a bit of both? It is hard for outsiders to judge. Perhaps mindful of this, the U.S. Environmental Protection Agency has begun to try to find ways to measure its enforcement activity against the state of compliance with the laws in relevant sectors. The Agency's "Operating Principles" for its enforcement programme pledge to continue to count enforcement activities as a measure of success, but the Agency has also undertaken to measure actual results and the environmental impact of these and other activities.[4] It intends to collect and analyse information about the response of regulated parties to enforcement and compliance assurance actions, the benefits to human health and the environment from such actions, and the level of compliance in industry sectors. Although this effort is in its very early stages, it would be well worth British environmental regulators keeping this initiative under review.

SPARE THE ROD?

One aspect of American criminal enforcement of environmental laws does not emerge clearly from the statistical record. In America, both lawmakers and environmental regulators are much more selective in their use of the criminal law than their opposite numbers in Britain. This is a matter of conscious choice and policy at both Federal and state levels in America, and it also reflects the availability as an alternative of much more sophisticated procedures for civil and administrative enforcement there.

Earl Devaney, Director of the EPA's Office of Criminal Enforcement, supports reserving criminal sanctions for cases involving serious harm to the environment or human health and safety, or the threat of it. He has said:

"I like our cases to be directed to companies who knew it was a crime and went ahead and did it anyway. Routine negligence suggests a civil remedy."[5]

Nancy Firestone, Deputy Assistant Attorney General at the U.S. Department of Justice, has made a similar point, remarking that:

"You want to make criminal offences serious, or criminality becomes meaningless."[6]

Roughly 3 percent of the cases handled by the Department of Justice's Environmental and Natural Resources Division in 1997 consisted of criminal enforcement, with the other 97 per cent being made up of administrative and civil enforcement cases.[7]

Very much the same picture is reflected in the extensive enforcement of environmental laws undertaken by the American states. Twenty-two of the 23 attorneys employed by the Texas state environmental regulator on legal enforcement work undertake primarily administrative enforcement: only one specialises in criminal environmental law enforcement.[8] Oregon's "Guidelines for Bringing Criminal Charges" and the way that they are applied by the state's Department of Environmental Quality reflect the same emphasis. Officials with Oregon's Department of Environmental Quality talk of prosecuting only the "dirty dozen".[9] Again, one reason that they are able to be so selective is that they have available the alternative of civil and administrative enforcement processes and tribunals, considered in more depth in the next chapter.

Some English solicitors and members of the United Kingdom Environmental Law Association may tell you privately that several of their clients would benefit from incarceration as an encouragement to take environmental laws more seriously. But in America, fierce talk about incarceration and criminal enforcement from environmental regulators ought not to obscure the fact that it is reserved for the worst environmental offences, usually with elements of deliberate intent, criminal negligence, or some aspect of corruption of the system, such as the provision of falsified data, and where the actual or potential harm to the environment or human health was serious.

A case in point was reported on 27 May 1998, when the Lousiana-Pacific Timber Corporation pleaded guilty to pollution violations, and agreed to pay $37 million in penalties, including the largest ever fine ($5 million) in the history of the Clean Air Act 1970. The additional $31 million in fines were reported to be for such offences as doctoring reports, tampering with pollution equipment and lying to inspectors. The company was warned that further violations could result in its being barred from future government contracts, including access to timber from national forests.[10]

This is in sharp contrast to the approach to the criminal law in England and Wales and in Scotland. Here there is a long tradition of enacting criminal offences to cover even minor infractions and violations of criminal statutes. There is relatively little difference between the approach to investigation of the most serious environmental offences in Britain and America. But for any given year, these offences could almost be counted on the fingers of one hand. The National Rivers Authority's landmark prosecution of Shell in 1990 for oil pollution of the Mersey,[11] with its fine of £1 million; Her Majesty's Inspectorate of Pollution's criminal case in 1996 against the Coalite company for illegal dioxin emissions, with a fine of £150,000 and £300,000 in costs;[12] the Secretary of State for the Environment's first prosecution, brought by the Drinking Water Inspectorate, for the criminal offence of supplying water unfit for human consumption, brought against Severn Trent Water PLC in 1995, with its fine of £45,000;[13] the Environmental Agency's prosecution of the ICI Chemicals and Polymers company for a major chloroform spill in Runcorn, Cheshire, in 1998 with a fine of £300,000[14]—these are all cases which in most jurisdictions with well developed environmental laws would result in criminal investigations and prosecutions. They were important cases in their fields. They sent strong signals to the industries concerned. But there did not need to be a large number of them to have that effect. The difference between Britain and America is in the handling of the large number of "second order" violations of environmental statutes.

Breaches of byelaws concerning the pollution of streams from vessels have been criminal offences in England and Wales under the Rivers (Prevention of Pollution) Act of 1951.[15] Breaches of a drought order made under the Water Resources Act of 1991 are a criminal offence.[16] Failure to undertake required removal of deposits and vegetation in rivers, under the same Act, is a criminal offence.[17] Failure to provide the proper receptacles for commercial or industrial waste is a criminal offence under the Environmental Protection Act of 1990.[18] Non-registration of an alkali works is made a criminal offence by the Alkali etc. Works Regulation Act of 1906.[19] Whenever secondary legislation is made under environmental laws (and it has been noted in Chapter 3 that such regulations are being made in quantity all the time) it is absolutely standard practice to provide that any breach of the regulations is a criminal offence, however trivial that might appear.

In some areas, such as water pollution, there is a long history in England and Wales of strict liability attaching even to criminal offences such as that of public nuisance. In *R. v. Medley*, for example, in 1834,[20] the Solicitor General himself prosecuted the directors of a gas works that polluted the river Thames, killing numerous fish and threatening the livelihood of local fishermen. It was held to be no defence that the directors claimed to have no knowledge of the actions or emissions of their servants or agents in operating the works, despite this being a criminal prosecution for the offence of causing a public nuisance. When 20 tonnes of aluminium sulphate were released into drinking water supply in Camelford in Cornwall in 1988,[21] there was found to be no statutory criminal offence to cover the crime,[22] and public nuisance was once again used as the basis for a criminal prosecution of the company responsible for the spill, South West Water.

During the passage of the Environment Act of 1995, a number of attempts were made to introduce amendments into the legislation which would have amounted to a "due diligence" defence. In other words, companies or individuals charged with the criminal offence of causing pollution to water would have had a defence if they could have shown that they had taken all reasonable steps to avoid causing such pollution. These amendments were resisted by the Government and environmental regulators, not so much on grounds of principle as on grounds of practicality.[23] Unlike, for example, air pollution from a factory, water pollution often results from activities which are not themselves authorised or regulated. If there were to be a "due diligence" defence of the sort proposed in the debates on the Environment Bill in 1995, it would make it much harder in practice for a regulator to construct a case against someone causing water pollution. The regulator would have to show whether or not the defendant had done everything that he reasonably could to avoid causing the pollution. This would entail being able to investigate and prove much more about the precise state of the operations undertaken by the defendant which led to the pollution, and the balance of "advantage" would shift to the defendant to proceedings.

For example, the Environment Agency for England and Wales would have to show, in a case involving pollution of a river by farm slurry, both that the slurry caused the pollution, and that the farmer was not "duly diligent" in the way he handled the containment of the slurry. At present, the effect of the law is that a criminal offence is made out if a link is established between the polluting activity and the resulting pollution; in this case between the escape of slurry and the resulting pollution.

The amendments proposed to the water legislation might have resulted in a fairer application of the criminal law if they had been accepted. But the decisive argument against them, apart from the long history of strict liability for criminal offences in the water pollution area referred to above, was that the tough provisions of the Water Acts of 1989 and 1991 were necessary for the protection of waters against pollution. Lord Crickhowell, Chairman of the National Rivers Authority, pointed out in the Parliamentary debates on the Environment Bill that serious water pollution incidents had decreased by half since these Acts were passed and the National Rivers Authority was set up.[24]

Arguments against a "due diligence" defence might have been much less persuasive if an effective and comprehensive system of civil and administrative enforcement had been available as an alternative to the criminal courts, which it was not. The objects of prosecutions for causing water pollution are presumably deterrence, some measure of punishment and provision of the means of restitution of rivers and streams and fish stocks where pollution has caused damage. All these objects could be achieved as well or better by means of the civil law enforcement process which would be open to regulatory authorities in America. There would then be no need to use sophisticated arguments to show why the use of the criminal law is appropriate where there is no intent, and in ordinary language, no fault.

Apart from the water pollution area, those looking for purpose or design in the way that English law has come to use the criminal law to enforce environmental statutes may look in vain. It has grown up that way piecemeal, and out of habit as much as by design. But the almost exclusive reliance on the criminal law is not without consequences.

The most intangible, but perhaps the most important, of these consequences may be the way in which the criminal law itself must lose something of its impact if it is used in a mass of trivial cases. When a company is taken to the Crown Court on indictment for a serious criminal charge, with the potential for unlimited fines or terms of imprisonment for company officers, it may take note. But who really benefits when a large company is brought for summary trial before a magistrates' court for some technical infraction of regulations, and fined £250? Ultimately, this is not a proper use of the concept of criminality. Regulations have to be enforced to have any effect at all, but in many cases the American model, which would determine a civil penalty based on any gain that the company may have made from non-compliance, with punitive elements, is much more closely aligned to what the company has done or failed to do, without the rather artificial assertion of criminal behaviour.

We may tend to weaken our criminal law by applying it to too many situations where ordinary members of the public would have difficulty recognising criminal behaviour. It is not necessarily right to accept that corporations should face criminal sanctions the basis of which would never be acceptable if applied to individuals. The fact that very many of the host of minor criminal offences which are placed on the statute book are seldom prosecuted does not resolve the issue of whether they should be there in the first place. It may rather speak to the practical difficulties of enforcement which reliance on the criminal law import.

INVESTIGATIVE CAPACITY

The first of these practical difficulties is the requirement that any criminal case must be capable of proof to the criminal standard (beyond a reasonable doubt), and the implications that has for the investigative capacity of enforcement agencies. Much depends on the complexity of the case, but some elements are fairly standard. Investigations have to be planned, and each element of the criminal offences being investigated has to be capable of strict proof. Investigators must have arrangements, powers and procedures for carrying out any necessary searches, for securing physical evidence, for managing and documenting documentary and other evidence, for conducting interviews under caution, sometimes on tape, for taking witness statements, for reviewing their evidence and "plugging gaps", and for ensuring that all of this is carried out in a timely fashion and before the evidence goes stale. With the increasing complexity of rules concerning interviews and searches and disclosure of "unused" material, early and continuing consultation with lawyers is a necessary part of the routine.

All of this may be well within the capacity of large regulatory agencies bringing a significant number of prosecutions, but it tends to make the task of any smaller agency, perhaps staffed with scientists or engineers rather than trained investigators, much more difficult. Reliance on the criminal law is not without implications for costs, resources, personnel and training, and training scientists or environmental engineers to be criminal investigators is quite possible, but not necessarily the best use of their time and expertise. It is notable that in the civil environmental law enforcement procedures in an American state like Oregon, when a civil penalty is assessed against a firm for violation of an environmental statute, an opportunity exists for informal negotiation over the basis of that assessment and the evidence to support it before it becomes final. One result is that much of the argument revolves around areas with which the enforcement staff of the environmental agency are entirely familiar, rather than procedures which are outside their training and expertise.

Whatever the jurisdiction, practical co-operation between agencies with overlapping jurisdictions is essential to the achievement of good results. The U.S. Attorney's Office in Oregon has set up an environmental and fraud unit[25] to try to ensure that in these areas of complex litigation such crimes are not pushed aside by the demands of more immediate crimes such as armed robbery. In practice, however, the Federal Department of Justice still relies heavily on other agencies such as the Environmental Protection Agency to investigate and prepare the cases on which its lawyers advise. Much of the success of such investigations clearly depends on working relations between various Federal and state agencies. Where these are good, investigations obviously run much more smoothly, and in some states informal groups of those agencies with a possible interest in investigating and prosecuting environmental crimes meet regularly.

The Texas Environmental Enforcement Task Force, for example, provides such a forum, and has improved working relations and co-operation between

Federal and State agencies investigating offences with jurisdictions which sometimes overlap.[26] In Oregon, three investigators from the Federal Environmental Protection Agency work in an office located inside the state Department of Environmental Quality, which goes far to improving lines of communication between both agencies.[27]

In Britain there is much that can be done, without much difficulty or expense, to ensure that regular informal meetings take place before problems arise between environmental regulatory agencies and the police, Crown Prosecution Service and other bodies with overlapping responsibilities. It would be useful for environmental agencies in Britain, the Environment Agency for England and Wales and the Scottish Environmental Protection Agency, "SEPA", to discuss with the Environmental Protection Agency possibilities for members of their staff to receive training at the Environmental Protection Agency's National Enforcement Training Institutes in America. There are few equivalents in Europe. It would also be worthwhile to arrange links between the laboratories used in forensic scientific work in British environmental law cases and their opposite numbers used by such agencies as the Environmental Protection Agency and the U.S. Fish and Wildlife Service. The investigative capacity of agencies can be enhanced by co-operation with others as well as by their own efforts.

The U.S. Environmental Protection Agency itself sees inter-agency co-operation, shared data and joint training as critically important to its most important intitiatives in the field of criminal environmental law. These initiatives include its San Diego Task Force, monitoring trafficking in hazardous waste and dangerous substances at the San Diego–Mexico border crossing, the Mississippi River Task Force focussing on polluters and waste dumpers along that river, and Operation "Cool Breeze" based in Miami which concentrates on trafficking and illegal trade in chlorofluorocarbons or "CFCs".[28] It would be wrong to assume that similar problems are unknown in Britain, and there is much scope to learn from the experience of the American agencies.

UNFAMILIAR TRIBUNALS

Another consequence of bringing a large number of minor environmental law cases before the criminal courts in England and Wales is that they are necessarily heard by tribunals with little or no relevant expertise. The majority of such cases will be brought as summary cases before magistrates' courts in England and Wales. Most such magistrates are lay members of the community, advised on matters of law by a clerk. They will typically hear long lists of cases involving plenty of drunks, driving offences, petty thefts and arguments in and around pubs. When suddenly confronted with a representative of, say, the Drinking Water Inspectorate, trying to explain the significance of regulation 28 of the Water Supply (Water Quality) Regulations 1989,[29] and why it matters that drinking water supply pipes are lined in a particular way, what are they to make of it? There will be little guidance for them on the seriousness of such offences. They must hear the facts and hazard a guess as to penalties.

PENALTY LOTTERY, AND SOME ALTERNATIVES

The penalty "lottery" of the criminal courts extends also to the Crown Courts for environmental law cases brought on indictment. For cases where charges are infrequently brought, there is unlikely to be guidance on sentencing from the Court of Appeal. The judge is confronted with a set of facts presented to him by a barrister, and must do the best that he or she can to determine how serious it is. Should the fine be £45,000, or £100,000? What is there to go on in the way of precedent or basis for such penalties where fines are potentially unlimited, and the factors to be taken into account in assessing them are left unstated in the legislation? Again, the contrast with the American civil enforcement system is striking.

The traditional duty of the prosecutor in an English court is to present the case for the prosecution fairly. He is not expected to conduct the mitigation for the defendant, but nor is he expected to go overboard or to exaggerate the severity of the offence described. To that extent, the adversarial system is tempered by the duty to present the facts fairly and clearly to the court. When, for example, a company is prosecuted for an environmental crime, its own advocate can be expected to recite all the mitigating factors. But the way in which the offence is described by prosecuting counsel, the selection of charges or the choice of details picked out for mention or emphasis can be highly important in determining the sentence. This can be more of an art than a science. It is probably best applied by the Treasury Counsel, who conduct the most serious criminal prosecutions at the Old Bailey in London and who are the most practised at giving a balanced account of a prosecution's case. But few environmental crimes are prosecuted at the Old Bailey, which is usually engrossed in more gory fare.

The U.S. Department of Justice used not to take positions on sentencing, maintaining a detachment similar to that shown by prosecutors in English courts. It is now reported that there is greater pressure for sentences to show a measure of restitution,[30] and doing more towards putting right the effects of a crime or paying for its consequences. This is reflected in the sentencing guidelines[31] used by the Department of Justice, which are also an interesting commentary on the American tendency to have a more structured purpose to the process of prosecution and sentencing than applies in Britain.

Importantly, the American Probation Service in Federal cases also files a pre-sentence report. The service provides input on how the sentencing guidelines ought to be applied, and recommendations are also made for corporations. The pre-sentence report will consider, for example, the scale of gravity of the offence against the scale of the offender's record, also weighing mitigating factors such as a plea of guilty. Those familiar with the way that companies' "antecedents" are dealt with at the conclusion of a criminal case in England and Wales will be aware of how much of the penalty is based on guesswork and unverified assumptions.

Fines in Britain are all paid into central government funds, instead of being applied or "hypothecated" to be used for restoration measures. So it cannot plausibly be argued that "clean up" or requiring restitution is a significant part of the object of criminal proceedings, although such orders are sometimes an incidental part of sentencing in criminal cases. Certainly the criminal process is a most inefficient way of requiring businesses or individuals to pay for their pollution. Procedures for requiring compensation to be paid under the criminal process are also unwieldy and difficult to apply. Where, for example, the real loser is that part of the environment which no one owns, such as the damaged ozone layer or polluted air, the criminal process is not effective at assessing compensation. Fines in America are also paid to the central Treasury, both in Federal courts and in state jurisdictions. There are constitutional limits to the extent to which agencies such as the Environmental Protection Agency in America can be seen to be "financing themselves" by recovery of fines, and there might be similar objections to the raising of taxes outside the authority of Parliament if British environmental agencies used fine recovery to finance their own operations.

But it is less clear what the objection would be to the use of some proportion of fines in criminal cases for the benefit of the environment affected by the environmental crime. At present, in both Britain and America there is no such benefit. The fact that a firm found guilty of an environmental offence is fined in itself does nothing for the environment affected by its actions, although there may be related orders for costs or even compensation.

This is not the case in Canada. Although Environment Canada, the Federal environmental agency, relies on criminal law almost exclusively for the enforcement of those environmental offences for which it has jurisdiction, and much of it Victorian criminal law at that, the handling of the criminal penalties is quite different from that in America or Britain, and much more sophisticated. For example, proceedings were brought in 1996 against two companies in British Columbia, Domtar Inc. and Stella-Jones Inc., under the Canadian Fisheries Act of 1868 for depositing wood preservative in streams. The companies faced eight counts of criminal offences, but the penalty was imposed by the judge after extensive negotiations between prosecution and defence, who eventually came to the judge with what amounted to an agreed order.[32]

The surviving company Stella-Jones Inc. was convicted on one count, and the other counts were stayed. The company was then fined $15,000. It was further ordered to pay $35,000 to the Receiver General for Canada for payment to the Department of Fisheries and Oceans. This was to be used for the conservation, enhancement and protection of fish and fish habitat as follows:

> $20,000 in the Nelson Creek and Brunette River watersheds by the Sapperton Fish and Game Club;
> $10,000 for conservation and environmental education programmes in the Coquitlam, Port Coquitlam and Port Moody watersheds by the Port Moody Ecological Society; and
> $5,000 for similar programmes in the Burrard Inlet watersheds by the Burrard Inlet Marine Enhancement Society.

The court orders in this case went on to require detailed undertakings from the company on the drainage systems and stormwater detention facilities it was to install, its operating procedures for wood treatment, its maintenance procedures for the collection of condensate from its chromated copper arsenate fixation tunnel, its monitoring requirements and even its employee training programmes.

The Canadian example shows that even old-established criminal laws can be used to tailor criminal penalties much more closely to the needs of the environment affected by an environmental crime and much more responsively to the needs of groups trying to address its effects. Canada is continuing to develop "Environmental Protection Alternative Measures" and included provisions allowing for this kind of agreed settlement of criminal charges in the Canadian Environmental Protection Bill brought forward in 1997.[33] There seems to be much good sense in this approach that would repay further study in Britain.

OREGON, AND A REVISED APPROACH TO THE CRIMINAL LAW

Oregon passed enhanced environmental crimes legislation in 1993. One factor in its doing so was its wish to take on responsibility for administration of a number of environmental law programmes which required that it have felony offences on its statute book for certain offences. However, once it passed that test, there was little guidance from the Federal agencies on how often or in what circumstances such felonies should be prosecuted.

In Oregon, there was remarkable bi-partisan support for the new and tougher environmental crimes legislation passed in 1993. An internal paper[34] from the state's Department of Environmental Quality states:

"The Environmental Crimes Act generated such overwhelming support because industry, small businesses, municipalities, and agricultural interests collectively recognized that certain environmental violations are so extreme that criminal prosecutions are warranted. Additionally, everyone recognized that significant criminal liability could certainly deter others from committing environmental offenses."

Another Department of Environmental Quality document[35] explains that:

"Before 1993, Oregon had little authority or capability to criminally prosecute violators of environmental law. At that time, Oregon could only seek misde-meanour penalties for even the most extreme environmental violations. In Oregon misdemeanours carry the least severe punishments. Furthermore, the State lacked the needed agency infrastructure to coordinate investigation and prosecution of environmental crimes. As a result, there was virtually no criminal prosecution of any kind of environmental violation."

The same document states that the inter-agency Environmental Crimes Co-ordination Team discussed over 100 potential crimes during 1995. Of these "approximately fifty were referred to law enforcement officers for crim-inal investigation and have led, so far, to the charging of approximately eigh-teen environmental crimes". The document lists three criteria for elevating an investigation of an environmental violation to the status of a possible criminal investigation. These criteria are:

"*   History of noncompliance—if the violator has a history of violating the envi-ronmental laws, criminal enforcement may be warranted as a punishment and deterrent;
  *   Violator's culpability—a criminal investigation may be warranted if the vio-lator was intentional, deceitful, deliberate or dishonest in committing the vio-lation;
  *   Results of the conduct—violators who cause a threat to public health or envi-ronmental damage are more likely to be prosecuted criminally than violators whose acts did not cause actual harm or threat of harm."

The most serious environmental offence on Oregon's statute book now is the crime of "environmental endangerment". It is plainly worded so as to be reserved for the most serious forms of misconduct. It is committed where a person:

"(a)   Knowingly commits the crime of unlawful disposal, storage or treatment of hazardous waste in the first degree, unlawful transport of hazardous waste in the first degree, unlawful air pollution in the first degree or unlawful water pollution in the first degree; and

(b) As a result, places another person in imminent danger or death or causes serious physical injury."[36]

This crime is a felony. An individual who commits it can be sentenced to a fine of a million dollars, 15 years' imprisonment or both. Corporations can be fined two million dollars. For second or subsequent convictions under this section, individuals can be sentenced to 30 years' imprisonment, and fines of five million dollars can be levied. It is difficult to imagine this crime being charged in other than the most serious cases of all, but it remains like an exclamation mark on the face of the statute. Where Oregon was one of the last states to introduce felony offences for environmental crimes, it has served notice that it does not want to be a haven for environmental criminals.

Oregon's statistics for investigation and prosecution of environmental crimes, and the criteria it uses for selecting them, make it clear that criminal sanctions are reserved for the worst environmental offenders. At a meeting with the Administrator for the Department of Environmental Quality's Northwest region, reference was made to the state's concentration on "the dirty dozen". A review of the lists of those prosecuted or referred for consideration for prosecution led to a similar conclusion. Examples given were an electroplating operation that had abandoned 43,000 gallons of highly toxic hazardous waste in a residential neighbourhood; a chrome-plating business that had repeatedly dumped its chrome waste on the ground, contaminating residential water wells with dangerous chemicals; an underground storage tank clean-up business which submitted falsified laboratory reports to the Department of Environmental Quality in order to conceal evidence of its misconduct. Most jurisdictions that are in any way serious about environmental enforcement would find this sort of violation to be criminal.

CONCLUSIONS

The criminal law remains both necessary and appropriate as a means for ensuring compliance with environmental laws by the small minority of businesses and individuals who set out to break those laws. But little would be lost, and much gained, by more effective and focussed enforcement in Britain of minor environmental violations under an administrative or civil process. The aims of the enforcement process could be better articulated. The penalties could be better calculated and more closely related both to any economic benefit gained by the violator and to the costs of restitution.

The enforcement process would gain in terms of reasonable predictability. Unpredictability is often cited by businesses as a complaint against environmental enforcement. More of the penalties levied could be used to put right any damage caused, in the same way that the Americans allow "supplemental environmental projects" to constitute part of civil penalty settlements. Fewer individuals and businesses would be dragged into the net of the criminal law. Less court time would be used up. And the weight and sanction of the criminal law would be reserved, as in Oregon and much of the rest of the United States, for the worst cases, where a violator's intent, or record, or the results of the violation were such that the most serious punishment and deterrence were called for. American civil and administrative penalties have developed in such a way that they do not need to be seen as an easy option or being "soft on polluters", as the next chapter describes.

But if Britain continues to rely to the present extent on the criminal law to enforce environmental obligations, there is still much scope for developing systems of penalties on the Canadian model which more closely reflect the damage actually done, and which allow it to be remedied more directly than by the payment of punitive fines to a remote central Treasury.

REFERENCES

1. EPA Enforcement and Compliance Assurance Accomplishments Report, FY 1995, EPA 300–R–96–006, July 1996, 2–3.
2. At the Fraud Investigation Group of the Director of Public Prosecutions' Office, which preceded the current Serious Fraud Office, the author and others always had at their fingertips statistics of cases under investigation, the value or amounts of money at risk, and impressive rates of conviction. While such statistics were entirely necessary in order to be able to argue for sufficient resources, personnel and equipment (including its first telex machine, only obtained 18 months after the Group was operational) for the Fraud Investigation Group, they were not necessarily a good indication of the inroads that were, or were not, being made into the control of fraud and corruption. Similarly, U.S. Environmental Protection Agency staff sometimes refer to their traditional approval to compiling enforcement statistics as "bean-counting".
3. N. 1 above, 3–11.
4. EPA Operating Principles for an Integrated Enforcement and Compliance Assurance Program, Office of Enforcement and Compliance Assurance, Interim Final, 18 Nov. 1996, under cover of a Memorandum from Steven Herman, Assistant Administrator dated 27 Nov. 1996 sent to the EPA Administrator, Department of Justice and all EPA Regions.
5. Meeting with Earl Devaney, EPA, Washington, D.C., 4 Feb. 1997.
6. Meeting with Nancy Firestone, U.S. Department of Justice, Washington D.C., 3rd Feb. 1997.
7. *Ibid.*
8. Meeting with John A. Riley, Divison Director, Litigation Support Division,

Texas Natural Resources Conservation Commission, Austin, Tex., 5 Nov. 1996.

9. Meeting with Tom Bispham, Administrator, Northwest District, Oregon Department of Environmental Quality, Portland, Ore., Jan. 1997. I hope one day to be able to write a short account of the different uses of the phrase "dirty dozen" in American environmental law circles. Reactions to this loaded phrase are mixed. In Silicon Valley, local newspapers published a list of the "dirty dozen" headed by IBM based on published toxic emissions data released to the public: IBM's response was to undertake to eliminate all freon from its processes within 3 years. But when a former Governor of Louisiana tried to publish a list of the "dirty dozen" top polluters in his state, one of the dozen gave $1 million to a successful campaign to have him replaced.

10. Associated Press, 27 May 1998, reported on "Greenlines", E-mail news service of Defenders of Wildlife.

11. *ENDS Report* 181, Feb. 1990, report of case at Liverpool Crown Court before Mars Jones J.

12. *ENDS Report* 253, Feb. 1996.

13. *ENDS Report* 243, Apr. 1995, 45. The company was fined £45,000 and ordered to pay costs of £67,000.

14. *ENDS Report* 278, Mar. 1998, 47.

15. S. 5.

16. S. 80, Water Resources Act 1991.

17. S. 90, Water Resources Act 1991.

18. S. 47.

19. S. 9(8).

20. Court of King's Bench, reported (1834), 2 C&P 292.

21. For accounts of later civil proceedings relating to this incident, see also *ENDS Report* 208, May 1992; *ENDS Report* 214, Nov. 1992; and (1993) 1 Env.LRep. 176, *AB* v. *South West Water Services Ltd* (1993) 1 Env.LRep. 266. South West Water Services Ltd was tried and convicted of the criminal offence of causing a public nuisance at Exeter Crown Court on 8 Jan. 1991.

22. Hence the origin of what is now s. 70, Water Resources Act 1991 and the offence of supplying water unfit for human consumption.

23. See speeches by Lord Dixon-Smith, H.L. Vol. 561, No. 40, Col. 611, the Earl of Onslow Col. 612, 14 Feb. 1995, Lord Jenkin of Roding at Col 613. See also Col. 614, and, for the Government reply, Viscount Ullswater at Col. 617.

24. *Ibid.*, Col. 614. Pt. I of the Environment Act 1995 set up the Environment Agency for England and Wales, which incorporated and took over the work of 3 earlier environmental regulators. These were the National Rivers Authority, Her Majesty's Inspectorate of Pollution and the waste regulation authority activities of local authorities.

25. Meeting with Frank Noonan, Chief, Criminal Division, U.S. Attorney's Office, (Federal) Department of Justice, Portland, Ore., 25 Sept. 1996.

26. Meeting with John A. Riley, Divison Director, Texas Natural Resources Conservation Commission, Austin, Tex., 5 Nov. 1996.

27. Meeting with Tom Bispham, Administrator, Northwest Region, Oregon Department of Environmental Quality, Portland, Ore., 3 Jan. 1997.

28. "The US Perspective on Environmental Criminal Law Enforcement with Special Focus on Operation 'Cool Breeze'", Presentation by Michael J. Penders, U.S. EPA at Department of the Environment seminar on Combating Environmental Crime, London, Dec. 1996.

29. Water Supply (Water Quality) Regs. 1989, S.I. 1989/1147.

30. N. 25 above.

31. Sentencing Commission Guidelines Manual, 1 Nov. 1995, Part Q Offenses Involving the Environment (statutory provisions 33 U.S.C. #1319(c)(3); 42 U.S.C. #6928(e)). These guidelines contain such interesting advice as "if death or serious bodily injury resulted, an upward departure may be warranted", and "if the offense involved a simple recordkeeping or reporting violation only, decrease by 2 levels".

32. File No. 42258C, Canada, Provincial Court, British Columbia, Judge W. J. Diebolt, Coquitlam, B.C., 4 Dec. 1996, *R. v. Domtar Inc. and Stella-Jones Inc.*, Proceedings at Plea and Sentence, and Order. I am indebted for this example to Digby R. Kier, Q.C., Department of Justice (Canada), and to R. Gordon Thompson, Head of Investigations and Beverley Hobby, Advocate, of Environment Canada, whom I met in Vancouver, B.C. on 17 Jan.1997.

33. Bill C, House of Commons of Canada: "An Act respecting pollution prevention and the protection of the environment and human health in order to contribute to sustainable development", 2nd Session, 35th Parliament, 45 Elizabeth II, 1996, ss. 295 *et seq.*, Environmental Protection Alternative Measures.

34. Tom Bispham *et al.*, "Environmental Crimes Guidance", unpublished paper produced by the Oregon Department of Environmental Quality, Portland, Ore., undated.

35. Tom Bispham, Holly Duncan and Leslie Carlough, "Oregon's Experience in Developing and Implementing a State Environmental Crimes Program", Oregon D.E.Q., Portland, Ore.

36. ORS 468.951.

7

Civil and Administrative Environmental Law Enforcement

"Le legge son: ma chi pon mano ad esse?"
Laws exist, but who is going to enforce them?

Dante

Within the European Community, as has been seen in Chapter 3, the Member States jointly negotiate and enact directives and regulations governing many aspects of their environmental laws. Failures of individual states to "transpose" Community directives into national law, or to enforce them in accordance with community law, are challenged by the European Commission, often in response to complaints by individual "citizens of the Union".[1] Failure by the Member State to put right any perceived breach of Community law results in the Commission bringing proceedings, under Article 169 of the Treaty of Rome, before the European Court of Justice.

By 1996, some 200 pieces of European Community environmental legislation had been adopted. In October of 1996, over 600 environmental complaints and infringement cases were outstanding against Member States of the Community, with 85 infringement cases awaiting determination by the European Court of Justice.[2] The European Commision has also made clear its intention to make full use of the "strong deterrent effect" of Article 171 of the Treaty of Rome, added by the Maastricht Treaty, which allows Member States to be fined for non-compliance with Community laws.

The European Commission has advocated the development of Community-wide minimum inspection criteria, enhanced investigation procedures to deal with environmental complaints within Member States and freer access to justice in national courts for the resolution of Community environmental law issues.

As a practical matter European Community Member States including Britain need to ensure that the methods of enforcement adopted in national laws implementing Community legislation are effective. If they are ineffective, this will only bring down on the Member State more challenges, often from its own citizens, more referrals to the European Court of Justice, more adverse judgments there, and now the exciting new possibility of being fined by European institutions.[3]

As a matter of European Community law, Member States of the European Community also have legal responsibilities when enacting Community legislation in their national laws, to make "whatever provision for enforcement is effective, proportionate and equivalent to that for member states' own laws".[4] Any Member State might be challenged if, to take extreme examples, there was only one environmental inspector for the whole country, if massive pollution offences could result in only trivial penalties or if there were stricter fines for breaching national laws than those enacting Community legislation. Within those parameters, in a further aspect of European Community law which the European Commission sometimes remembers and sometimes does not, Member States retain the discretion to choose which methods of law enforcement deliver the required results.

This retained power of Member States to choose different methods of law enforcement is potentially very important. It allows Member States at least some discretion to be innovative, to select methods of enforcement which match their own circumstances. Provided that Member States can validly defend different enforcement methods as proportionate and effective, there seems no reason for the European Commission to try to replace this flexibility with a more rigid and prescriptive approach.

To some European Commission staff, it looks untidy to have 15 Member States with even limited discretion to use enforcement methods of their own. The Commission has to police a joint body of law, to ensure that agreed common standards are not lowered or distorted by one or more Member States, which in turn often face the real political and economic costs of enforcing legislation long after they have negotiated it, and the Member States will sometimes twist and turn in an effort to escape from the costly realities. The need for even and fair application of Community law within the single market of the Community is another powerful driver towards uniformity. The understandable tendency of the European Commission will therefore be to look with suspicion at new approaches or anything that looks like a "let out" in terms of community environmental obligations.

But in the long term it is essential to have new and different approaches being tried out, as a response to the bewildering variety and intractable nature of environmental problems. European industry needs to be competitive: if more cost-effective ways of ensuring compliance with environmental standards can be found, should they not be adopted? The environment is not necessarily protected by methods of law enforcement that may not have moved on while the environmental problems and regulated technologies have changed beyond recognition. The next chapter considers the implications for regulation of rapidly developing "high tech" industries for which traditional regulation seems almost irrelevant.

One potential strength of American environmental law is that once Federal minimum standards have been established, implementation is taking place in 50 different states, each able to experiment with very different approaches. In any given field there are "market leaders" and states with innovative programmes. The patchwork may look like a weaker system of enforcement, and there are certainly wide variations and some states lag behind. The *New York Times* in June 1998[5] reminded its readers of some examples of lax state enforcement. These included the U.S. Environmental Protection Agency's fine of $125 million of Smithfield Foods for dumping hog wastes in a Virginia river, which was really also a rebuke to the Virginia environmental regulator for its inactivity; New Mexico's failure to inspect half of its bad air polluters from 1990 to 1996; and the Agency's own Pacific Northwest office based in Seattle, which the paper accused of overlooking pollution in Alaska and Idaho. But in the long term, the American approach may yield better results than uniformity. The strength of variety within the state system is particularly apparent in the field of pollution prevention, examined in the next chapter. European regulators might benefit from considering how to take advantage of diversity rather than trying to blot it out.

This chapter and the previous one, on the use of the criminal law, suggest that a more effective method of enforcing environmental laws in Britain might be to develop systems of civil and administrative environmental law tribunals of the sort to be found in America. For this shift from reliance on the criminal law to take place, it would have to be shown that civil and administrative law tribunals were capable of delivering enforcement that was effective, proportionate and equivalent to that for Britain's own national laws. To do that it is necessary to look in some detail at the uses to which American environmental regulators put the civil law.

FEDERAL ENFORCEMENT: FIRST PRINCIPLES

In America, rightly, there is no embarrassment about the idea that laws once passed should be enforced robustly. The U.S. Environmental Protection Agency's "Operating Principles for an Integrated EPA Enforcement and Compliance Assurance Program" sets the tone:[6]

> "America's last twenty-five years of environmental improvements are attributable to a strong set of environmental laws and an insistent and enforced expectation of compliance with those laws."

It helps to try to be clear (this is not something that English regulators are good at) precisely what enforcement is supposed to achieve. Enforcement of civil and criminal environmental laws, according to the Environmental Protection Agency:[7]

* "* remedies the environmental harm caused by environmental violations and prevents future environmental harm from occurring;
* * addresses conditions which may present an imminent and substantial endangerment to human health, welfare or the environment;
* * addresses violations of the law and ensures that all necessary steps are taken to achieve and maintain compliance with the applicable requirements of federal environmental laws and regulations;
* * deters others from similar illegal behaviour;
* * 'levels the economic playing field' by ensuring that those who violate the law do not enjoy an economic advantage over those who comply;
* * recovers the government's costs for environmental response actions . . . ;
* * implements site remediation provisions of the environmental laws."

When the Environment Agency for England and Wales was established, its Management Statement had this to say about its aims and objectives:[8]

"Ministers expect the Agency to implement environmental regulations in ways which deliver environmental objectives while not imposing unnecessary burdens on those it regulates. To do so, the Agency should seek constructive relationships with regulated bodies (or whose business activities are otherwise affected by its work) and their representatives. This should include provision of advice on regulations, including its approach to enforcement and how to comply with requirements.

The Agency should develop a Code of Practice on the exercise of its regulatory responsibilities. This should promote fairness, proportionality, transparency and consistency of enforcement. It should reflect the principles of the Government's code for enforcement agencies ('Working with Business') and Schedule 1 of the Deregulation and Contracting Out Act 1994, while enabling the Agency to maintain effective environmental protection and to take immediate enforcement action where this is justified."

FEDERAL POLICY TO SETTLE CIVIL CASES AND LIMIT LITIGATION WHERE POSSIBLE

Despite having a clear policy on the enforcement of environmental laws that has not become too tangled up in its other management objectives, the Environmental Protection Agency, like other Federal agencies in America, is subject to an explicit requirement to try to settle more civil cases out of court wherever possible. This takes the form of a Presidential Executive Order[9] which states that whenever feasible, claims should be resolved through informal discussions, negotiations and settlements rather than through any formal court proceeding.

Where their use is warranted, the U.S. President's Executive Order recommends alternative dispute resolution "ADR" techniques and processes. The Executive Order also prescribes revision of the ways in which legislation and regulations are prepared. In response to Executive Order 12988, the Federal Department of Justice has created the position of "Senior Counsel for Alternative Dispute Resolution" and requires all of its attorneys whose practices are substantially civil to attend "a comprehensive basic training program in negotiation and ADR".[10] The Environment and Natural Resources Division at the Department of Justice headquarters in Washington, D.C., which handles much of the Department's most significant environmental enforcement cases, has developed its own alternative dispute resolution criteria for use by its attorneys.[11]

FEDERAL CIVIL PENALTIES

In fiscal year 1995, the U.S. Environmental Protection Agency reported that civil penalties of more than $70 million had been assessed in its cases. On the judicial side, nearly $35 million in penalties were assessed, with nearly one third of these under the Clean Air Act. Administratively assessed penalties totalled more than $36 million, with more than one third assessed under the Resource Conservation and Recovery Act.

In assessing penalties, the Agency seeks a fair distribution of the burdens of environmental regulations between all regulated businesses and entitties, and usually seeks to recapture, at least, the economic benefits of non-compliance. In this it is assisted by sophisticated computer modelling of such benefits, which has resulted in a sixfold increase in fines levied by courts as the courts have come to accept the evidence of financial gain.[12] The formulae by which civil penalties are assessed in American states, and the elements which they contain, are detailed in the legislation and therefore predictable by all parties. In addition, the Federal Environmental Protection Agency, and most states, operate two computer programs, the BEN and ABEL systems.

The BEN system allows a detailed assessment to be made of the economic gain achieved by companies in violating environmental laws or in avoiding compliance. Recovery of this gain is usually one of the principal objectives of American regulators in enforcing environmental laws. The ABEL system is used to assess companies' claims of economic hardship when they are faced with civil penalty assessments, and how much they can afford to pay in penalties without having to cease trading. As with all computer systems, these systems are not infallible, but they do allow for more objective consideration of both areas.

The Environmental Protection Agency seeks to deter violators and to ensure that those who do not comply do not achieve a competitive advantage over those who have invested time and money in achieving compliance.

The Agency notes[13] that:

> "Much of the success of other tools, such as compliance assistance and compliance incentives, relies on a general expectation in the regulated community that violations discovered by government will be the subject of enforcement actions with sanctions. . . .
> . . . voluntary compliance for all facilities and entities will likely improve greatly when the regulated community expects enforcement penalties as a response to violations".

In other words, not all regulated firms and individuals will take time and spend money on the steps necessary to achieve compliance with environmental regulations unless they really believe that there will be robust enforcement action taken against them if they fail to do so. A wish that commercially motivated bodies would be altruistic is not enough, even if some of them are.

SUPPLEMENTAL ENVIRONMENTAL PROJECTS, "SEPS"

Supplemental Environmental Projects, "SEPs", are defined as "environmentally beneficial projects which a defendant/respondent agrees to undertake in settlement of an enforcement action, but which the defendant/respondent is not otherwise legally required to perform".[14] These projects are used both by the Federal Environmental Protection Agency and individual states as a useful part of the civil enforcement process, but most commentators agree that the Federal Agency's own SEPs policy is more sophisticated and better thought out than most of its state equivalents,[15] and therefore a better model.

The Environmental Protection Agency only allows supplemental environmental projects where it has formally identified a violation, and is able to help shape the proposed project before its implementation. Projects involving pollution prevention are preferred over other types of reduction or control strategies.

To be accepted, projects must be sufficiently related to the violation ("adequate nexus"). They must advance at least one of the declared objectives of the environmental statutes at issue. Neither the Environmental Protection Agency nor any other Federal agency will accept a role in managing or controlling funds to administer a SEP. There is a signed settlement agreement setting out the nature and scope of the project. SEPs are not allowed as a substitute for any of the Agency's statutory duties, or to provide it with extra funds. This would involve constitutional problems similar to those which would result from any appropriation of funds by an agency in Britain which took place without the necessary Parliamentary authority.

The Environmental Protection Agency lists seven categories of projects which can qualify as SEPs. They are public health; pollution prevention; pollution reduction; environmental restoration and protection; assessments and audits; environmental compliance promotion; and emergency planning and preparedness.

There are strict rules as to how penalties and the costs of SEPs are to be calculated, what can properly be offset and what will be permitted to mitigate a penalty. Use of SEPs to address "environmental justice" issues is welcomed and encouraged, and a number of commentators such as Professor Robert Kuehn of Tulane University, New Orleans, see SEPs as one important way in which such concerns can be addressed. There are also provisions to prevent companies from using SEPs in ways which would constitute advertising or to detract from their character as part of a civil penalty.

The Environmental Protection Agency gives the following examples of direct environmental benefits from the use of SEPs in its civil enforcement process:[16]

" * Total reduction of 637,000 pounds of non-halogenated organics, including toluene and xylene (9 cases)
  * Total reduction of 483,000 pounds of halogenated organics, including solvents (6 cases)
  * Total reduction of 4,000 tons per year of sulfur dioxide air emissions
  * Total reduction of 104,000 pounds per year of volatile organic compounds (VOCs) air emissions (2 cases)."

Civil enforcement of environmental laws is probably the least developed of all the options available to regulators in England, and there is much to be learned from the way that the Environmental Protection Agency and Federal Department of Justice apply environmental laws and penalties through civil and administrative tribunals and cases. But it should not be overlooked that a great deal of the civil enforcement effort in America is taking place at the state level. For example, the office of the Federal Department of Justice in the State of Oregon estimates that about 90 per cent of the time of its civil practitioners is spent defending Federal departments and agencies against civil suits filed by other groups: only about 10 per cent of their time would typically be spent working directly on civil enforcement cases, and the most important of these would be likely to be referred the headquarters of the Federal Department of Justice (so called "Main Justice") in Washington,

D.C.[17] The Federal Department of Justice may account for some of the biggest cases of civil law enforcement, but these cases will only account for a very small percentage of all the actions brought to enforce environmental laws. The rest are part of the very large portfolio of responsibilities of state environmental agencies and departments of justice.

STATE ENFORCEMENT: OREGON'S CIVIL ENFORCEMENT PROCESS

In many states in America, the lion's share of the enforcement of environmental laws is made up by administrative enforcement and civil law procedures. In Oregon, such administrative cases are brought before each agency's administrative law court or tribunal. There are hearings officers, similar to the administrative law judges found at federal level. Cases are adversarial, but with less formality than in a full court. They are held on the record, but without recourse to the full jury rights of other American civil law cases. The system is supposed to be cheaper and quicker, and to allow, for example, for much self-representation. Final orders can be appealed directly to the state Court of Appeals. This system is also used for permit appeals by permit holders or applicants.[18] Oregon's system of civil environmental law enforcement is well thought out, and it is one of two states whose civil and administrative environmental law procedures are being studied by Canadian provinces as a possible model for a similar approach. Canada, like Britain, has traditionally relied much more heavily on a variety of criminal offences for the enforcement of its environmental laws.

When the Oregon Department of Environmental Quality assesses a civil penalty, an appeal lies to the Environmental Quality Commission, the board to which the Director of the Department reports. Such appeals are relatively rare. The Environmental Quality Commission, as a state body, receives legal advice from the state's Assistant Attorney General, and the proceedings on an appeal are somewhat judicial in nature (for example with references to affidavits and transcripts). Appellants may be represented by outside lawyers. The Department of Environmental Quality will typically present its own case itself, and over-reliance by either party on procedural points, such as the incorrect captioning of filings, is met with a discouraging response from members of the Commission, some of whose members are foresters or farmers as well as lawyers. Table 7.1 shows the layout of a Commission appeal hearing which took place in the course of one of its regular meetings in Portland, Oregon, on 10 January 1997.

Table 7.1

OREGON ENVIRONMENTAL QUALITY COMMISSION
LAYOUT OF COMMISSION HEARING:
COMMISSION
(Appointed by Governor)

Linda McMahon (Scientist/ law degree)	Tony van Vliet (Professor, forester, Former State Legislator)	Henry Lorenzen (Chairman, farmer, lawyer)	Carol Whipple (Vice Chair, cattle rancher)	Melinda Eden (Rancher, lawyer)

ADVISORS:
Larry Knudsen
Assistant Attorney-
General, Oregon
Department of Justice
(Legal advisor to the
Dept. of Environmental
Quality and Commission)

DEQ OFFICIALS SPEAKING TO AGENDA ITEMS

Langdon Marsh
Director, Dept of
Environmental Quality

PUBLIC _____

Secretary/
Stenographer/
Tape Recorder

The goal of enforcement under Oregon's civil process, set out in the Administrative Rules adopted by the state's Department of Environmental Quality, is to:

"(a) obtain and maintain compliance with the Department's statutes, rules, permits and orders;

(b) protect the public health and the environment;

(c) deter future violators and violations; and

(d) ensure an appropriate and consistent statewide enforcement programme."[19]

Where there is an alleged permit violation, a Notice of Permit Violation is served on the permittee. This sets out the violation that is supposed to have occurred and states that a civil penalty will be imposed unless the permittee submits one of the following within five working days:[20]

"(a) a written response acceptable to the Department certifying that the permitted facility is complying with all the terms of the permit, with sufficient information for that to be verified;

(b) a written proposal, acceptable to the Department, to bring the facility into compliance, with—

   (A) a detailed plan and time schedule for achieving compliance in the shortest practicable time;

   (B) a description of the interim steps to be taken to reduce the impact of the permit violation;

   (C) a statement that the permittee has reviewed all other conditions of the permit have been reviewed without other violations being discovered;

(c) where a compliance schedule provides for compliance within a period over six months, the Department incorporates the compliance schedule into a formal Order with stipulated penalties for any noncompliance;

(d) certification required by these provisions is to be made by a Responsible Official of the permitted facility, defined in such a way as to ensure that full responsibility is taken by that entity for the plan.[21]"

Advance notice prior to notification of a civil penalty is not required (that is, the Department can issue a Notice of Civil Penalty Assessment) if:

"(a) the violation is intentional;

(b) the water or air violation would not normally occur for five consecutive days; or

(c) there has been a Notice of Permit Violation, or other formal enforcement action concerning permit violation at the facility in the period of 36 months preceding the documented violation."

Various violations of federal environmental protection programmes, state air contamination rules and other circumstances allow the assessment of a penalty without advance notice.[22]

Notices of Non-compliance are issued for all classes of documented violations, under the direction of a Department of Environmental Quality manager or his authorised representative. The Notice of Non-compliance informs a person of the violation, and the consequences of it or of continued non-compliance. It may state the actions required to resolve the violation and a time within which compliance is to be achieved. The Rules also prescribe when and at what level of seniority the Department may issue a Notice of Permit Violation, a Notice of Civil Penalty Assessment or an Order. These Notices are set out within the Department's public Administrative Rules. They are predictable, and relate to specific categories of descriptions of violations or levels of seriousness within such categories. While discretion is specifically retained, therefore, for the department to seek other legal or equitable remedies, the public at large and the regulated business community know in advance when they can expect a formal notice to issue, and what steps they are required to take on its receipt. This alone is in some ways preferable to the issue of criminal proceedings in England, which will not of themselves ensure that a violation of environmental laws or regulations is put right, and which are largely unpredictable in their outcome.

The Oregon Department of Environmental Quality's Administrative Rules, in a pattern common to many of the states, then provide civil penalty schedule matrices. Civil penalties under this scheme are not hazarded like English fine payments in criminal cases, but are worked out according to quite complex formulae. The Rules[23] provide that:

> "In addition to any liability, duty, or other penalty provided by law, the Director may assess a civil penalty for any violation pertaining to the [Environmental Quality] Commission's or Department's statutes, rules, permits or orders by service of a written notice of assessment of civil penalty upon the Respondent."

With minor exceptions, civil penalties apply to violations grouped within four matrices, the $10,000 Matrix, the $2,500 Matrix, the $1,000 Matrix and the $500 Matrix. Within these four matrices, violations are further grouped into three classes of seriousness. The $10,000 Matrix looks like this:

Table 7.2 Magnitude of violation

Class of Violation	Major	Moderate	Minor
Class I	$6,000	$3,000	$1,000
Class II	$2,000	$1,000	$500
Class III	$500	$250	$100

If this table looks something like the fines on the standard scale to be found in schedules of summary criminal offences against provisions of English statutes, the impression is dispelled by the next provision of the Administrative Rules. This makes it clear that no civil penalty issued by the Director pursuant to this matrix shall be less than $50 or more than $10,000 for *each day of each violation*. Clearly significant civil penalties assessed for several related violations which are continuing could quickly amount to sums far in excess of anything on the Standard Scale for English summary offences.

The $10,000 Matrix covers relatively serious violations of statutes, rules, permits or orders concerning such matters as air quality, water quality, underground storage tanks, hazardous waste, certain types of oil spill, PCB management and disposal, environmental clean-up, noise control, solid waste and failure to provide recycling opportunities. It is clear from this list that if any similar regime were to be applied in England, not only large numbers of summary offences (tried in magistrates' courts) or those triable either way (in magistrates' or Crown Courts) would be transferred from the jurisdiction of the criminal courts to that of administrative tribunals, but matters transferred would also include whole categories of statutory nuisance now dealt with in England before the magistrates' courts.

The $2,500 Matrix limits the total civil penalty which may be levied for each day to $2,500. The Matrix covers such matters as violations of open burning rules and open burning of tyres. The $1,000 matrix covers violations of laws and rules on rigid plastic containers. The $500 Matrix covers violations of certain woodstoves laws and rules, various recycling provisions and some financial assurance requirements for ships transporting hazardous materials and oil. In other words, once a scheme is in place, a very wide variety of violations of environmental statutes, regulations and permits can be brought within its framework.

In an English criminal courtroom where a company is found or pleads guilty to a significant environmental offence, counsel for the prosecution outlines the facts, counsel for the defence turns in his mitigation, and then the judge or magistrates ponder the appropriate sentence. It is a tense moment, and few people can fairly claim to know what to expect in the way of a penalty. Fines in offences tried on indictment can be unlimited. Defence counsel may hope that the court will take the view that it was a technical offence, long ago and far away and long since rectified. Perhaps prosecuting counsel hope that an example will be made of the company, and see their own names in reports of fines exceeding a million pounds. But for the judge in his chambers considering the appropriate penalty for infrequently prosecuted or new environmental offences, there is little guidance to be derived from practice or precedent.

This may be contrasted with the civil penalty determination procedure in the Oregon Department of Environmental Quality's Administrative Rules, which requires the Director[24] to:

"(a) Determine the class and magnitude of each violation."

Violations are classed by the Rules themselves, and their magnitude is determined by reference to detailed criteria, including, for example "the degree of deviation from the Commission's and Department's statutes, rules, standards, permits or orders, concentration, volume, percentage, duration, toxicity, and the extent of the effects of the violation".

The Director must then:

"(b) Choose the appropriate base penalty (BP) established by the matrices of [Oregon Administrative Rules] 340–12–042 after determining the class and magnitude of each violation" and then

"(c) Starting with the base penalty, determine the amount of penalty through application of the formula:

$$BP + [.1 \times BP(P + H + O + R + C)] + EB \ldots".$$

In this scheme of things, "P" is whether the respondent has any prior significant actions relating to statutes, rules, orders and permits pertaining to environmental quality or pollution control. It can range from "0" for no prior significant actions or insufficient information on which to base a finding, to "10" if "the prior significant actions are nine Class Ones or equivalents" and so forth. Criminal practitioners in England and Wales might prefer to think of "P" as being based on the offender's "Previous"!

"H" is the past history of the respondent in taking all feasible steps or procedures necessary or appropriate to correct any violations cited in previous significant actions.

"O" is whether the violation was repeated or continuous, with a value of two if it lasted for more than a day or recurred on the same day.

"R" is whether the violation resulted from an unavoidable accident, or a negligent, intentional or flagrant act of the respondent.

"C" is the respondent's co-operativeness and efforts to correct the violation.

"EB" is the approximated dollar sum of the economic benefit that the respondent gained through non-compliance. Across the United States, recovery of a polluters' economic benefit gained through non-compliance is regarded as one of the main purposes of enforcement action. To assess this benefit, the Oregon Department of Environmental Quality uses the Federal Environmental Protection Agency's BEN computer model "as adjusted annually to reflect changes in marginal tax rates, inflation rate and discount rate". Introduction of this computer model has, according to the EPA, resulted in a sixfold increase in the assessment of federal civil penalties, as tribunals are made better aware on the basis of rational and defensible information of the real economic gains made by avoidance of compliance with relevant laws.

The Department of Environmental Quality may reduce any penalty based on the respondent's inability to pay the full penalty amount. Here the onus is on the respondent to raise and prove the issue of inability to pay, and once again the Department is assisted by a further computer program derived from the Federal Environmental Protection Agency's ABEL computer model. Arguments over means and ability to pay before English criminal tribunals would probably benefit from the use of similar resources to provide a measure of objectivity to the claims and counter-claims and hastily researched and sometimes scrappy information about a defendant's means.

Particular kinds of violations, particularly those involving wilfulness or negligence may qualify for additional civil penalties. These also apply[25] where a person discards hazardous waste which results in the destruction, through food and water contamination, of various species of wildlife.

In the debates over what is now section 39 of the Environment Act 1995, the duty of the new environment agencies in England and Wales and Scotland to have regard to costs and benefits in exercising their powers, opponents of the provision often asked how you could set a value on a species.

Mr Sam Galbraith M.P. demanded to know how the Scottish Environment Protection Agency would take account of the value of a Blackthroated Diver, in these terms:[26]

> "Take the example of the Blackthroated Divers in Loch Shin, Sutherland, that has been mentioned before. One reason they are in danger is that the water level varies because of hydro-electric activity. Were we to insist that the hydro-electric industry keep the water at a prescribed level, it might say that would cost 5 million pounds a year. But the benefit would be saving a threatened species—the Blackthroated Divers. How can that benefit be quantified against the 5 million pounds? How do we make that judgement, who makes it and using what criteria? Many people will not know about the Blackthroated Divers and many more will not care. Is their preservation an important benefit? How do we decide?"

It is not a complete answer to all the questions raised by Mr Galbraith, but it is interesting to note that this section of the Oregon Administrative Rules puts a dollar value on individual animals destroyed through these means for the purposes of assessing civil penalties:

> "(b) Each mountain sheep or mountain goat, $3,500.
> (c) Each elk $750
> . . .
> (f) Each wild turkey, $50
> . . .
> (h) Each salmon or steelhead trout, $125".

The attempt to put a monetary value on individual animals has not been entirely successful. For example, where a value is put on individual salmon killed, the real cost of a spill or chemical contamination incident may lie in the destruction of other species, plants or invertebrates necessary to support fish life in an affected stream.

Intentional or reckless violations of provisions carry further enhanced civil penalties. The Rules conclude with a very detailed classification of violations of provisions relating to each environmental medium into the classes which fit the means of assessing penalties.

CONCLUSIONS

Anecdotal evidence suggests that in the system of civil and administrative tribunals operated in Oregon, most cases brought are uncontested, and the apparatus for contesting civil penalty assessments and appealing them to the Environmental Quality Commission or the state's Court of Appeals is relatively seldom used. More careful studies would have to be made of relative costs before this system could be recommended as a possible alternative to large numbers of "second order" criminal cases. But the small number of contested cases and appeals suggests that the formulaic but predictable criteria for levying civil penalties has become understood and accepted in the state. It is almost certainly significant that there is a high degree of transparency in the enforcement process. Civil penalty assessments are published (indeed, the attendant publicity is an important part of the penalty), and contested hearings take place in public.

Penalties are much more closely linked to recovery of any economic gain that has been made by offending firms or individuals, and to the real costs of damage to the environment. Civil penalties under this system are frequently much higher than the English criminal law equivalent for similar circumstances. The element of artificiality, in asserting intentional criminal behaviour, is missing, which perhaps more accurately reflects how the majority of violations of environmental laws arise. It would be hard to argue that a system such as Oregon's is incapable of dealing effectively and logically with violations of environmental laws. The system of "supplemental environmental projects" operated by American Federal authorities offers even more scope for matching offences with action to remedy harm done. Civil and administrative tribunals seem to have much to recommend them.

REFERENCES

1. Art. 8 of the Treaty of Rome; Part Two of the Treaty of Rome was inserted by Art. G(C) of the Treaty on European Union (Maastricht).
2. European Commission, *Implementing Community Environmental Law, Communication to the Council of the European Union and the European Parliament* (European Commission, Brussels, 22 Oct. 1996), COM 96/0500 Final.
3. See Art. 171 of the Treaty of Rome, as amended by Art. G(51) of the Treaty on European Union (Maastricht): and Cases C–121 and 122/97, *Commission v. Germany*, basing a proposed fine on a proportion of Germany's Gross Domestic Product.
4. Art. 5 of the Treaty of Rome, as interpreted by the European Court of Justice in Case 68/88, *Commission v. Greece* [1989] ECR 2965, points 23 and 24.

5. *New York Times* leader, "Soft on Pollution", carried in the *International Herald Tribune* on 12 June 1998.
6. Interim Final, 18 Nov. 1996: U.S. EPA Office of Enforcement and Compliance Assurance, 1.
7. *Ibid.*, 3.
8. The Environment Agency: Management Statement, Annex to Enforcement Policy, "Version 1", May 1996.
9. Executive Order 12988 of 5 Feb. 1996, Presidential Documents, Federal Register Vol. 61, No. 26, Wednesday, 7 Feb. 1996.
10. Order OBD 1160.1, Attorney General Janet Reno, U.S. Department of Justice, "Promoting the Broader Appropriate Use of Alternative Dispute Resolution Techniques", Apr. 1995.
11. Federal Register, Vol. 61, No 136, Monday, 15 July 1996, Notices, 36908.
12. The EPA's BEN computer model calculates a violator's economic benefit from non-compliance; its ABEL model evaluates a violator's solvency and ability to pay clean-up and compliance costs or a civil penalty while still remaining in business.
13. N. 6 above.
14. EPA, *Interim Revised Supplemental Environmental Projects Policy*, effective 8 May 1995 (Office of Enforcement and Compliance Assurance, Washington, D.C.).
15. For comparisons, see Oregon Department of Environmental Quality, Internal Management Directive—Civil Penalty Mitigation for Supplemental Environmental Projects (17 Nov. 1995); or Texas Natural Resources Conservation Commission Supplemental Environmental Project (SEP) Information Sheet, 23 Jan. 1996.
16. EPA Enforcement and Compliance Assurance Accomplishments Report, FY 1995, EPA 300–R–96–006, July 1996, 3–13.
17. Meeting with Judith Kobbervig, Chief, Civil Division, US Attorney's Office (Federal Department of Justice), Portland, Ore., 25 Sept. 1996.
18. Meeting with Larry Knudsen, Assistant Attorney General, Oregon Department of Justice, Portland, Ore., Sept. 1996.
19. Oregon Administrative Rules, hereafter "OAR", Ch. 340, Division 12— Oregon Department of Environmental Quality, OAR 340–12–026.
20. OAR 340–12–040.
21. This procedure is closely similar to the system of undertakings provided for in ss. 18–20 of the Water Resources Act 1991, whereby water undertakers in England and Wales are formally bound to achieve compliance with water quality standards and to take prescribed steps to that end on a fixed timetable. Undertakings were challenged unsuccessfully by Friends of the Earth in national litigation that went as far as the Court of Appeal, with leave to appeal further refused by House of Lords. The English courts held that while there was a requirement in European law to remedy any breach as quickly as possible, it had not been shown that the system of undertakings would fail to achieve that objective. The Government argued that such undertakings would in fact

achieve compliance quicker than a system of contested court enforcement orders.

22. N. 20 above.
23. OAR 340–12–042.
24. OAR 340–12–045.
25. OAR 340–12–049.
26. H.C., House of Commons Official Report, Standing Committee B, Environment Bill [Lords], Ninth Sitting, Col. 283, Thursday, 18 May 1995.

8

An End to Pollution and Waste?

"The Congress hereby declares it to be the national policy of the United States that pollution should be prevented or reduced at source whenever feasible; pollution that cannot be prevented should be recycled in an environmentally safe manner, whenever feasible; pollution that cannot be prevented or recycled should be treated in an environmentally safe manner whenever feasible; and disposal or other release into the environment should be employed only as a last resort and should be conducted in an environmentally safe manner."

Section 13101(b), US Pollution Prevention Act of 1990

DEREGULATION V. POLLUTION PREVENTION?

In Britain in the early 1990s, government concern at the burden of regulation on businesses led to the passage of the Deregulation and Contracting Out Act of 1994. Teams of civil servants from the Department of Trade and Industry, with assistance from businessmen, began to trawl through the statute book proposing lists of unnecessary or burdensome regulations. Deregulation units were set up within each Whitehall department to speed the process of identifying this legislative dead wood.[1] The Act allows for deregulation orders to be proposed to Parliament, and for ministers to remove or replace unnecessarily burdensome regulations where it can be shown that to do so would not remove necessary protection.[2]

The British statute book is, no doubt, liberally supplied with examples of unnecessary regulation. But the deregulation initiatives of the early 1990s suffered from two important drawbacks. First, there was little evidence of a strategy to seek to influence the legislative programme in Europe and the passage of new regulations at the European level, despite the fact that that is where perhaps 80 per cent of British environmental regulations originate. Regulations in place as a result of a requirement of European law, for example in transposing into national law the provisions of a European Community directive, cannot simply be revoked: effect must still be given to the European Community law.

The second feature of the deregulation initiative, as it affected the environmental field, was that it operated in isolation. It considered only one aspect of environmental laws and regulations, namely their burden on business. It confronted all vested interests in the making of those laws and regulations head on, from environmental groups to the Department of the Environment. The "deregulators" therefore risked being seen as representing one interest group to the exclusion of others, to lack a real commitment to environmental protection.

Where the process or deregulation becomes little more than the collection of statistics, it must be observed that there is a virtually inexhaustible supply of minor regulations of questionable significance with which to feed the flames of bonfires of red tape. But pursuit of that process on its own achieves little, either for the environment or for the process of lifting the burden from business. It addresses symptoms but not causes.

POLLUTION PREVENTION IN AMERICA

America is not short of proponents of deregulation and smaller government. It has a constitutional and historical bias against all taxes and government in general, and against Federal government in particular. As has been seen in Chapter 2, there are from time to time suggestions from the political right to do away with the Federal Environmental Protection Agency altogether, and to replace it with enhanced state bodies.[3] But back in the political mainstream, some of the energy that in Britain was put into the deregulation initiative has been channelled in America into support for pollution prevention.

One immediate difference between British deregulation and American pollution prevention is that the latter attracts political and practical support and participation from every side of the political debate and all interest groups. Whereas in Britain, environmental groups are generally suspicious and critical of moves towards deregulation of environmental laws, in America they are enthusiastic supporters of pollution prevention and reduction of waste at source. In Britain the interests of government departments are divided, between those who see their success as to be judged by the number of regulations put on the bonfires of red tape and those who see effective protection of the environment as more important. But in America, the emphasis on pollution prevention has brought out some of the best and most original thinking within Federal and state governments, and in some cases has achieved what perfectly functioning markets were supposed to achieve, but did not.

It seems clear that the potential of pollution prevention is limitless as long as any pollution and waste occurs, and there is more future in an approach around which all parties and interests can unite.

FOUR FEDERAL PROGRAMMES

Green Lights

The Green Lights Programme was launched by the Environmental Protection Agency on 16 January 1991. The Agency noted that new energy saving lighting technologies which promised big savings were not being widely taken up by institutions. Individually, it appears that savings from lower energy costs were not great enough to command much attention from senior managers, while building managers who took the relevant decisions had no incentive to interrupt the efficient running of their buildings.[4] The programme invented a contract between government and facilities which required the attention of senior management. Participants are required to survey their domestic facilities and upgrade lighting only wherever it is profitable to do so (based on an internal rate of return of at least 20 per cent or more) and where lighting quality would be improved or maintained.

On average, Green Lights participants achieve rates of return of nearly 50 per cent, and achieve 50 per cent energy saving from their lighting. By 1995 there were 1,900 participants in the programme. By 17 March 1997, this number had grown to 2,313 participants, from schools, companies, banks, the states of Michigan, Missouri and Montana, cities like Houston, Texas and Cincinnati, Ohio, hospitals and branches of the National Guard.[5] The cumulative savings to participants at 28 February 1997 were estimated to be some $ 282.4 million, and the energy saved was estimated to be 3.759 million Kilowatts.[6] All this was set in motion by an initial staff on the programme of three.

The Green Lights Programme has a number of particular features which seem to have contributed to its astonishing success. It had very specific targets and was focused on readily achievable results. It made an accurate assessment of the management levels within institutions that had to be reached before different decisions were taken. It emphasised not only the abstract benefits of energy saving but the commercial advantages to participants. It provided plenty of information but little regulation, and only required a one page report annually from participants. And in a feature common to many of the most successful pollution prevention programmes, it was readily able to demonstrate both results and benefits.

The 33/50 Programme

Another highly successful voluntary programme operated by the Environmental Protection Agency was the 33/50 Programme. Again launched in 1991, the programme focused on 17 of the most toxic chemicals and their compounds on the public Toxics Release Inventory,[7] and started with a direct approach from the then EPA Administrator William K. Reilly to the 600 companies with the largest discharges of these chemicals to the environment. Thousands of other companies were encouraged to participate voluntarily as well. The companies were invited to achieve reductions in releases of the target chemicals of 33 per cent by the end of 1992, and 50 per cent by the end of 1995, using 1988 as a baseline. How they did so was left up to them. The programme was entirely voluntary except where some other legislative provision applied.

By 1994, the Environmental Protection Agency was reporting that 1,300 companies were participating in the programme. Industry had reduced releases of the 17 target chemicals by 100 million pounds in excess of the 1992 target of 33 per cent, and a further 100 million pound reduction was achieved in 1993, representing a total reduction of 686 million pounds or 46 per cent, just short of the 50 per cent target for 1995.[8] In the iron and steel industries, for example, releases and transfers of the 33/50 chemicals were 58,862,594 pounds in 1988, but by 1994 the 233 facilities involved had reduced this to releases and transfers of 15,862,423 pounds, a reduction of 73 per cent.[9] A year later, the Agency was able to report that since 1988, participating companies, (which represented 98 per cent of the reductions in releases and transfers recorded for the preceding year) had cut releases and transfers of the 33/50 chemicals by 57 per cent.[10]

The editor of *Chemical Engineering*, writing in August 1995 declared:[11]

"33/50 has been one of the smartest things EPA has done regarding the environment, it has set national priorities by putting 17 of the 316 TRI chemicals on a hit list. This has helped companies in the chemical process industries decide on what to target first."

Clearly where the issue is legal compliance with a requirement, such as achievement of an emission limit, it is difficult for a regulatory agency to set priorities in this way, however helpful that might be to industry. It is hard to say that industry needs to comply with this requirement, but need not concern itself with that. The approach of a voluntary programme allows for priorities to be indicated without upsetting the legislative framework that requires compliance. But it can also be seen that the 33/50 programme shared with the Green Lights Programme the setting of very clear objectives, in this case tied to firm timetables, while allowing a great deal of latitude as to how the objectives were achieved. Considering the Toxics Release Inventory and the 33/50 Programme, Malcolm Sparrow has written that "The lessons . . . are that an informed public can be a formidable ally, and that appeals for voluntary cooperation represent a valuable addition to the compliance toolkit".[12]

At the conclusion of the programme, there was plenty of recognition for the participant companies and their achievements. The Environmental Protection Agency was not at all shy of publishing the names of the companies and congratulating them on their contributions. This seems not only fair, but very American. It is very much part of the American culture in all sorts of walks of life to thank people, both warmly and publicly, for good work or notable contributions to the community. Outstanding students, generous college alumni, long-serving postmistresses, safe truck drivers and in-house winners of the Pulitzer Prize are very publicly honoured and thanked. President Clinton devotes the first page and a half of many of his speeches to singling out, boosting and thanking local politicians, officials and achievers: it goes down well. For companies in a programme such as the 33/50 Programme, there is obviously some commercial value to such recognition, and that is explicitly used by regulatory agencies as a means to promote pollution prevention initiatives. And there are some programmes where "eco-friendly" logos and materials and congratulations are perhaps too readily dispensed without the companies participating being asked to do enough.[13] But it is human nature to like to have hard work and real achievements recognised, and in this area it is suggested that American exuberance has the edge on British reserve.

The Common Sense Initiative

The Environmental Protection Agency's Common Sense Initiative has been a more broad-ranging attempt to get round regulatory costs and inflexibility by reviewing regulations across the board for six selected industries. These are automobile manufacturing, computers and electronics, iron and steel, metal finishing, petroleum refining and printing. In launching the initiative, there was much talk of a "new generation of environmental protection". It was noted that U.S. businesses spent nearly $30 billion on environmental compliance in 1992 but still released over three billion pounds of toxic emissions. The document launching the initiative lamented the stifling of initiative and common sense by overly complicated and rigid environmental regulation, and the resulting conflict, gridlock and adversarial relationships between environmental protection and a healthy economy.[14]

Perhaps inevitably with such a general diagnosis, the search for a cure, even with industry-specific teams, has not been easy. The philosophy of the Common Sense Initiative seems to have been to combine a wide range of interests in one room—industry representatives, environmentalists and so on—and hope that consensus could be hammered out, for example on reducing duplicated reporting requirements and streamlining permitting processes. The document introducing the initiative talks of 150 subcommittee and work-group meetings held in the Common Sense Initiative's first year, with 37 projects initiated to test new approaches and develop policy recommendations. But this is a very heavy workload to place on any organisation, let alone senior executives from industry who have to justify their attendance at such meetings in terms of clear objectives and tangible results.

As recently as March 1997 the petroleum refiners and the American Petroleum Institute decided to withdraw from participation in the Common Sense Initiative. They expressed support for the aims of the initiative, but cited as reasons for not pursuing it a lack of clear direction, too many meetings with no clear outcome, lack of regular participation by Environmental Protection Agency staff of appropriate seniority and participation from the outset by environmental interests with a track record inimical to their industry.[15] It is striking that very similar criticisms are made of the Common Sense Inititative by participants from the field of electronics regulation.[16]

It may also be worth noting that the petroleum refining subcommittee was working on rewriting the Environmental Protection Agency's rules to consolidate, streamline and simplify air emissions reporting requirements for oil refineries, at a time when the Agency was bringing forward new and stricter air emissions standards for ozone and particulates. Voluntary initiatives which propose flexibility without tackling the underlying laws which make requirements of regulated entities are doomed to a certain amount of frustration. Where a law, say on emission limits, represents a mandatory requirement, the U.S. Environmental Protection Agency itself does not have unlimited scope to get round it, and could indeed face legal challenges for failing to implement it, however much it might want to introduce flexibility in applying the law.

A closely similar dilemma faces any European Union government that wants to introduce regulatory flexibility from any requirement that is based on European Union environmental law. Whenever and wherever the Member State can be said not to be fully implementing European Union law, it runs the risk of challenge either from one of its own nationals in national courts or the European Court of Justice, or infraction proceedings under Article 169 of the Treaty of Rome brought by the European Commission. Regulators who want to make good on a promise of wholesale flexibility in the application of environmental laws may have to be prepared to sponsor legislation to permit it, and in the British case this would probably mean European legislation.

Project XL

There cannot be many pollution prevention initiatives that have received quite as much publicity as Project XL. It has been called the flagship[17] of all the efforts described by President Clinton and Vice President Gore in their document "Reinventing Environmental Regulation".[18] This in turn was an important component of Vice President Gore's programme of reinventing government, finding ways to cut down on unnecessary paperwork, reporting requirements and regulations.

In 1995, President Clinton declared:[19]

" . . . we will provide the flexibility to test alternative strategies to achieve environmental goals. The most notable of these projects is *Project XL*. This program will give a limited number of responsible companies the opportunity to demonstrate *eXcellence* [*sic*] and *Leadership*. They will be given the flexibility to develop alternative strategies that will replace current regulatory requirements, while producing environmental benefits."

It was clear then from the outset that this was not a programme to apply across the board, but a series of experiments which may or may not produce models for other industries and facilities to follow.

In his State of the Union Address on 23 January 1996, President Clinton said:

"To businesses this administration is saying: if you can find a cheaper, more efficient way than government regulations require to meet tough standards, do it . . . as long as you do it right."

That was the philosophy, and that was the message reflected in the descriptions of Project XL given during the Presidential election campaign in 1996. Yet as at 9 May 1996, 14 proposals had been submitted for participation in Project XL,[20] which compares with over 1,000 participants in the EPA's 33/50 Programme and nearly 2,000 participants in its Green Lights programme by the same date.

Applicants to join Project XL are promised a short application form of ten pages. Yet they have to be able to demonstrate "superior environmental results", that is, better results from their proposed approach than would be achieved simply by their compliance with existing environmental regulations. They must also demonstrate the cost savings and paperwork reductions to be achieved, steps taken to encourage "stakeholder support", for example from affected communities, innovation and multi-media pollution prevention, the transferability of their proposals, their feasibility, arrangements for monitoring, reporting and evaluation, and the absence of shifting of the risk burden from one environmental medium to another.[21]

It is clear that some applicants think that they can still achieve better results by pursuing this initiative than by being required to comply with existing environmental regulations. But consideration of project applications is proving anything but straightforward, in part because of the legislative limits on the government's ability to be flexible in its application of existing laws. This is the same problem as faces the participants in the Environmental Protection Agency's Common Sense Initiative.

The official line put forward in testimony to Congress by the Environmental Protection Agency's Deputy Administrator, Fred Hansen, is that the Agency sees no need for Federal legislation to give it the flexibility it needs to make the most of Project XL. But more junior officials at the Agency's headquarters[22] suggest that this reluctance to see Federal legislation in the area has as much to do with what else Congress might add to the legislation. This is hardly surprising. By the time the Alaskan delegation to Congress had done its worst, both the legislation and the Agency itself might be unrecognisable. The political balance in Washington has therefore resulted in a reluctance in the part of the Environmental Protection Agency to take all the powers it might need to be able to deliver on the promise of regulatory flexibility.

Project XL is about a series of experiments, and it is probably therefore unfair to compare it directly to the Agency's 33/50 Programme. But in at least one feature it is strikingly different. The 33/50 Programme was directly based on the public information on toxic chemical releases on the Toxics Release Inventory. It focused on one part of those releases and targeted the companies and facilities releasing most of the chemicals which were the subject of the programme. By contrast, Project XL makes no direct reference to the Toxics Release Inventory data and does not target particular participants.

An analysis of the Environmental Protection Agency's Toxics Release Inventory Report for 1994 shows that the "Top 50" facilities releasing or transferring reportable toxic chemicals were responsible for no less than 32.7 per cent of all such releases or transfers in the United States.[23] One company, Dow Chemical, with one facility on this list at Freeport, Texas (number 39), has applied to participate in Project XL. For its plant in Freeport, Texas, Midland, Michigan, and Plaquemine, Louisiana, Dow Chemical proposed regulatory relief from the Resource Conservation and Recovery Act, "RCRA", the Clean Water Act, "CWA", the Clean Air Act, "CAA", and the Comprehensive Environmental Response, Compensation and Liability Act, "CERCLA" (Superfund).[24] Specifically, Dow Chemical sought flexibility with respect to permitting, monitoring, reporting and record-keeping requirements under these Federal laws and some state laws. Perhaps the Dow Chemical shopping list for regulatory flexibility gives some clue why applications to participate in Project XL take so much time for regulators to consider.

More generally, it seems legitimate to ask why, if Project XL is the key to reinventing environmental regulation, there is apparently so little participation by the other 49 facilities which between them account for about a third of all reported releases and transfers of toxic chemicals in the United States.

As the Federal government has found itself constrained in proposing legislation to support this programme, the initiative has passed to the states. A number of states have brought forward legislation allowing them to accord flexibility in compliance with environmental regulations in return for superior environmental performance. The emphasis of these state laws reflects the very different political constituencies from which they come, and the expectations for a clean environment of the different state electorates.

Illinois proposed to introduce rules for "a market-based emissions reduction, banking and trading system that will enable stationary sources to implement cost-effective compliance options".[25] Wisconsin intended to proceed cautiously with a pilot programme of "not more than 10 cooperative agreements to evaluate innovative environmental regulatory methods" which must "provide at least the same level of protection of public health and the environment" as existing regulations.[26] Washington state proposed an act "to create a voluntary program authorizing environmental excellence agreements . . . that use innovative environmental measures or strategies not otherwise recognized or allowed under existing laws and rules to achieve results that represent environmental excellence".[27] The Washington state bill emphasised the vital role of "stakeholder participation", and the fact that civil and criminal penalties for the violation of legal requirements are to remain the same. Legislation from the state of Louisiana placed more emphasis on "regulatory flexibility", and the proposed power of the Secretary of the Louisiana Department of Environmental Quality to exempt qualified participants from regulations promulgated by that department, insofar as that is consistent with federal law and regulation.[28] No doubt there will be ample scope for litigation and court challenges to explore how far state legislation to allow for regulatory flexibility is consistent with Federal environmental laws.

OTHER STATE POLLUTION PREVENTION INITIATIVES

It would be difficult in the space of a few pages to do justice to the full range of American state initiatives on pollution prevention, and to the energy and inventiveness with which they are applied. Each state is a laboratory of different approaches, and the best ideas are exchanged not only on the Internet and state and Federal agency web pages, but at important conferences such as those held by the National Pollution Prevention Roundtable which can attract as many as 500 participants, not nearly enough of them from Europe.[29] It seems that states are a size of governmental unit particularly well adapted to successful pursuit of this objective, and that this is one of the happiest areas of co-operation between states and Federal government and between industry and other interests such as environmental groups.

State programmes often feature high levels of state recognition of worthwhile efforts by state companies, and many states have Governor's awards programmes for excellence in pollution prevention. Pennsylvania, for example, publishes an annual book of Governor's Awards for Environmental Excellence, commending actions as diverse as the "Mouthwash Waste Minimization Initiative" of the Warner Lambert company and the contribution as an individual to environmental education of James W. Johnson.[30] Some states such as Colorado have also found it useful to use the Governor to cajole their top polluters into doing more to reduce their pollution.[31] The Colorado Governor hosted a reception for the state's top 50 polluters and challenged them to do more. Those that did received technical assistance, with a visit from a state environmental agency engineer. This mixture of recognition, rewards, technical assistance and a bit of embarrassment at the local level was reported to have had spectacular results.

Many states work with the companies within their boundaries to promote the technological innovations and fixes that are so dear to American hearts, publishing the results in a series of very comprehensive reports. A good example of these states is Texas, which has a particularly active and effective pollution prevention programme, and has written pollution prevention into the mission statement for its state environmental regulator.[32] The Office of Pollution Prevention and Recycling at the Texas Natural Resources Conservation Commission sees part of its mission as combating the philosophy that "we're going to create waste whatever we do".[33]

Texas is also interesting in having integrated its pollution prevention programme closely with its enforcement activity. Legislation to permit companies certain exemptions for carrying out environmental audits is administered by the Litigation Support Division. This division also conducts investigations and enforcement. The Director of Litigation Support, a former Brooklyn District Attorney with experience of murder investigations, is not an obvious candidate for being "soft" on polluting industries, but sees the agency's ability to promote self-auditing as important. It allows him to allocate enforcement resources to where they are most needed, while bringing more companies into compliance by encouraging them to clean up their own processes.[34] With 700 personnel monitoring 200,000 regulated entities, it is clear that the TNRCC has needed to find ways to address the most pressing problems first.

Both states and the Federal government are highly active in spreading the word of the benefits of pollution prevention. The Federal Environmental Protection Agency pours invaluable information onto the Internet, notably in its "Enviroene" programme and on other Web sites and factsheets aimed at transferring new technology to where it is needed.[35] Many states maintain effective programmes for assisting businesses and the environment at the same time, such as the New Jersey Technical Assistance Programme "NJTAP", or the Toxics Use Reduction Programmes of the Massachusetts Department of Environmental Protection. Between 1987 and 1994, New Jersey reduced its hazardous waste by 50 per cent. Massachusetts between 1990 and 1994 reduced toxic chemical use by 17 per cent and hazardous waste generation by 25 per cent,[36] so it is not surprising that both states have come to be regarded as leaders in the field.

"ZERO POLLUTION, ZERO WASTE"

The world of pollution prevention in America is a place of high achievements and great optimism about what is possible. But it has not yet fully embraced the next logical step, which is that the aim should not just be processes which *reduce* pollution and waste at source, but methods of production which produce *no* pollution and *no* waste.

William McDonough, the "Green Dean" of the School of Architecture at the University of Virginia, and his business partner, German chemist Dr Michael Braungart, have argued forcefully that the mentality of design is "still in the steamship mode" in failing to factor out waste and pollution altogether. McDonough has said that we should think of recycling not first but last, in a series of activities beginning with redesigning. The goal should simply be to eliminate the concept of waste, on the ground that "pollution and toxicity are always and irrevocably products of inefficiency. They are not the inevitable outcome of human interaction with the environment but the built-in results of the design of our system. Designing manufacturing and living systems that create no waste is both economical and prosperous."[37]

Is this challenge to current thinking merely Utopian? The President's Council on Sustainable Development has declared:

> "Just as the manufacturing sector has adopted a goal of zero defects, the nation can aspire to the ideal of a zero-waste society through more efficient use and recycling of natural resources in the economy and more efficient use of public and private financial resources in the regulatory system."[38]

Bodies considering sustainable development do tend to say things like that, but could industry ever be brought to share this aspiration? It is instructive to consider the case of DuPont.

The DuPont Company, properly E. I. du Pont de Nemours & Company, owns no fewer than four of the top 50 facilities with the largest total releases of toxic chemicals in the United States—numbers 1, 2, 6 and 10 on that list in 1994—at Pass Christian, Mississippi, New Johnsonville, Tennessee (recently subject to an Environmental Protection Agency civil enforcement action), Beaumont, Texas, and Victoria, Texas. DuPont's Pass Christian plant in Mississippi has the dubious distinction of recording the highest releases of reportable toxic chemicals in the whole of the United States in 1994, almost three times as much as its next competitor (also owned by DuPont).

Yet the DuPont Company has said that it wishes to move away from a focus on compliance to a focus on pollution prevention and elimination. It has adopted an in-house slogan that "the goal is zero", as a challenge to the "mindset" that achievement of numerical goals for reduction of pollution and waste is enough. All DuPont's plant in Texas, manufacturing petro-chemicals, agricultural chemicals, ethylene and adiponitrile have joined the Texas state's Clean Industries 2000 programme, which requires a commit-ment to a reduction of TRI chemical releases and/or hazardous waste gener-ation by 50 per cent or more from 1987 levels by the year 2000.[39] Perhaps after all the highest goal of all, production that is free of all pollution and waste, with a balanced use of natural resources, is achievable if one of the greatest polluters in the United States has adopted it as an aim and taken steps towards it.

THE ENVIRONMENT AND THE AMERICAN COMPUTER INDUSTRY

If any industry could reasonably be expected to be leading the rest in terms of "zero pollution, zero waste" methods of production, it ought surely to be the American computer industry. This is the industry with the newest facto-ries, the newest technologies, and a large number of extremely clever people involved in it. It is the opposite of a rust belt industry. Its reputation is that of a clean, high-tech alternative to the old behemoths of the past.

The manufacture of computers, and especially of printed circuit boards and computer chips, is in fact a very dirty process, involving huge quantities of contaminated water, acids, solvents and other pollutants, notably those used to etch and clean the circuit boards. The Campaign for Responsible Technology, part of an environmental ginger group called the Silicon Valley Toxics Coalition in San Jose, California, claims that on average, the produc-tion of an eight-inch wafer uses the following:

4,267 cubic feet of bulk gases
3,787 gallons of waste water
27 pounds of chemicals

29 cubic feet of hazardous gases
9 pounds of hazardous waste
3,023 gallons of de-ionized water.[40]

In many places, the industry has done considerable harm to the environment around it. Its use and contamination of massive amounts of water alone should be cause for concern in the dry states where so much of its growth has occurred, such as California, Texas and Arizona. It is making progress in achieving cleaner and safer production methods. But it is sometimes slow to apply pollution prevention techniques already successfully used elsewhere. With an industry that expects to spend between $1 billion and $2 billion on each new semiconductor manufacturing plant or "fab", and to have all the equipment in that plant obsolete within three to five years, something different is called for in terms of regulation.

Not a Cottage Industry

Thomas W. Armstrong, President of the Semconductor Industry Association has said:

> "It is difficult to resist the words 'surging', 'dramatic' and 'impressive' in describing the unprecedented growth in the global semiconductor industry."[41]

Computers and electronics in America are not exactly a cottage industry. The American lead in research and development has been seen by the United States government as a strategic necessity. When Japan took the lead in semiconductor sales in 1984, the Americans responded with SEMATECH, the central research project based in Austin, Texas. With $1 billion in Federal subsidies and $5 billion more from the top 14 semiconductor manufacturers, this collaborative research effort has produced the "national technology roadmap", a proposed national plan for the research necessary to retain the technological lead. The Semiconductor Industry Association is also responsible for the Semiconductor Research Corporation in Research Triangle Park in North Carolina. This dominance in research and development is credited with re-establishing the U.S. lead in semiconductor manufacturing, spawning a huge range of new and related industries, and being partly responsible for the recent phenomenal growth in and around Silicon Valley. After a bruising but successful round of trade disputes with Japan, America in 1997 had over 20 per cent of the Japanese semiconductor market, and 43.4 per cent of worldwide semiconductor market share, compared to 40.1 per cent for Japan.

While the semiconductor industry leads the economic charge in Silicon Valley, it pulls along with it a whole range of new and related industries supplying parts, software and new products such as microcomputers for the automobile industry. One example of many is the Read-Rite Corporation of Milpitas, California, which makes "recording heads, head gimbal assemblies and head stack assemblies for disk drives and magnetoresistive heads for tape drives". A disk drive is about the size of two fingers, and the parts made by Read-Rite are roughly the size of a pea and four or five grains of rice. The company employs 21,000 people in Japan, California, Thailand, Malaysia, the Philippines and Singapore, and has revenue of $1 billion.

Not Quite Clean

In Silicon Valley, the first sign that the electronics and computer industry might not be as clean as it appeared came with the discovery of major groundwater contamination at the Fairchild site. In the 1980s, 23 electronics-related sites in Santa Clara county alone were added to the Superfund "national priority list" of worst contaminated sites, making a total of 29 sites in all for the county, the highest number of any county in America.

Industry trade bodies in Silicon Valley, such as the Semiconductor Industry Association and the Silicon Valley Manufacturing Group, complain that these Superfund listings were political and unfair, as the industry has never dodged its responsibility to clean up its contamination. And they make the fair point that many of the problems arose from compliance with the fire regulations then in force, which required that stores of chemicals be put in underground tanks, which later leaked, contaminating groundwater. Modern "just-in-time" production methods have greatly reduced the amounts of chemicals stored at fabrication plants, and there is no doubt that since the 1980s the industry has taken the threat of pollution much more seriously, and pollution abatement equipment such as double-lined pipes and tanks for hazardous chemicals is now standard at semiconductor manufacturing plant.

Nevertheless, one may take with a pinch of salt the Californian view that the 1980s are so long ago as to be "like the Middle Ages". Groundwater, once contaminated, is not easily cleaned up, although some firms are trying. Twenty firms in the Santa Clara Valley were involved in groundwater clean-up projects in 1997. In 1995, 11 of these companies pumped and treated one billion gallons of groundwater, re-injecting 303 million gallons to the aquifer, and spending an estimated $116 million in the process.[42]

In Washington state, a report by the state environmental regulator on the printed circuit board sector showed that "waste quantities have increased faster than production" and concluded that "the data suggests that the benefits of implementing pollution prevention techniques have not been fully realised". In 1991 and 1994 respectively, the printed circuit board industry in Washington state produced 2,776,109 pounds and 4,406,788 pounds of "Dangerous Waste", and 253,993 pounds and 488,055 pounds of "Extremely Hazardous Waste". The same report noted that seven out of 11 sector facilities had violated their wastewater discharge permits, with 44 violations and fines totalling $203,489 between 1991 and 1994. Most of these violations were for exceeding limits for copper and lead in wastewater.[43]

Down at the other end of the pipe, the City of Palo Alto's Regional Water Quality Control Plant has been struggling to meet copper emission limits for discharges to San Francisco Bay. A special ordinance was introduced applying to printed circuit board manufacturers and metal finishers, requiring further pollution prevention measures to be taken by July 1996. By the autumn of 1996, one printed circuit board manufacturer remained out of compliance with these requirements.[44] These may be signs that the huge expansion of production in the American industry has put strains on its compliance with environmental standards.

Slow to Adopt Best Practice?

What is also clear is that despite the industry's notable improvements in some areas, it can be very slow to pick up on pollution prevention ideas being successfully applied even elsewhere in America. Motorola's Oak Hill Facility in Austin, Texas, used to use hydrofluoric acid for etching wafers in its semiconductor manufacturing. In 1992 it generated 680 tons of hydrofluoric acid "HF" waste, which it used to dispose of by deep well injection. It has now installed a fluoride waste treatment system, which neutralises this hazardous waste stream completely by adding lime. The result is a 99 per cent reduction in HF waste, and a 46 per cent reduction of total hazardous waste generation at the site.[45] Another Motorola site in Austin Texas has found a way to clean and recycle 95 per cent of its sulphuric acid. But hydrofluoric acid waste is still produced by many other semiconductor plants, and sulphuric acid is not universally recycled.

Both the Computer Circuitry Company in Grand Prairie, Texas,[46] and Velie Circuits of Colorado Inc in Broomfield, Colorado,[47] have found ways of eliminating formaldehyde from the manufacturing process for circuit boards. Yet formaldehyde remains part of the production process in many other parts of the United States. IBM undertook to phase out the use of all freons within three years, after topping a list of the "dirty dozen" polluters published by a California newspaper when public right-to-know laws were introduced and emissions made public. But freons will still part of the processes at a number of other plants under construction in America.

Like many industries, the American computer industry has tended to concentrate on the environmental problems that seem most pressing rather than to spend time on addressing the whole of their environmental impacts. For example, glycol ethers have been implicated in reproductive hazards to workers employed in fabrication plants that use them, and the industry has moved fairly rapidly to phase out their use. Large amounts of CFCs used to be released by computer manufacturing plants, but these emissions have been vigorously tackled because of the publicity about their effect on global warming. Less well known hazardous chemicals with less well researched effects continue to be used.

In some cases, technological advances which offer tantalising possibilities of cleaner production are still being tested while computer chip manufacturing plant are still being built. The U.S. Environmental Protection Agency is currently funding a demonstration project to test a dry cleaning system for semiconductor wafers. It would use laser-assisted cleaning of the wafers, sweeping away contaminants with flowing gas. This might offer the potential to replace whole categories of processes using and contaminating water and generating hazardous wastes.[48] The process is being tested at Motorola's Corporate Research Laboratory in Phoenix, Arizona, and at the Rutherford Appleton Laboratory in Chilton, England.

Even the computer industry cannot always anticipate technological progress. But it could clearly do more to pick up on and apply pollution prevention lessons that have already been learned and demonstrated in other states, or even the same state. An IBM plant in California, for example, discovered traces of zinc in its wastewater discharges. After a long investigation, it traced the source to the wastewater discharges from its laundry. Four or five years later another company a short distance away discovered exactly the same problem, and had to undergo the same investigation to locate the source. An industry that devotes as much time and effort as this one telling the rest of us about the importance for the next century of information and networks could usefully practise what it preaches.

One factor that may prevent the industry from applying best practice in pollution prevention techniques more systematically is its competitiveness. Ted Smith of the Silicon Valley Toxics Coalition put it like this in evidence to the United States Congress in 1992:

> "Chip production is intensely competitive, so companies focus almost all their manufacturing technology efforts on cutting costs and increasing reliability. . . . These firms may be well situated to introduce new methods, but since they don't currently pay the price of pollution or pollution-control, they have no incentive to explore alternatives."[49]

The WaferTech company in 1997 was building a new semiconductor plant in Camas in Washington state. It planned to spend $500 million on buildings, and $800 million on equipment that it expected to have to replace entirely in about five years. It believed that its pollution control and abatement equipment at the time of construction was state-of-the-art and capable of exceeding any regulatory requirement that might be placed upon it. It may be right. With that sort of investment, it is scarcely worth quibbling about some necessary piece of pollution abatement equipment. Companies will do what they have to do, and spend what they have to spend, to get into production quickly and to stay in production continuously. Every day's lost production is seen as costing a fabrication plant between $1 million and $2 million.

Anything that holds up the issue of permits becomes a major issue. Lawrence Cowles, Environmental Health and Safety Manager for Read-Rite and Chair of the Environmental Committee of the Silicon Valley Manufacturing Group, has remarked that "three months can kill you".[50] As that company's disk drive products have a technological shelf-life of only eight months, it is possible to see how the traditional approach to formulating regulations may be irrelevant either to the needs of this industry or to the needs of the environment that it affects.

Lawrence Cowles also noted the importance of the help given to the company by the city of Fremont in California when the company was planning a new manufacturing plant. The city streamlined the permitting process, appointing one contact to co-ordinate all the permissions necessary, and within one week convened a meeting of all the utilities and agencies involved, so that the company could ensure that it met all their requirements at one time.

Regulating High-tech

There are two powerful interests at stake here with the potential for conflict between them. The first is the American computer industry itself, a huge engine of growth, and a financially powerful and impatient lobby. People want it to succeed. They want the prospect of jobs with a future that it seems to offer, and communities, towns, states and even countries, including Britain, compete for the investment that it brings. On the other hand, the second interest is that of the public in a clean environment. People also want, and need, unpolluted water, air and land, and less reliance on very hazardous chemicals which can injure those working with them and produce unmanageable toxic wastes.

With an industry whose technology is developing as rapidly as this one, it makes little sense for regulations to focus on how environmental objectives are to be achieved, as opposed to what the objectives should be. Most regulatory agencies are not going to be in a position soon to hire enough of the best brains from Silicon Valley to help them second-guess how its computer firms should achieve pollution prevention targets.

Isao Kobashi, Pollution Manager of Santa Clara County's pollution prevention programme, put the issue in this way:[51]

> "You have to go back to the purpose. Why are you regulating? You make your list of concerns known, then make sure they are understood. For frontier technologies, you put it back on industry, with performance or outcome goals, leaving it to them how to achieve them."

Publicity and the public "right-to-know" legislation have been highly effective in achieving reductions of toxic emissions in Silicon Valley. The Silicon Valley Manufacturing Group claims that reportable emissions have fallen by 89 per cent since this legislation allowed the public to know what pollution was being produced.

Voluntary pollution prevention programmes have also been successful, particularly where the target was specific and well defined. Silicon Valley contributed to the U.S. Environmental Protection Agency's "33/50 Programme", which, as has been seen, exceeded its target of reducing emissions of 17 priority chemicals by 50 per cent within four years, leaving the means to achieve this up to the industries concerned. But the continued expansion of this industry may in the end overtake its pollution prevention achievements, rather as increasing traffic volume may overtake the benefits of cleaner engine technologies and catalytic converters. There is room for a fundamentally different approach to the issue of pollution.

CONCLUSIONS

Pollution prevention in America provides rich pickings of good ideas that could and should be applied elsewhere. Pollution prevention, or "P2" as it is sometimes known, benefits greatly from the almost universal support that it receives from government, industry and environmentalists. Some of the most successful initiatives have been those which are highly specific, with clear and measurable targets, little prescription about how to achieve them and plenty of recognition to those who succeed in meeting them.

Traditional regulation seems highly unlikely to reconcile the difference between the needs of new industries for growth and speed of response and the needs of the public for effective environmental protection. By the time the regulations were formulated and discussed in the usual way, it would almost be time for the computer manufacturing plant to throw away its machinery and start again.

Perhaps the answer is for this industry and others like it to embrace the goals of "zero pollution and zero waste", to make itself the leader in clean production technologies that it ought by rights to be. In both America and Britain there has been a move to explore alternatives to "command and control" environmental regulation. An industry that wants to be free of the worst effects of regulation should show itself fully capable of delivering a better alternative.

But the issue of "regulating high tech" is not only one for the industries concerned, but one for governments and regulators. It might be a good time to devise an "incentive jackpot" in terms of regulations and taxes for those shown capable of delivering the benefits of high tech industries like computers and electronics without the costs of their pollution and wastes.

The goal of "zero pollution, zero waste" would be such an enormous benefit to society and the environment, such a marked advance, that it would justify the greatest rewards that government and regulators could offer: the most regulatory flexibility, the most generous tax incentives, the highest recognition. This, surely, is where the pollution prevention movement should focus next. Businesses able to increase production with no pollution, no waste and a sustainable use of natural resources are the way of the future. They should receive every encouragement that the system of legislation and regulation can devise.

REFERENCES

1. Since the election of the Labour government in Britain in May 1997, in a change which George Orwell would surely have appreciated, the "Deregulation Unit" of the Department of Trade and Industry changed its name to the "Better Regulation Unit".
2. S. 1 of the Deregulation and Contracting Out Act 1994 (c.40) allows ministers to repeal or amend enactments by order where the enactments, in the minister's opinion, impose a burden affecting any person in the carrying on of any trade, business or profession "or otherwise", and if it would be possible to amend or repeal the enactment to remove or reduce the burden "without removing any necessary protection" (s. 1(1)(b)).
3. See e.g. David Schoenbrod, Professor of Law, New York Law School, "Why States, Not EPA, Should Set Pollution Standards", in 4 *The Cato Review of Business and Government*, entitled "Regulation".
4. I am grateful for some of the facts in this section to Jessica Mathews, Senior Fellow at the Council on Foreign Relations, Washington, D.C., who kindly gave me a copy of her article "Look Before You Lop" on the Green Lights Program from the *Washington Post*, 27 Mar. 1995.
5. See also EPA, *Green Lights and Energy Star Buildings Programs Participant*

List, 17 Mar. 1997: also U.S. EPA Air and Radiation Division, *Green Lights and Energy Star Buildings Update*, Winter 1997, and *Partnerships in Preventing Pollution—A Catalogue of the Agency's Partnership Programs* (U.S. EPA Office of the Administrator, Washington, D.C., Spring 1996). For contact information on this and other programmes referred to in this ch., see below.

6. Telephone call to EPA Green Lights Programme, 10 Apr. 1997.

7. The 17 chemicals groups were Benzene; Cadmium and Cadmium Compounds; Carbon Tetrachloride; Chloroform; Chromium and Chromium Compounds; Cyanide and Cyanide Compounds; Lead and Lead Compounds; Mercury and Mercury Compounds; Methylene Chloride; Methyl Ethyl Ketone; Methyl Isobutyl Ketone; Nickel and Nickel Compounds; Tetrachloroethylene; Toluene; 1,1,1-Trichloroethane; Trichloroethylene; Xylenes.

8. U.S. EPA Office of Pollution Prevention and Toxics, "33/50 Programme Company Profiles: Reduction Highlights" (EPA, Washington, D.C., Oct. 1994).

9. U.S. EPA factsheet, "Iron & Steel Industry & the 33/50 Program", 1994.

10. U.S. EPA Office of Pollution Prevention and Toxics, "EPA's 33/50 Programme Sixth Progress Update—Continuing Progress Toward Ultimate Reduction Goal" (EPA, Washington, D.C., Sept. 1995).

11. *Chemical Engineering*, Aug. 1995, Editor's Page, Richard J. Zanetti, Editor-in-Chief.

12. Malcolm K. Sparrow, *Imposing Duties—Government's Changing Approach to Compliance* (Praeger, Westport, Conn., 1994).

13. E.g. participation in the Louisiana Environmental Leadership Programme requires participants to indicate support for some guiding principles, submit a brief plan describing their reduction goals for selected waste and emission streams and to commit to sharing information about progress towards the goals, and generally about their successes in pollution prevention. In return, participants receive a letter and certificate from the Louisiana Department of Environmental Quality, a seat on the Leadership Council with senior LDEQ staff and eligibility to compete in the LDEQ Secretary's Awards for Environmental Excellence (Louisiana Environmental Leadership Pollution Prevention Program Enrolment Package). This seems, on the whole, unlikely to clean up the Mississippi.

14. U.S. EPA, "The Common Sense Initiative—A new Generation of Environmental Protection" (EPA, Washington, D.C., Apr. 1996).

15. Telephone interviews with American Petroleum Institute staff, Mar. 1997, meetings with API staff member, Apr. 1997.

16. Meeting with Isao Kobashi, Programme Manager, Pollution Prevention, County of Santa Clara, Cal., San Jose, Cal., 6 May 1997.

17. Meeting with Keith Laughlin, Associate Director, Executive Office of the President, Council on Environmental Quality, Washington, D.C. 3 Feb. 1997.

18. 16 Mar. 1995.

19. *Ibid*.

20. Environmental Briefing, Supplementary Papers, 21 and 22 May 1996, Keith Mason U.S. EPA, London, England.

21. Project XL for Facilities, Industry Sectors, and Government Agencies, EPA leaflet, Mar. 1996.

22. Interviews, Feb. 1997.

23. Toxics Release Inventory, U.S. EPA, 1994, 38, table, "Top 50 TRI Facilities with the Largest Total Releases".

24. N. 20 above.

25. An Act relating to environmental protection, Public Act 89–465, signed 13 June 1996,

26. Wisconsin draft Act relating to the budget, State of Wisconsin 1997–1998 Legislature, LRB—0625/1.

27. State of Washington, 55th Legislature, House Bill 1866, by Representatives Chandler and Linville.

28. Draft Louisiana Environmental Regulatory Innovations Act, Regular Session 1997, R.S. 30:2043.

29. At the National Pollution Prevention Roundtable Spring Conference in Denver, Colo. in Apr. 1997 the author, a lawyer, was apparently the only British participant apart from an academic bookseller. There was no one from the Environment Agency, the Scottish Environment Protection Agency or the European Environment Agency. Americans sometimes exhibit a marked lack of curiosity in good ideas from Europe, but in this area it seems pointless to reciprocate by ignoring so many ideas and so much useful information.

30. 1996 Governor's Awards for Environmental Excellence, Commonwealth of Pennsylvania Department of Environmental Protection, Office of Pollution Prevention and Compliance Assistance.

31. Presentation by Patti Shwayder, Executive Director, Colorado Department of Public Health and Environment, NPPR Spring conference, Denver, Colo., 2 Apr. 1997.

32. See e.g. Texas Natural Resource Conservation Commission, Office of Pollution Prevention and Recycling, "Pollution Prevention Ideas from Texas Industries—a Case Study Compendium" (TNRCC, Austin, Tex., Mar. 1996).

33. Meeting with Andrew Neblett, Director, Office of Pollution Prevention and Recycling, TNRCC, Austin, Tex., 5 Nov. 1996.

34. Meeting with John A. Riley, Division Director, Litigation Support Division, Texas Natural Resources Conservation Commission, Austin, Tex., 5 Nov. 1996.

35. See e.g. the U.S. EPA's "Technology Transfer Highlights", issued periodically by the office of Research and Development, and its *Design for the Environment* publications series from its Pollution Prevention Information Clearinghouse. Industries that overlook these sources are missing a very big, and free, trick: sometimes it commands more attention to be required to pay large sums for information!

36. Carolyn Hartman, US Public Interest Research Group, "USPIRG", presentation at National Pollution Prevention Roundtable Spring Conference, Denver, Colo., 2 Apr. 1997.

37. See: Robert Frenay, "Biorealism—Reading Nature's Blueprints", *Audubon*,

Sept.–Oct. 1995; William Mcdonough, "A Boat for Thoreau", *Business Ethics*, May/June 1993; "Industrial Revolution II—William Mcdonough's New Way of Thinking", *Interiors and Sources*, May 1995; Paul Hawken and William McDonough, "Seven Steps to doing Good Business", *Inc*, Nov. 1993. McDonough Braungart Design Chemistry can be contacted at 619 East High Street, Charlottesville, Virginia 22902, tel. (804)–295–1111, fax (804)–295–1500, or contacted on the Internet at http://www.mbdc.com

38. Sustainable America—A New Consensus for Prosperity, Opportunity and a Healthy Environment for the Future, the President's Council on Sustainable Development, Feb. 1996, 28.

39. The facilities will also be required to have source reduction and waste minimisation plans consistent with the requirements of the Texas Waste Reduction Policy Act of 1991: Clean Industries 2000 Program Description, Texas Natural Resource Conservation Commission.

40. Campaign for Responsible Technology, "Communities and Workers Beware!!" (San Jose, Cal.).

41. Message from the President, Semiconductor Industry Association, Status Report and Industry Directory, 1996–7.

42. Santa Clara Valley Manufacturing Group, "What we are Doing for the Environment", *Santa Clara Valley Industry Environmental Report*, June 1996, 11.

43. Washington State Department of Ecology, "Measuring Pollution Prevention: Analysis of the Printed Circuit Board Fabrication Sector in Washington State", Publication No. 96–409, May 1996, 36, 37, 33 and 12.

44. Regional Water Quality Control Plant, *Clean Bay Plan 1997*, Summary (City of Palo Alto, Palo Alto, Cal., 1997).

45. Texas Natural Tesources Conservation Commission, "Pollution Prevention Ideas from Texas Industries—a Case Study Compendium", Mar. 1996, Office of Pollution Prevention and Recycling.

46. *Ibid.*, 159.

47. J. Canterbury and N. Kolwey, *Colorado Pollution Prevention Case Studies Compendium* (Colorado Department of Public Health and Environment Pollution Prevention Program, Sept. 1996), 67–8.

48. *U.S. EPA Pollution Prevention News*, Oct.–Nov. 1996, Technology update.

49. Ted Smith, Chair, Campaign for Responsible Technology, evidence to House Science, Space and Technology Committee, 15 Sept. 1992: Meeting with Ted Smith, San Jose, Cal., 6 May 1997.

50. Meeting with Lawrence Cowles, Fremont, Cal., 6 May 1997.

51. N. 16 above.

9

Keeping Hope Alive

Calvinist Protestantism traditionally held that people were divided by pre-destination into two very distinct groups. There were the Elect (those on a fast track to Paradise) and the Damned (those with a ticket to the Other Place). This thinking finds echoes in two very different views of environmental issues and environmental laws: nineteenth-century confidence, and late twentieth-century doubts. A fair account of the state of the environment may be one that avoids the excesses of either view. There is enough to be concerned about without representing that all the news is bad. And if public support is to be enlisted for environmental laws, then in the long term people have to be persuaded not only that the laws are necessary but also that their contribution makes a real difference.

THE ELECT: NINETEENTH-CENTURY CONFIDENCE

Victorian Britain was a confident place. There seemed no end to the possibilities of new science and technology, from Brunel's railways and steamships to all the other inventions of the Industrial Revolution. Victorian buildings in every town and city reflected the civic pride and confidence of the era. When architects of the day were called on to restore Saxon or Norman churches, they did not hesitate to tear out old features and replace them with modern ones, which they were sure were better. The country was militarily strong, the fleet unrivalled, the Empire covered a third of the globe. Lady Eden's account of her progresses around India with her brother, the Governor General in the 1830s, with hundreds of elephants, thousands of retainers and cases of jewels to dispense to Maharajahs certainly make modern government officials appear mousy by comparison.

The laws reflected the times. Many of the more remarkable Victorian laws, such as those put forward by the great reforming Earl of Shaftesbury to bring little children out of the mines and down from the chimneys of Britain, were motivated by the strong religious faith then widespread and by a particular view of the value of individual human souls. Laws governing aspects of what we would now call the environment reflected the clear view that resources appeared to be limitless, and the only aspects of the natural world worth protecting were those that were useful to man. The nineteenth-century game laws in Britain extended strict protection to "useful" game species in order to make them available for hunting and shooting, but allowed free rein for the control of "pest" species like owls and hawks. Selective protection of limited numbers of species was a feature of the laws made by the British for many parts of their Empire. The Canadian Fisheries Act of 1868, still in force today, confines the protection it affords to waters containing fish which are used by man: there is no protection of the waters, or the fish, for their own sakes. In the international field, the Convention for the Protection of Birds Useful to Agriculture of 1902 is a fine example of the genre.

Before the Civil War, nineteenth-century America too was a confident place. Lewis and Clarke had shown the way across the huge continent, and others were not slow to follow. J. C. Calhoun, setting out the claims of the United States to the Oregon Territory in a document in Washington, D.C., in September 1844 wrote:

> "There can be no doubt, now that the operation of the same causes which impelled our population westward from the shores of the Atlantic across the Alleghany to the Valley of the Mississippi will impel them onward with accumulating force across the Rocky Mountains into the Valley of the Columbia, and that the whole region drained by it is destined to be peopled by us."

An advertisement of the day for agricultural machinery declared:

> "Westward the course of empire takes its way—with McCormick reapers in the van!"

Like Victorian Britons, nineteenth-century Americans seemed to enjoy a prospect of limitless resources. The plains of America teemed with buffalo and antelope. Land grants tempted the pioneer wagons westward. The mountains were full of minerals, and their slopes with stands of old growth timber. What was needed was brave folk to settle and tame the wilderness, and to take part in the three great western enterprises of logging, ranching and mining. The laws to encourage this movement of settlers were not full of references to sustainable development. Development was a benefit in its own right. America's Mining Act of 1872, still in force, still offers cheap concessions on Federal lands to mining companies and, which is almost as important today, virtual freedom from responsibility to clean up after their operations.

Socialist countries have preserved an essentially nineteenth-century view of the environment well into the twentieth century. The Soviet Union put the interests of man (as represented by industrial development and military strength) first and those of the environment a long way second, but, as has been noted, this ultimately resulted in falling life expectancy for Russian citizens. China's determination to build the Three Gorges Dam across the Yangtze River, or Slovakia's construction of the Nagymaros dam on the River Danube, reflect a similar view of the proper priorities.

In western countries, nineteenth-century thinking has persisted for longest in the sparsely populated areas where it has been possible to hold on to the illusion that resources may still be limitless, and where there seems enough wilderness to spare. In Alaska, proposals to drill for oil in National Wildlife Refuges, to put roads across wilderness areas or to log national forests are keenly pursued. In Montana, mining companies propose a huge cyanide leach pit mine in the valley of the Blackfoot River. In Idaho, it is planned to construct a bombing range in the Owyhee Canyonlands.

Where people are convinced that they are numbered among the Elect and that the world is there for their exploitation, there has always been the problem of whether any incentives exist for good behaviour in the meantime. The Scots writer of adventure stories, John Buchan, wrote one of his finest tales, *Witch Wood*, about a community in the Borders of Scotland in the seventeenth century who had concluded that they were all of the Elect. Being guaranteed a passage to Paradise, they found nothing inconsistent with being stern Calvinists by day and practising witchcraft in the forest nearby at night. In environmental terms, those who have acted from a confident view of the primacy of man's interests over all others have inflicted some of the heaviest blows on the state of the natural environment, often without intending that effect. Those who diverted the rivers from the Aral Sea in Russia were trying to grow cotton over a wider area, not to create the contaminated wasteland that resulted. The African countries that have erected hundreds of miles of game fences across the migration routes of wild animals were trying to protect their beef herds from foot and mouth disease so as to encourage exports to the European Community, not to decimate 99 per cent of the Kalahari wildebeeste.

THE DAMNED: LATE TWENTIETH-CENTURY DOUBTS

From the bull-necked confidence of the nineteenth-century view that all human development was an unqualified good, we seemed to have arrived at the brink of the new Millennium with a collection of contrary doubts. The religious faith that sustained the Victorians has waned. Some commentators have remarked that it appears to have been replaced by belief in topics such as environmentalism, which they describe as a new religion, an end in itself and not a means to achieve something else like human happiness.

It has become clear that many resources are not limitless. The Stockholm Conference of 1970, which was a turning point in the modern environmental movement, was followed in 1973 by the first oil shock. This brought home to many the finite nature of non-renewable energy resources. The last three decades have emphasised the finite nature of many other resources that the Victorians could have counted as unlimited. Exploration of space, and films such as NASA's *Blue Planet* showed the Earth's atmosphere to be a thin blue line surrounded by a limitless black void. Damage to the ozone layer, and now global warming due to the burning of fossil fuels, are issues which will continue to occupy the next century. The rate of extinction of species has accelerated dramatically, in step with the disappearance of so much habitat, and with the pressures of the greatest ever increase in human population.

Species extinction and biodiversity are common parlance today, in a way which Victorians would have found eccentric. Lady Eden, who described as "a great blessing for the country they are in" the fact that members of her party had shot 26 tigers, several of them man-eaters, would have been astonished at the desperate efforts to save the last of this species. The Endangered Species Act in America and the international Biodiversity Convention result in environmentalists and governments being engaged in great efforts to save species, not simply because they are useful to man, but because they are there. Nature, which in the nineteenth century was something to be subjugated and turned to useful and productive purposes, is today something to be protected for its own sake. There probably is a case for trying to save Preble's Jumping Mouse, or Desmoulin's Snail, but making that case in economic terms is always going to be difficult.

The world has read about air pollution samples taken from Mount Everest, of fish affected by detergents under the North polar ice cap, of melting ice floes in Antarctica, and hermaphrodite polar bears in the Arctic that have accumulated polychlorinated biphenyls. For many, the effect has been, on a world scale, equivalent to the change in national perceptions in America that came with the closing of the frontier. Few people today can expect to discover an untamed wilderness, or, like Wilfred Thesiger, to cross the Empty Quarter of the Sahara and find it untouched by man. We have to decide what kind of care we intend to exercise over the environment nearer to home.

Nowhere has the change in thinking between the nineteenth- and twentieth-century views on environmental issues been greater than over Man's place in the natural order. Where the Victorian would have put him at the top, and insisted that the natural world should operate for his benefit, to environmentalists in the late twentieth century, man is the problem. To hear some environmental commentators discuss the world's population, you would think they were discussing a pest species. Environmental groups and non-governmental organisations in particular are much given to a world view that is rather hostile to the human race. Like Gulliver in Lilliput, humans are made to feel like huge engines of destruction, blighting whatever parts of the natural world they turn up in. In a way, the misplaced confidence that Man in general, western Man in particular, was of the "Elect" has been turned on its head. From being the "Elect", Man is now seen as the "Damned". The problem is that this too offers few incentives to "good behaviour" in the time allotted to us before the arrival of an asteroid or galactic implosion renders the entire debate academic.

THE CASE FOR OPTIMISM

A view of Man as all of the problem and none of the solution risks overlooking some important factors. It tends to minimise the real achievements of individuals in the field of environmental protection, which is a pity, because those achievements are considerable. Without David Brower's leadership of the Sierra Club and founding of Friends of the Earth, the Grand Canyon would probably be a reservoir by now, and countless other battles would have been lost. Miriam Rothschild in Britain has made the production of wildflower seed and butterfly and dragonfly conservation mainstream and welcome activities. At the age of 89, she still campaigns from her wheelchair for Wildlife Trusts and nature reserves. Ian Player in South Africa led the effort that saved the white rhino, and taught many the value of wilderness. Wangari Maathai in Kenya led the Green Belt Movement there which has planted over 12 million trees. And everywhere the scale of environmental problems is matched by the determination and energy of the next generations of Browers and Rothschilds of Players and Maathais, armed with new knowledge and new technology.

The development of environmental law since 1970 in Britain, America and Europe is a necessary part of this story. There are always ways, which this book has tried to explore, of making environmental law more effective. But environmental laws have had a major impact on the control and reduction of pollution of water, air and land. They have established the agencies and institutions by which we propose to take this work forward. If there is ever going to be an effective response to environmental problems, environmental law is going to be one of the main means by which it is delivered.

THE NEED FOR HOPE

The distinguished palaeontologist and conservationist, Richard Leakey, has said in his book *The Sixth Extinction*[1] that he believes that there is an ethical imperative to protect and not harm other species, because of our intimate connection with the rest of nature in terms of our origins. He wrote that this is our duty "not because we are the one sentient creature on Earth, which bestows some kind of benevolent superiority on us, but because in a fundamental sense *Homo sapiens* is on an equal footing with each and every other species here on Earth".

The biologist Richard Dawkins regards us as a collection of "selfish genes", programmed by DNA and dancing to its tune, in a form of biological predestination with strong echoes of Calvinism. This school of biologists would have us believe that altruism is a mere biological and genetic function to be expected in the higher primate, at least within its immediate family circle. So if we want to make the world a better place for our children, that is only natural behaviour for late twentieth-century hominids. Religious people, of course, have fewer problems with these questions. It is easier for them to accept the duty of stewardship over a divine creation as natural and sensible.

Wherever they start from, people need to have hope and to have optimism if they are to be motivated to contribute to environmental protection. By and large, many of us are less confident than we might have been in the nineteenth century of being the Elect, with the whole of creation displayed for our benefit and use. But we should not be persuaded, by environmentalists or anyone else, that we are collectively damned, that it is all too late and that nothing we do can make a difference. One theme of this book has been a search for ways to reconnect the environmental law-making process with the concerns of the wider public. If our laws too are to reflect our times, they must not only seek to manage decline, but to reflect our wider beliefs that a better environment for ourselves and our children is possible and within our reach.

REFERENCE

1. Richard Leakey, *The Sixth Extinction* (Weidenfeld & Nicolson, London, 1996).

Bibliography

ADAMS, JOHN, *Risk* (University College London Press, London, 1995).

ALLISTON, GERALDINE, *et al.*, *Review of the Implementation and Enforcement of EC Law in the UK* (Department of Trade and Industry, London, 1993).

BADEN, JOHN A., *et al.*, *Environmental Gore: A Constructive Response to Earth in the Balance* (Pacific Research Institute for Public Policy, San Francisco, Cal., 1994).

BATES, DAVID V., *Environmental Health Risks and Public Policy: Decision Making in Free Societies* (University of Washington Press, Seattle, Wash., 1994).

BRIDGES, OLGA, and JIM, *Losing Hope: The Environment and Health in Russia* (Avebury Studies in Green Research, Aldershot, 1996).

BULLARD, ROBERT, *Dumping in Dixie: Race, Class and Environmental Quality* (Westview Press Inc, Boulder, Colo., 1994).

CANTERBURY, J., and KOLWEY, N., *Colorado Pollution Prevention Studies Compendium* (Colorado Department of Public Health and Environment Pollution Prevention Program, Denver, Colo., September 1996).

CARSON, RACHEL, *Silent Spring* (Hamish Hamilton, London, 1963).

CLINTON, PRESIDENT BILL, and GORE, VICE PRESIDENT AL, *Reinventing Environment Regulation* (U.S. Government, Washington, D.C., 16 March 1995).

COHEN, RICHARD E., *Washington at Work, Back Rooms and Clean Air* (Macmillan, New York, 1992).

COHRSSEN, JOHN J., and COVELLO, VINCENT T., *Risk Analysis: A Guide to Principles and Methods for Analyzing Health and Environmental Risks* (Council on Environmental Quality, Washington, D.C., 1989).

COLBORN, THEO, DUMANOWSKI, DIANNE, and MYERS, JOHN PETERSON, *Our Stolen Future—Are We Threatening Our Fertility, Intelligence and Survival? A Scientific Detective Story* (Penguin, New York, 1997).

COUNCIL ON ENVIRONMENTAL QUALITY, U.S., EXECUTIVE OFFICE OF THE PRESIDENT, *Environment Quality—25th Anniversary Report* (Council on Environmental Quality, Washington, D.C., 1996).

DICKERSON, JANICE F., and WARD, ROGER K., *Environmental Justice in Louisiana— The Louisiana Department of Environmental Quality's Environmental Justice Program* (Louisiana DEQ, Baton Rouge, Lou., 1996).

DOWIE, MARK, *Losing Ground—American Environmentalism at the Close of the Twentieth Century* (Massachusetts Institute of Technology Press, Boston, Mass., 1995).

ENVIRONMENT AGENCY FOR ENGLAND AND WALES, *A Guide to Information Available to the Public* (Environment Agency, Bristol, 1996).

ENVIRONMENT, DEPARTMENT OF, ENGLAND, *Indicators of Sustainable Development 1996* (Department of the Environment, HMSO, London, 1996).

—— *The UK Environment* (HMSO, London, 1992).

ENVIRONMENT, TRANSPORT AND THE REGIONS, DEPARTMENT OF, ENGLAND, *Digest of Environmental Statistics No. 19, 1997* (DETR, HMSO, London, 1997).

ENVIRONMENTAL PROTECTION AGENCY, U.S., *Toxics Release Inventory* (U.S. EPA, Washington, D.C., paper and on CD-Rom, annually).

——*EPA Enforcement and Compliance Assurance Accomplishments Report, FY 1995* (U.S. EPA, ref. 300–R–96–006, Washington, D.C., July 1996).

GENERAL ACCOUNTING OFFICE, U.S., *Siting of Hazardous Waste Landfills and their Correlation with Racial and Economic Status of Surrounding Communities* (U.S. GAO, Washington, D.C., 1983).

GOLD, HEATHER L., and THORPE, KENNETH E., *Louisiana Health Care Data Book* (Tulane, New Orleans, Lou., 1996).

GORE, AL, *Earth in the Balance: Forging a New Common Purpose* (Earthscan, London, 1992).

HARR, JONATHAN, *A Civil Action* (Vintage Books, New York, 1995).

HEALTH AND SAFETY EXECUTIVE, U.K., *The Tolerability of Risk from Nuclear Power Stations* (HMSO, London, revised 1992).

HORTON, TOM, and EICHBAUM, WILLIAM M., *Turning the Tide: Saving the Chesapeake Bay* (Island Press, Washington, D.C., 1991).

HOUSE OF LORDS EUROPEAN COMMUNITIES COMMITTEE—SUB-COMMITTEE F (ENVIRONMENT), *Enquiry on Implementation and Enforcement of EC Environmental Legislation* (HMSO, London, October 1991).

HUMPHREYS, JAMES, *Negotiating in the European Union: How to Make the Brussels Machine Work for You* (Century, London, 1997).

INTERGOVERNMENTAL PANEL ON CLIMATE CHANGE, *The Second Assessment Report* (U.N. Environment Programme, Nairobi, 1995).

JEFFERSON, THOMAS, *Autobiography*, in Adrienne Koch and William Peden (eds.), *The Life and Selected Writings of Thomas Jefferson* (Random House, New York, 1993).

KEMMIS, DANIEL, *Community and the Politics of Place* (University of Oklahoma Press, Norman, Okla., 1990).

LEAGUE OF WOMEN VOTERS OF COLORADO EDUCATION FUND, *Your Role at Rocky Flats—A Guide to Public Participation Opportunities at Rocky Flats Environmental Technology Site* (League of Women Voters of Colorado, Denver, Colo., 1995).

LEAKEY, RICHARD, *The Sixth Extinction* (Weidenfeld & Nicolson, London, 1996).

MARCY, RANDOLPH B., *The Prairie Traveller* (Perigee, New York, undated facsimile edition, ISBN 0–399–51865–7) (first published 1859).

MARIN, A., *Risk Analysis, Perception and Management* (Royal Society, London, 1992).

MINTZ, JOEL A., *Enforcement at the EPA* (University of Texas Press, Austin, Tex., 1995).

OREGON, STATE OF, *State of Oregon Voters' Pamphlet* (State of Oregon, Portland, Ore., 5 November 1996), i and ii.

PALO ALTO, CITY OF, REGIONAL WATER QUALITY CONTROL PLANT, *Clean Bay Plan 1997* (City of Palo Alto, Palo Alto, Cal., 1997).

PRESIDENT'S COUNCIL ON SUSTAINABLE DEVELOPMENT, *Sustainable America—A New Consensus for Prosperity, Opportunity and a Healthy Environment for the Future* (President's Council on Sustainable Development, Washington, D.C., February 1996).

RIPON OF HEXHAM, LORD (Chairman of Commission), *Making the Law: The Report of the Hansard Society Commission on the Legislative Process* (Hansard Society for Parliamentary Government, London, 1993).

RISSLER, JANE, and MELLON, MARGARET, *The Ecological Risk of Engineered Crops* (Massachusetts Institute of Technology and Union of Concerned Scientists, Boston, Mass., 1996).

ROYAL COMMISSION ON ENVIRONMENTAL POLLUTION, *Eighteenth Report, Transport & the Environment*, Cm 2674 (HMSO, London, 1994).

SEMICONDUCTOR INDUSTRY ASSOCIATION, *Status Report & Industry Directory 1996–1997* (Semiconductor Industry Association, San Jose, Cal., 1997).

SPARROW, MALCOLM K., *Imposing Duties—Government's Changing Approach to Compliance* (Praeger, Westport, Conn., 1994).

TENNER, EDWARD, *Why Things Bite Back: Technology and the Revenge of Unintended Consequences* (Knopf, New York, 1996).

TEXAS NATURAL RESOURCES CONSERVATION COMMISSION, *Pollution Prevention Ideas from Texas Industries—a Case Study Compendium* (Texas Natural Resources Conservation Commission, Office of Pollution Prevention and Recycling, Austin, Tex., March 1996).

TROMANS, STEPHEN, and FITZGERALD, JAMES, *The Law of Nuclear Installations and Radioactive Substances* (Sweet & Maxwell, London, 1997).

UNITED CHURCH OF CHRIST, COMMISSION FOR RACIAL JUSTICE, *Toxic Wastes in the United States: A National Report on the Racial Socio-Economic Characterisation of Communities with Hazardous Waste Sites* (United Church of Christ, New York, 1987) and *Toxic Waste and Race Revisited* (United Church of Christ, New York, 1994).

VOGEL, DAVID, *National Styles of Regulation: Environmental Policy in Great Britain and the United States* (Cornell University Press, Ithaca, NY, 1986).

WASHINGTON STATE DEPARTMENT OF ECOLOGY, *Measuring Pollution Prevention: Analysis of the Printed Circuit Board Fabrication Sector in Washington State* (Washington State Department of Ecology, Seattle, Wash., May 1996).

WASSERSTROM, ROBERT F., and WILES, RICHARD, *Field Duty—U.S. Farmworkers and Pesticide Safety* (World Resources Institute, Washington, D.C., 1985).

Index